ACCOUNTING & VALUATION GUIDE

Assets Acquired to Be Used in Research and Development Activities

Preface

About This AICPA Accounting and Valuation Guide

This AICPA Accounting and Valuation Guide has been developed by the AICPA IPR&D Task Force (task force) and AICPA staff. This guide provides guidance and illustrations for preparers of financial statements, independent auditors, and valuation specialists[1] regarding the initial and subsequent accounting for, valuation of, and disclosures related to acquired in-process research and development (IPR&D) assets. The valuation guidance in this guide is focused on measuring fair value of IPR&D assets for financial reporting purposes.

The financial accounting and reporting guidance contained in this guide has been reviewed and approved by the affirmative vote of at least two-thirds of the members of the Financial Reporting Executive Committee (FinREC), which is the designated senior committee of the AICPA authorized to speak for the AICPA in the areas of financial accounting and reporting. Conforming changes made to the financial accounting and reporting guidance contained in this guide will be approved by the FinREC Chair (or his or her designee). Updates made to the financial accounting and reporting guidance in this guide exceeding that of conforming changes will be approved by the affirmative vote of at least two-thirds of the members of FinREC.

This guide

- identifies certain requirements set forth in the Financial Accounting Standards Board (FASB) *Accounting Standards Codification®* (ASC).

- describes FinREC's understanding of prevalent or sole practice concerning certain issues. In addition, this guide may indicate that FinREC expresses a preference for the prevalent or sole practice, or it may indicate that FinREC expresses a preference for another practice that is not the prevalent or sole practice; alternatively, FinREC may express no view on the matter.

- identifies certain other, but not necessarily all, practices concerning certain accounting issues without expressing FinREC's views on them.

- provides guidance that has been supported by FinREC on the accounting, reporting, or disclosure treatment of transactions or events that are not set forth in FASB ASC.

---

[1] Although this guide uses the term *valuation specialist*, Statement on Standards for Valuation Services No. 1, *Valuation of a Business, Business Ownership Interest, Security, or Intangible Asset* (AICPA, *Professional Standards*, VS sec. 100), which is a part of AICPA *Professional Standards*, defines a member who performs valuation services as a *valuation analyst*. The term *valuation specialist*, as used in this guide, is synonymous to the term *valuation analyst*, as used in AICPA *Professional Standards*.
When referring to the valuation specialist in this guide, it is commonly presumed that the valuation specialist is an external party, but if individuals within the entity possess the abilities, skills, and experience to perform valuations, they can also serve in the capacity of a valuation specialist.

Accounting guidance for nongovernmental entities included in this AICPA Accounting and Valuation Guide is a source of nonauthoritative accounting guidance. FASB ASC is the authoritative source of U.S. accounting and reporting standards for nongovernmental entities, in addition to guidance issued by the SEC. AICPA members should be prepared to justify departures from U.S. generally accepted accounting principles, as discussed in Rule 203, *Accounting Principles* (AICPA, *Professional Standards*, ET sec. 203 par. .01). In addition, AICPA members who perform engagements to estimate value that culminate in the expression of a conclusion of value or a calculated value are subject to the requirements of the AICPA's Statement on Standards for Valuation Services.

This guide does not include auditing guidance;[2] however, auditors may use it to obtain an understanding of the accounting requirements and the valuation process applicable to IPR&D assets.

Recognition

IPR&D Task Force (2009–2013)

(members when this edition was completed)	*(past members who contributed to this edition)*
Anthony V. Aaron, *Co-Chair*	Ying (Vivian) Liu
Val R. Bitton, *Co-Chair*	
Matthew C. Coffland	
Jeffrey P. Draper	
David C. Dufendach	
Randolph Green	
Robert Laux	
Andreas Ohl	
Brad Pursel	
Stephanie Shepherd	

---

[2] In October 2011, the AICPA Auditing Standards Board (ASB) issued Statement on Auditing Standards (SAS) No. 122, *Statements on Auditing Standards: Clarification and Recodification* (AICPA, *Professional Standards*), which contains 39 clarified SASs and supersedes all outstanding SASs through SAS No. 121, except for 8 SASs. SAS No. 122 represents the redrafting of existing SASs to apply the ASB's clarity drafting conventions and converge with International Standards on Auditing. SAS No. 122 is effective for audits of financial statements for periods ending on or after December 15, 2012. Refer to individual sections for specific effective date language.

AU-C section 540, *Auditing Accounting Estimates, Including Fair Value Accounting Estimates, and Related Disclosures* (AICPA, *Professional Standards*), addresses the auditor's responsibilities relating to accounting estimates, including fair value accounting estimates and related disclosures, in an audit of financial statements. This section supersedes AU section 342, *Auditing Accounting Estimates* (SAS No. 57), and AU section 328, *Auditing Fair Value Measurements and Disclosures* (SAS No. 101). AU-C section 540 combines the requirements and guidance from AU section 342 (SAS No. 57) and AU section 328 (SAS No. 101), but it does not change or expand those standards in any significant respect.

Auditors may also find it helpful to refer to the AICPA Audit Guide *Special Considerations in Auditing Financial Instruments*, which, among other things, addresses the auditor's responsibilities relating to auditing accounting estimates, including fair value accounting estimates, and related disclosures.

The AICPA and the IPR&D Task Force gratefully acknowledge the following individuals for their assistance in development of this guide: Kristin D. Bauer, Brian Blisard, Jonathan K. Duong, Amanda Guanzini, Ryan Kaye, Christopher Krawtschuk, Chade Lowe, Elsye Putri, and Nisha Sheth.

Guidance Considered in This Edition

Authoritative guidance issued through May 1, 2013, has been considered in the development of this edition of the guide.

This guide includes relevant guidance issued up to and including the following:

- FASB Accounting Standards Update No. 2013-11, *Income Taxes (Topic 740): Presentation of an Unrecognized Tax Benefit When a Net Operating Loss Carryforward, a Similar Tax Loss, or a Tax Credit Carryforward Exists (a consensus of the FASB Emerging Issues Task Force)*

- AICPA's Statement on Standards for Valuation Services No. 1, *Valuation of a Business, Business Ownership Interest, Security, or Intangible Asset* (AICPA, *Professional Standards*, VS sec. 100)

Readers of this guide should consider guidance issued subsequent to those items listed previously to determine its effect on entities covered by this guide. In determining the applicability of recently issued guidance, its effective date should also be considered.

AICPA.org Website

The AICPA encourages you to visit its website at www.aicpa.org and the Financial Reporting Center at www.aicpa.org/FRC. The Financial Reporting Center supports members in the execution of high-quality financial reporting. Whether you are a financial statement preparer or a member in public practice, this center provides exclusive member-only resources for the entire financial reporting process and provides timely and relevant news, guidance, and examples supporting the financial reporting process, including accounting, preparing financial statements, and performing compilation, review, audit, attest, or assurance and advisory engagements. Certain content on AICPA websites referenced in this guide may be restricted to AICPA members only.

TABLE OF CONTENTS

Contents

Introduction

.01 Financial Accounting Standards Board (FASB) *Accounting Standards Codification* (ASC) 805, *Business Combinations*, provides guidance on the accounting and reporting for transactions that represent a business combination or an acquisition by a not-for-profit entity[1] (thereafter collectively referred to as a *business combination*) to be accounted for under the acquisition method. FASB ASC 805-20-25-1 requires that at the acquisition date, the acquirer "recognize, separately from goodwill, the identifiable assets acquired, the liabilities assumed, and any noncontrolling interest in the acquiree."[2] During its deliberations of FASB Statement No. 141(R), *Business Combinations*, FASB concluded that "in-process research and development acquired in a business combination generally will satisfy the definition of an asset . . ."[3] As such, an acquirer is required to recognize all tangible and intangible assets acquired in a business combination[4] that are to be used in research and development (R&D)

---

[1] The Financial Accounting Standard Board (FASB) *Accounting Standards Codification* (ASC) glossary defines an *acquisition by a not-for-profit entity* as a transaction or other event in which a not-for-profit acquirer obtains control of one or more nonprofit activities or businesses and initially recognizes their assets and liabilities in the acquirer's financial statements.

    It should be noted that certain acquisitions by a not-for-profit entity are not within the scope of FASB ASC 805, *Business Combinations*. Specifically, FASB ASC 805-10-15-4(e) indicates that the guidance in FASB ASC 805 does not apply to a transaction or other event in which a not-for-profit entity obtains control of a not-for-profit entity but does not consolidate that entity, as permitted or required by FASB ASC 958-810-25. FASB ASC 805 also does not apply if a not-for-profit entity that obtained control in a transaction or other event in which consolidation was permitted but not required decides in a subsequent annual reporting period to begin consolidating a controlled entity that it initially chose not to consolidate.

[2] The FASB ASC glossary defines a *business combination* as a "transaction or other event in which an acquirer obtains control of one or more businesses." A *business* is then defined as an "integrated set of activities and assets that is capable of being conducted and managed for the purpose of providing a return in the form of dividends, lower costs, or other economic benefits directly to investors or other owners, members, or participants." Additional implementation guidance regarding what constitutes a business is available in paragraphs 4–9 of FASB ASC 805-10-55.

[3] FASB Statement No. 141(R), *Business Combinations*, was codified in FASB ASC 805. The quoted language is an excerpt from paragraph B152 of FASB Statement No. 141(R). Paragraph B152 was part of the "Basis for Conclusions" section, none of which was codified in FASB ASC. However, the IPR&D Task Force (task force) believes that paragraph B152 provides helpful guidance and, therefore, decided to incorporate it into this guide.

[4] On July 1, 2013, FASB issued for public comment several Private Company Council (PCC) proposals that address private company stakeholder concerns raised about the relevance and complexity of certain aspects of U.S. generally accepted accounting principles (GAAP).

    One of the proposals, proposed Accounting Standards Update (ASU) *Business Combinations (Topic 805): Accounting for Identifiable Intangible Assets in a Business Combination (a proposal of the Private Company Council)*, which is derived from PCC Issue No. 13-01A, *Accounting for Identifiable Intangible Assets in a Business Combination*, would not require private companies to separately recognize certain intangible assets acquired in a business combination. The proposal enables private companies that elect the accounting alternative within GAAP to recognize only those intangible assets arising from noncancelable contractual terms or those arising from other legal rights. Otherwise, an intangible asset would not be recognized separately from goodwill even if it is separable.

    Another proposal, proposed ASU *Intangibles—Goodwill and Other (Topic 350): Accounting for Goodwill (a proposal of the Private Company Council)*, which is derived from PCC Issue No. 13-01B, *Accounting for Goodwill Subsequent to a Business Combination,* would permit amortization of goodwill and a simplified goodwill impairment model. This would enable private companies that elect the accounting alternative within GAAP to amortize goodwill on a straight-line basis over the useful life of the primary asset acquired in a business combination, not to exceed 10 years. Goodwill would be tested for impairment only when a triggering event occurs that would indicate that the fair value of an entity may be below its carrying amount. Moreover, goodwill would be tested for impairment at the entity-wide level as compared to the current requirement to test at the reporting unit level.

    Please refer to the FASB website for the latest information regarding the status of this project at www.fasb.org/cs/ContentServer?c=Page&pagename=FASB%2FPage%2FSectionPage&cid=1351027243076.

activities, regardless of whether these assets have an alternative future use by the acquirer. FASB ASC 805-20-30-1 requires that these assets be measured at their acquisition-date fair values. FASB ASC 820, *Fair Value Measurement*, defines *fair value* as the "price that would be received to sell an asset or paid to transfer a liability in an orderly transaction between market participants at the measurement date."

.02   After initial recognition, tangible assets acquired in a business combination that are used in R&D activities are accounted for in accordance with their nature. After initial recognition, intangible assets that are used in R&D activities, including specific in-process R&D (IPR&D) projects (subsequently referred to as *IPR&D assets*), acquired in a business combination are accounted for in accordance with FASB ASC 350-30. FASB ASC 350-30 requires that these assets be classified as indefinite-lived until the completion or abandonment of the associated R&D efforts,[5] at which time the entity would determine the assets' appropriate useful life. R&D expenditures incurred subsequent to the business combination related to the acquired capitalized IPR&D assets are generally expensed as incurred unless they represent costs of materials, equipment, or facilities that have alternative future uses.

.03   In a business combination, the recognition of assets used in R&D activities can significantly affect the financial reporting of current and future operating results of the reporting entity. Before the effective date of FASB Statement No. 141(R), an acquirer was required to measure and immediately expense tangible and intangible assets acquired to be used in R&D activities (including specific IPR&D projects) that had no alternative future use. (However, as discussed in paragraph .08, tangible assets were generally capitalized because they were presumed to have an alternative future use.) This reduced the amount of excess purchase price that would otherwise be recorded as goodwill, as well as decreased net income of the reporting entity in the period following acquisition. Under the current guidance contained in FASB ASC 805, an entity no longer expenses assets to be used in R&D activities that have no alternative future use immediately after the acquisition date, but recognizes them at their acquisition-date fair values.

.04   In a transaction other than a business combination (subsequently referred to as an *asset acquisition*), accounting guidance for assets acquired for use in R&D activities remains unchanged. In accordance with FASB ASC 730-10, such assets are capitalized only if they have alternative future uses; otherwise, such assets are expensed. As a result, assets used in R&D activities acquired in a business combination and those acquired in an asset acquisition are still subject to different accounting treatment. Similar to business combinations, R&D expenditures incurred subsequent to the asset acquisition related to the acquired capitalized IPR&D assets are generally expensed as incurred unless they represent costs of materials, equipment, or facilities that have alternative future uses.

---

[5] The requirement to classify in-process research and development (IPR&D) assets acquired in a business combination as indefinite-lived resulted from FASB Statement No. 141(R), which superseded FASB Interpretation No. 4, *Applicability of FASB Statement No. 2 to Business Combinations Accounted for by the Purchase Method*, and amended FASB Statement Nos. 2, *Accounting for Research and Development Costs*, and 142, *Goodwill and Other Intangible Assets*. This requirement was subsequently codified in FASB ASC 350-30.

History and Organization of This Guide

.05 Until the early 1990s, amounts allocated to specific IPR&D projects in business combinations were not significant. Later, however, amounts assigned to acquired IPR&D became an increasing portion of the total acquisition price—in some instances, more than 75 percent of the total acquisition price. Financial reporting constituents in the software, electronic devices, and pharmaceutical industries expressed concern about (a) the lack of comparability among entities for the definition of what constitutes assets acquired to be used in R&D activities, including specific IPR&D projects; (b) methodologies and assumptions used to value specific assets acquired to be used in R&D activities, including specific IPR&D projects; and (c) level of disclosures provided for amounts allocated to assets acquired to be used in R&D activities, including specific IPR&D projects. In addition, some, including SEC staff, were concerned about valuations of assets acquired to be used in R&D activities, including specific IPR&D projects, that appeared to be unreasonable determinations of fair value, and some were concerned about the adequacy of procedures employed in audits of financial statements that included a charge for the assets acquired to be used in R&D activities, including specific IPR&D projects. As a result, on September 9, 1998, the chief accountant of the SEC released a letter to the chair of the AICPA SEC Regulations Committee citing a number of issues relating to the valuation of assets acquired in a business combination that the SEC staff noted in its review of public registrant filings.

.06 The AICPA responded to these concerns by forming a task force comprising representatives from various constituencies to study the issues and prepare a best practices publication that would benefit all parties interested in the financial reporting of assets acquired to be used in R&D activities, including specific IPR&D projects, in the software, electronic devices, and pharmaceutical industries (though accounting principles generally accepted in the United States of America [GAAP] underlying the best practices apply to all industries). The original guidance was published in 2001. It was issued in the form of a practice aid, *Assets Acquired in a Business Combination to Be Used in Research and Development Activities: A Focus on Software, Electronic Devices & Pharmaceutical Industries* (subsequently referred to as *the original practice aid*).

.07 Since the issuance of the original practice aid, there have been significant additions and amendments to GAAP. This guide has been updated to reflect the latest guidance, including the guidance in FASB ASC 820. In the original practice aid, an entire chapter was devoted to the concept of fair value. Since then, FASB has established guidance that defines fair value, as well as lays out a framework for measuring and disclosing fair value. This updated guide does, however, provide incremental best practices and examples, as determined by the IPR&D Task Force (task force), related to the valuation techniques and practices used to measure the fair value of IPR&D assets with the focus on the software, electronic devices, and pharmaceutical industries.[6]

---

[6] In this guide, it is commonly presumed that valuation is performed by an external valuation specialist. However, if management has appropriate credentials and experience, they can also serve in the capacity of a valuation specialist. It should also be noted that regardless of whether fair value measurements are developed by management or a third party, management is responsible for the measurements that are used to prepare the financial statements and for underlying assumptions used in developing these measurements.

.08 This guide has also been updated to reflect the issuance of FASB Statement No. 141(R), which significantly amended the guidance on accounting for a business combination. Specifically, the requirement to capitalize assets acquired in a business combination to be used in R&D activities, regardless of whether those assets have an alternative future use, had a significant effect on accounting for intangible assets (that is, IPR&D assets). Under the old guidance, those assets were often expensed due to lack of alternative future use. However, the capitalization requirement did not result in a significant change in practice for tangible assets because under the old guidance, these assets were generally presumed to have an alternative future use and, therefore, were usually capitalized. As a result, this guide mostly focuses on intangible assets (that is, IPR&D assets). This guide has also been updated to reflect the guidance of other relevant pronouncements.

.09 The guide provides incremental conclusions about what the task force members perceive as best practices related to initial accounting for (chapters 2–3), disclosing (chapter 5), and valuing (chapters 1 and 6) IPR&D assets, including specific IPR&D projects. In addition, this guide discusses best practices with respect to accounting for acquired IPR&D assets subsequent to the acquisition date (chapter 4). Although this subject was not included in the original practice aid, the task force believes that such information is needed due to the requirement to capitalize IPR&D assets acquired in a business combination.

.10 Given different accounting treatment of assets used in R&D activities acquired in a business combination and those acquired in an asset acquisition, this guide also addresses considerations related to assets acquired in an asset acquisition that are to be used in R&D activities (chapter 3).

.11 This guide is based on GAAP and does not address International Financial Reporting Standards (IFRSs). Although efforts have been made to converge GAAP and IFRSs in the areas of fair value (FASB ASC 820 and IFRS 13, *Fair Value Measurement*)[7] and business combinations (FASB ASC 805 and IFRS 3 [revised], *Business Combinations*), significant differences still remain in the areas of impairment (FASB ASC 350, *Intangibles—Goodwill and Other*, and 360, *Property, Plant, and Equipment*, versus International Accounting Standard [IAS] 36, *Impairment of Assets*) and accounting for IPR&D assets (FASB ASC 350-30 and 730-10 versus IAS 38, *Intangible Assets*).

---

[7] International Financial Reporting Standard 13, *Fair Value Measurement*, is effective for annual periods beginning on or after January 1, 2013, with earlier application permitted.

Chapter 1

Valuation Techniques Used to Measure Fair Value of In-Process Research and Development Assets

Introduction

1.01   As indicated in paragraph .04 of the AICPA's Statement on Standards for Valuation Services (*SSVS*)[1] No. 1, *Valuation of a Business, Business Ownership Interest, Security, or Intangible Asset* (AICPA, *Professional Standards*, VS sec. 100), in the process of estimating value, the *valuation specialist* applies valuation approaches and valuation methods[2] and uses professional judgment. The use of professional judgment is an essential component of estimating value. Also, it is important for the valuation specialist to consider facts and circumstances specific to the asset being valued.

1.02   Valuation approaches used to measure the *fair value* of an asset may be classified broadly as cost, market, or income.[3] FASB ASC 820-10-35-24 states that a "reporting entity shall use valuation techniques that are appropriate in the circumstances and for which sufficient data are available to measure fair value, maximizing the use of relevant observable inputs and minimizing the use of unobservable inputs." Therefore, when valuing an asset, all three approaches should be considered, and the approach or approaches that are appropriate under the circumstances should be selected.

1.03   Each of the three approaches can be used to measure fair value of an asset acquired in a business combination, asset acquisition, or, subsequently, for impairment testing and measurement purposes. As provided in FASB ASC 820-10-35-24B

> [i]n some cases, a single valuation technique will be appropriate...In other cases, multiple valuation techniques will be appropriate...If multiple valuation techniques are used to measure fair value, the results (that is, respective indications of fair value) shall be evaluated considering the reasonableness of the range of values indicated by those

---

[1] Words or terms defined in the glossary are set in italicized type the first time they appear in the body of this guide.

[2] Financial Accounting Standards Board (FASB) *Accounting Standards Codification* (ASC) 820, *Fair Value Measurement*, refers to valuation approaches and valuation techniques. However, Statement on Standards for Valuation Services (SSVS) No. 1, *Valuation of a Business, Business Ownership Interest, Security, or Intangible Asset* (AICPA, *Professional Standards*, VS sec. 100), refers to valuation approaches and methods (not techniques). SSVS No. 1 (which is discussed in chapter 6, "Valuation of In-Process Research and Development Assets") defines *valuation method* as "within approaches, a specific way to determine value." This definition is consistent with the meaning attributed to valuation techniques in FASB ASC 820. Also, in practice, many valuation techniques are referred to as *methods* (for example, discounted cash flow method, multiperiod excess earnings method, relief from royalty method, Greenfield method, real options method, and so forth.) As a result, this guide uses the terms *technique* and *method* interchangeably to refer to a specific way of determining value within an approach.

[3] Note that while the discussion of the various approaches in this guide are focused only on fair value, as defined in FASB ASC 820, of in-process research and development (IPR&D) assets for financial reporting purposes, these approaches can, and frequently are, used for other assets or under other valuation premises or standards (for example, fair market value, liquidation value, investment value, and so forth).

results. A fair value measurement is the point within that range that is most representative of fair value in the circumstances.

1.04   For purposes of measuring the fair value of *in-process research and development (IPR&D) assets*, the *cost approach* is applied only in limited circumstances. For example, the cost approach may be used to value dedicated, single purpose fixed assets used in research and development (R&D) activities, assets that can be substituted effectively through replacement or reproduction, or *IPR&D projects* that are in initial stages of development in which robust *prospective financial information* (PFI) does not exist. The *market approach* is seldom used to value IPR&D assets due to the lack of observable market values for similar assets, except in certain cases in which there may be sufficient observable asset pricing data. In most instances, however, the *income approach* is used to value IPR&D assets.

1.05   The classification of valuation methods and approaches used in this guide reflects the views of the IPR&D Task Force (task force). However, the task force acknowledges that there is some diversity in views in the valuation profession regarding certain characterizations. For instance, although this guide classifies the *relief from royalty method* as a method under the income approach, some practitioners believe that it is a form of the market approach. There are likely other examples of different views on characterizations. However, the task force believes that categorization does not change the substance of the application of these methods or their results. It should be noted that this guide does not intend to definitively determine which method falls within which approach or which method is a subset of another method.

Cost Approach

1.06   As discussed in paragraphs 3D–3E of FASB ASC 820-10-55, the cost approach reflects the amount that would be required currently to replace the service capacity of an asset (often referred to as *current replacement cost*). From the perspective of a *market participant* seller, the price that would be received for the asset is based on the cost to a market participant buyer to acquire or construct a substitute asset of comparable utility, adjusted for obsolescence.

1.07   There is some dispute in the valuation profession regarding whether replacement cost is a pretax or an after-tax measure. This issue is beyond the scope of this guide. However, for purposes of valuing the assembled workforce in the comprehensive example (see paragraphs 6.185–.199 and related schedules), it is assumed to be pretax.

1.08   The task force recognizes that the cost approach is widely used for valuing assets in general. However, it is less commonly used to value IPR&D assets because the goal of R&D is generally to develop commercial products (that is, income-producing assets), which are intended to generate profits (that is, the value derived from those assets is expected to exceed costs incurred in developing those assets). Therefore, for assets to be used in R&D activities, including IPR&D projects, there may be little or no relationship between historical cost expended and fair value. For example, a great invention may cost little, in which case, fair value may far exceed cost. Conversely, an R&D project may last for years without producing a commercially viable product, in which case, the cost approach may overstate the fair value of the technology.

1.09 Because many assets used in R&D activities are unique or proprietary and cannot be reproduced or otherwise replaced, the task force believes that the cost approach will generally not be appropriate for valuing such assets as the intangible portion of an IPR&D project. However, the use of a cost approach may be appropriate in limited circumstances, including the valuation of (a) single purpose fixed assets, (b) assets that can be substituted effectively through replacement or reproduction, or (c) specific IPR&D projects in which the stage of development, although substantive, is so early that reliable information about anticipated future benefits does not exist.

Market Approach

1.10 As stated in FASB ASC 820-10-55-3A, the market approach uses prices and other relevant information generated by market transactions involving identical or comparable (that is, similar) assets, liabilities, or a group of assets and liabilities, such as a business.

1.11 The prices in recent transactions of comparable technology may be a reasonable basis for estimating the fair value of an early-stage technology. In such circumstances, the valuation specialist would study the characteristics of the asset and the stage of its development to ensure that the subject and comparable assets are reasonably similar. However, sales prices of comparable IPR&D assets are seldom available because either (a) IPR&D assets typically transfer with the sale of a business, not individually, or (b) when they do transfer individually, they may not be comparable to the subject asset. Therefore, the market approach seldom is used to value IPR&D assets, unless exchanges of individual assets comparable to the subject asset can be observed.

1.12 In some cases, estimates of fair value may be based on the prices of single-technology or single-product companies that are publicly traded. There may also be markets for the purchase of early-stage discoveries from academic institutions or businesses. Markets are evolving for the exchange of intellectual property, and prices from such markets may also be a useful input. These prices may provide indications of fair value for similar early-stage discoveries. Besides market prices for comparable assets, market-derived data can provide inputs to valuing an asset using the income approach (for example, royalty rates derived from licensing arrangements). It should be noted, however, that the terms in these transactions may include an upfront lump-sum payment with certain contingent payments or ongoing royalties based on future success and revenue. Difficulty converting the transaction terms to either a single lump-sum amount or a blended effective royalty rate may be an obstacle in benchmarking the value of the subject asset, in addition to other issues of comparability.

Income Approach

1.13 As stated in FASB ASC 820-10-55-3F, the income approach converts future amounts (for example, cash flows or income and expenses) to a single current (that is, discounted) amount. When the income approach is used, the fair value measurement reflects current market expectations about those future amounts.

1.14 The term *income*, as used when referring to techniques under this approach, implies anticipated future benefits (sometimes referred to as *economic earnings* as opposed to the notion of accounting earnings or net income), in the form of *net cash flows*. Net cash flows differ from reported net earnings in that net cash flows are net of earnings reinvested to fund asset growth or development and adjusted for noncash expenses, such as depreciation and amortization. The income approach involves two basic steps. The first is development of prospective net cash flows[4] expected to accrue to an investor resulting from ownership of an asset or collection of assets. The second step involves discounting the prospective cash flow to a present value.

1.15   The income approach generally may be broken down into two methods: (*a*) single-period capitalization and (*b*) multiperiod discounted cash flows. The single-period capitalization method is used primarily in the valuation of small businesses, professional practices, certain types of real property, mature companies with steady growth, or stable growth intangible assets that are expected to exist over an indefinite future period. This method is rarely of use in the valuation of assets used in R&D activities because the assumptions of indefinite existence and continuous growth would be inappropriate. A variation of the multiperiod *discounted cash flow method*, the *multiperiod excess earnings method*, is the most commonly used valuation technique under the income approach to value IPR&D assets. It requires forecasting cash flows for a discrete period and discounting those amounts to present value at a rate of return that considers the risk of the cash flows. These methods are conceptually the same in that they both convert prospective net cash flows expected to accrue to an investor resulting from ownership of an asset or collection of assets to a present value. The main distinction between these methods is that the single-period capitalization method is most commonly used to perform an entity-type valuation, whereas the multiperiod discounted cash flows method, due to its greater flexibility, can address, for example, valuation scenarios with nonconstant growth rates and margins, and, thus, can be used to value a much wider range of subject assets, including entities, segments of entities, groups of assets, and individual assets.

1.16   The following are the most commonly used methods and techniques under the income approach to value IPR&D assets:

- Multiperiod excess earnings
- Relief from royalty[5]
- Decision tree analysis
- "Split" methods (that is, revenue, cash flows, or profit split)

1.17   Other methods and techniques under the income approach that might be used to value IPR&D assets are as follows:

- Monte Carlo analysis

---

[4] Typically, net cash flows are considered in the income approach and discounted to present value. However, in certain instances and depending on the unit of account determination, certain cash outflows, such as licensing fees or royalties, may need to be presented as a separate liability or contingency. If this is the case, the estimated future gross cash flows will be discounted to their present value to determine the fair value of the asset versus the liability. See the "Questions and Answers—Recognition of IPR&D Assets Acquired in a Business Combination" section in paragraphs 2.14–.15 for further discussion.

[5] Although SSVS No. 1 categorizes the relief from royalty method as a method under the market approach, other sources of valuation literature classify it under the income approach. However, the IPR&D Task Force (task force) believes that categorization does not change the substance of the application of this method. See paragraph 1.05 for further discussion.

- Options-based methods
- Manufacturing cost savings
- Incremental revenue or profit (for example, price premium)
- "With and without" analysis
- Greenfield method

1.18 The stream of cash flows from each of these methods is discounted to present value, including, as appropriate, any tax benefits derived from amortizing the intangible asset for tax purposes,[6] to estimate the fair value of the intangible asset.

1.19 The valuation specialist should apply income-based method(s) or technique(s) that most accurately captures the benefit of owning the IPR&D asset, given the nature of the asset and availability of required inputs.

1.20 *Multiperiod excess earnings method*. In cases when there is an identifiable stream of prospective cash flows for a collection of assets, a multiperiod excess earnings method may provide a reasonable indication of the value of a specific asset. Specifically, under the multiperiod excess earnings method, the estimate of an intangible asset's fair value starts with the PFI associated with a collection of assets, rather than a single asset. *Contributory asset charges*, also referred to as *economic rents*, are then commonly deducted from the net (or after-tax) cash flows for the collection of the associated assets to isolate remaining or "excess earnings" attributable solely to the intangible asset being valued. The contributory asset charge is a deduction for the contribution of supporting assets (for example, net working capital, fixed assets, customer relationships,[7] trade names, and so on) to the generation of the prospective cash flows. Contributory asset charges should be applied for all assets, including other intangible assets, which would be required by market participants to generate the overall cash flows of the collection of assets. The excess earnings, net of the charges for contributory assets, are ascribed to the asset being valued and discounted to present value. The multiperiod excess earnings method is discussed in detail in chapter 6, "Valuation of In-Process Research and Development Assets."

1.21 *Relief from royalty*. The premise of the relief from royalty method is that ownership of the subject asset *relieves* the owner of the need to license the asset from a third party. Thus, by owning the intangible asset, the owner avoids the royalty payments required to license the asset. The relief from royalty is cash flow savings that are discounted to present value. The present value of the prospective after-tax royalty payments are commonly used to approximate the fair value to the investor of owning the intangible asset. When selecting a royalty rate, one needs to consider whether it is licensor or licensee that is responsible for costs associated with various functions. For instance, when valuing IPR&D assets using the relief from royalty method, it may be appropriate to consider costs to complete, probability of completion, postcompletion

---

[6] The need to include the benefits of tax amortization will depend on which tax jurisdiction the intangible asset is located, or would be located, from a market participant perspective. Also, as further discussed in paragraph 6.123, the task force believes that tax amortization benefit should be included regardless of whether the actual transaction is a taxable transaction in which the buyer will receive a step-up in basis for tax purposes.

[7] The inclusion of customer relationships in the contributory asset charge indicates that a different methodology would need to be used to value customer relationships in order to avoid cross charges. For further discussion regarding cross-charges, see paragraphs 3.5.04–.07 in the Appraisal Foundation document setting forth best practices for *The Identification of Contributory Assets and the Calculation of Economic Rents* (the Appraisal Foundation document).

maintenance R&D costs, and so on. For further discussion, see paragraphs 3.5.03 and 3.6.04 in the Appraisal Foundation document setting forth best practices for *The Identification of Contributory Assets and the Calculation of Economic Rents* (the Appraisal Foundation document).

1.22 A relief from royalty method is often appropriate for certain types of intangible assets. For instance, trademarks and trade names, patents, and *developed product technology* are examples of intangible assets that frequently are licensed in exchange for a royalty payment. A critical element of this method is the development of a royalty rate that is comparable to ownership of the specific asset (for example, a rate that equates to worldwide, exclusive rights to use that asset in perpetuity in any manner desired). Therefore, if a properly supportable royalty rate that corresponds to the rights and responsibilities represented by the asset being licensed cannot be obtained due to the nature of the asset, then the relief from royalty method should not be used, and other, more appropriate methodologies should be considered instead.

1.23 Generally, the relief from royalty method is applied in situations in which

- the importance of the intangible asset to a business or product is similar to that of a comparable, licensed asset (for example, pharmaceutical compounds that are licensed).
- the intangible asset can be reasonably separated from other assets, and it is practical and possible to license it separately.
- the rights of ownership can be compared to the rights under a license (for example, similar geographic market coverage, duration, exclusivity, limitation, technology, and type of customer).
- royalty rates can be observed, including rates for agreements that confirm comparable economic rights for similar intellectual property.

1.24 Typically, the best source of royalty rate information would be other licensing agreements for comparable technologies made by one of the companies in a transaction. When such information is not available, it may be appropriate to use industry average rates or other broad benchmarks with reasonable justification. Royalty rates would also need to consider the qualitative drivers of comparability. Truly comparable rates may be difficult to find for most IPR&D assets and, therefore, simulated or adjusted royalty rates taking into consideration qualitative value drivers of the subject intangible asset could be used. The relief from royalty method is discussed in detail in chapter 6.

1.25 *Decision tree analysis.* Decision tree analysis is an income-based method that explicitly captures the expected benefits, costs, and probabilities of contingent outcomes at future decision points, or nodes. In general, these nodes are points at which a major investment decision will be made, such as whether a pharmaceutical company will proceed to a phase III clinical trial. At that point, management can decide whether to make an additional investment based on the benefits and costs expected from that point forward. If the expected present value of the asset at that time is less than the required investment, then the investment is avoided. This is the key difference between decision tree analysis and the previously discussed methods—the ability to analyze future values, change course, and potentially avoid future investment costs that are not expected to produce an adequate return. In contrast, other income approach-based methods often assume that such contingencies are resolved favorably and that future development costs are incurred. Methods such as the multiperiod excess earnings, relief from royalty, and other income-based methods may attempt to account for the risk of failure in the estimation of the risk-adjusted *discount rate*. Decision tree analysis is particularly applicable to the valuation of assets subject to risks that are not correlated with the market, such as the risk that a particular technology will succeed or fail. Risks that are correlated with external markets can be estimated discretely when a decision tree analysis is employed. In summary, the decision tree analysis provides the valuation specialist an ability to analyze costs, risks, and contingent outcomes at various stages.

1.26 An example of a decision tree analysis appears in chapter 6 of this guide. In this example, the market risks are modeled using two potential outcomes—a high market potential and a low market potential. It is important to note that this method will capture the aggregate value of an investment opportunity, including the values of primary and contributory assets. The adjustments required to isolate from the assemblage of assets the values of specific assets (for example, a specific IPR&D asset) are discussed in the example in chapter 6.

1.27 *"Split" methods.* Splitting revenues, cash flows, or profits among assets, or collections of assets, can be a useful technique for isolating cash flows and avoiding double counting when measuring fair value. Such methods may be used to fully isolate the cash flows of a particular asset (for example, a relief from royalty method could be characterized as a form of a profit-split technique) or in combination with other methods (such as multiperiod excess earning) to reduce reliance on the calculation of contributory asset charges as a necessary adjustment to avoid double counting. It should be noted that splitting of revenues, cash flows, or profits would need to be based on a reasonable set of assumptions (for example, profitability of various functions represented) as opposed to being arbitrary. For further discussion, please refer to paragraph 3.5.06 in the Appraisal Foundation document.

1.28 *Monte Carlo analysis.* The Monte Carlo technique can be used in the application of income-based methods previously discussed. The term *Monte Carlo* refers to computer-generated simulations of numerous PFI scenarios. This type of analysis is consistent with the present value techniques described in paragraphs 4–20 of FASB ASC 820-10-55. The Monte Carlo technique can be used for estimating the fair value of IPR&D assets. Also, many assumptions can be simulated using this technique and incorporated into other valuation methods. The details of the Monte Carlo technique are beyond the scope of this guide.[8]

---

[8] The nature of Monte Carlo analysis theoretically would lend itself well to the valuation of IPR&D assets. However, the task force observes that, as of the writing of this guide, this methodology was not commonly used in practice to value IPR&D assets. The task force has observed, however, the use of this methodology in the valuation of contingent consideration under FASB ASC 805, *Business Combinations*. For information on the Monte Carlo and other numerical simulation and scenario analysis techniques, readers may refer to the following publication: Johnathan Mun, *Modeling Risk: Applying Monte Carlo Risk Simulation, Strategic Real Options, Stochastic Forecasting, and Portfolio Optimization* (Hoboken, New Jersey: John Wiley & Sons, Inc., 2010). Less technical discussions scenario valuation approaches can be found in the following two publications: Francis Clauss, *Corporate Financial Analysis with Microsoft Excel* (McGraw-Hill Companies, 2010) and Tim Koller, Marc Goedhart, and David Wessels, *Valuation: Measuring and Managing the Value of Companies* (Hoboken, New Jersey: John Wiley & Sons, Inc., 2010). Furthermore, Richard Razgaitis' book *Dealmaking Using Real Options and Monte Carlo Analysis* (Hoboken, New Jersey: John Wiley & Sons, Inc., 2003) is also a useful reference for Monte Carlo and real options techniques.

1.29 *Options-based methods.* Like decision tree analysis, options-based methods (commonly referred to as *real options* and *real options analysis*) are income approach-based techniques that capture explicitly the expected benefits, costs, and probabilities of contingent outcomes at future decision points. Again, like decision tree analysis, a real options analysis considers the stages at which an investment decision will be made.

1.30 Real options analysis differs from decision tree analysis in one key respect: "Market" risks are addressed inside the model using option pricing concepts. The details of options-based methods are beyond the scope of this guide.[9]

1.31 *Manufacturing cost savings.*[10] An intangible asset may afford its owner a cost savings (that is, a reduced or eliminated cash outflow) over the best alternative to the asset. These cost savings represent the value of ownership of the intangible asset. The present value of the cost savings is fair value of the intangible asset, provided the cost savings would be available to market participants if they owned the intangible asset.

1.32 *Incremental revenue or profit.* An intangible asset may allow for premium pricing (that is, higher cash generation) if it provides utility beyond that of competitive products or services. The premium price is a measure of the benefit derived from ownership of the intangible asset. The present value of incremental cash flows resulting from premium pricing is the fair value of the asset, provided that market participants would also be able to take advantage of premium pricing if they owned the intangible asset.

1.33 *"With and without" analysis.* Fair value of some assets may best be measured in a general sense by calculating the difference between a scenario that reflects the benefits of the asset being in place versus a scenario of not having the asset in place. There are a number of specific forms of this technique.

1.34 *Greenfield method.* This direct value method lends itself to valuing key assets in certain industries (such as broadcast, wireless, and cable industries), as discussed in FASB ASC 805-20-S99-3. Conceptually, the Greenfield method and multiperiod excess earnings method accomplish the same objective. The Greenfield method is not commonly used to value IPR&D assets.

---

[9] The task force cannot point to any specific examples of using real options analysis for the valuation of IPR&D assets in financial reporting, even though the nature of this methodology also theoretically would lend itself well to the valuation of IPR&D assets. For information on the real options method, readers may refer to the following publications: AICPA Guide *Valuation of Privately-Held-Company Equity Securities Issued as Compensation* (see appendix G, "Real Options"); Thomas E. Copeland and Vladimir Antikarov, *Real Options, Revised Edition: A Practitioner's Guide* (London, UK: Texere, 2003); Martha Amram and Nalin Kulatilaka, *Real Options: Managing Strategic Investment in an Uncertain World* (Boston: Harvard University Press, 1999); Johnathan Mun, *Real Options Analysis: Tools and Techniques for Valuing Strategic Investments and Decisions* (Hoboken, New Jersey: John Wiley & Sons, Inc., 2002); and Timothy Luehrman, *Investment Opportunities as Real Options: Getting Started on the Numbers* (*Harvard Business Review*, July 1998).

[10] Manufacturing costs savings is a part of the broader cost savings method. However, the task force believes that research and development activities would be mainly focused on applying technology to saving costs in the manufacturing process.

Chapter 2

Definition of and Accounting for Assets Acquired in a Business Combination That Are to Be Used in Research and Development Activities

Introduction

2.01 This chapter sets forth what the IPR&D Task Force (task force) believes are best practices in defining assets acquired in a business combination that are to be used in research and development (R&D) activities, including specific in-process R&D (IPR&D) projects, for purposes of applying Financial Accounting Standards Board (FASB) *Accounting Standards Codification* (ASC) 805, *Business Combinations*. The task force notes that business combinations involving the software, electronic devices, and pharmaceutical industries have traditionally exhibited the greatest proportional amount (in terms of total value) of assets acquired to be used in R&D activities. Accordingly, this guide focuses on those industries.

2.02 This chapter's "Introduction" and "Key Concepts" sections are supplemented by the "Explanatory Comments" section, which expands on the discussion and sets forth the task force's support for the determination of best practices. In addition, this chapter includes questions, and the task force's answers, which are intended to aid in the application of the best practices.

2.03 In this guide, an R&D project that has not yet been completed is referred to as an *IPR&D project*. Intangible assets that are to be used or are used in R&D activities, including specific IPR&D projects, are referred to as *IPR&D assets*. In other words, an IPR&D project is an example of an IPR&D asset. However, in some cases, an IPR&D project may comprise several IPR&D assets. In this chapter, unless indicated otherwise, the term *IPR&D asset* refers to an IPR&D asset acquired in a business combination.

2.04 FASB ASC 730-10 excludes from its scope assets acquired in a business combination that are to be used in R&D activities. However, it sets forth broad guidelines regarding what constitutes R&D activities. FASB ASC 805-20 requires that an acquirer recognize and measure at fair value, separately from goodwill, the identifiable assets acquired in a business combination. Identifiable assets acquired that are to be used in R&D activities are separately recognized and measured at fair value regardless of whether those assets have an alternative future use. Separately identifiable assets include both tangible and intangible assets, including intangible assets representing specific IPR&D projects to be pursued by the reporting entity. The task force believes that acquired IPR&D projects must have been the result of R&D activities undertaken by the acquired business, the costs of which qualified as R&D costs under FASB ASC 730-10.

2.05 The following diagram illustrates an overall description of assets acquired in a business combination. This guide provides guidance on the assets that are *italicized* and in **bold type**. See the "Used in R&D Activities Criteria" section in paragraphs 2.08–.10 for further discussion.

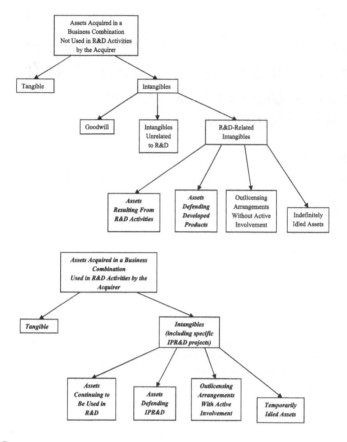

Key Concepts

Recognition of Assets Acquired in a Business Combination

Asset Recognition Criteria

2.06 Based on guidance in paragraphs 1–3 of FASB ASC 805-20-25, to qualify for recognition as part of applying the acquisition method

- assets acquired (and liabilities assumed) in a business combination must meet the definition of an asset (and liability) in FASB Concepts Statement No. 6, *Elements of Financial Statements*,[1] at the acquisition date.

- assets acquired (and liabilities assumed) must be part of what the acquirer and the acquiree (or its former owners) exchanged in the business combination transaction rather than the result of

---

[1] It should be noted that the Financial Accounting Standards Board (FASB) Concepts Statements were not codified. However, the IPR&D Task Force (task force) believes that FASB Concepts Statement No. 6, *Elements of Financial Statements*, provides relevant guidance and, therefore, included references to it in this guide. The FASB Concepts Statements are available at www.fasb.org/jsp/FASB/Page/SectionPage&cid=1176156317989.

separate transactions. (Refer to paragraphs 20–22 of FASB ASC 805-10-25 for additional guidance.)[2]

- an asset must be identifiable.

2.07 According to the FASB ASC glossary, an asset is *identifiable* if it meets either of the following criteria:

> *a.* It is separable, that is, capable of being separated or divided from the entity and sold, transferred, licensed, rented, or exchanged, either individually or together with a related contract, identifiable asset, or liability, regardless of whether the entity intends to do so.
>
> *b.* It arises from contractual or other legal rights, regardless of whether those rights are transferable or separable from the entity or from other rights and obligations.

Used in R&D Activities Criteria

2.08 The task force believes that an asset acquired in a business combination that is to be "used in R&D activities" by the acquirer is distinguishable from other acquired assets because the acquirer has specifically identified an IPR&D project that is expected to incur R&D costs within the scope of FASB ASC 730-10 that will use the acquired asset. As discussed further in paragraph 2.39, paragraphs 3–5 of FASB ASC 730-10-15 set forth broad guidelines on the activities whose costs are and are not to be classified as R&D. Although the use of the asset need not necessarily be limited to identified IPR&D projects, its use in, or contribution to, identified R&D projects should be more than minor. The exclusion of an IPR&D project from future spending plans for R&D or internal lists of projects on which the company is actively working are examples of factors that may indicate that a company is not planning to use the acquired intangible asset in R&D activities.

2.09 The task force observed that it would not be appropriate to characterize goodwill (or elements of acquired value ascribed to goodwill) as "assets used in R&D activities."

2.10 The task force has considered the following categories of intangible assets acquired in a business combination in connection with the "used in R&D activities" criteria:

- *R&D efforts of acquiree to be continued by the acquirer.* These assets represent R&D acquired in a business combination that will continue to be actively pursued by the acquirer in its ongoing R&D activities. Such assets would clearly be considered "used in R&D activities."

- *Defensive.* If the reporting entity intends to hold (or lock up) an acquired intangible asset to prevent others from obtaining access to the asset in order to "defend" the value of other intangible assets used in R&D activities, the task force believes that such asset would be considered "used in R&D activities." This is because such asset will be used in R&D activities indirectly by defending assets that the reporting entity utilizes in its R&D activities.

---

[2] When evaluating whether an individual transaction is a part of a business combination, it may also be helpful to consider guidance in FASB *Accounting Standards Codification* (ASC) 810-10-40-6. This paragraph discusses whether multiple arrangements should be accounted for as a single transaction as it relates to a parent ceasing to have a controlling financial interest in a subsidiary.

However, if an acquired intangible asset will be defending a developed product, the task force believes that such asset would not be considered "used in R&D activities" because it will not be associated with R&D. (See the "Defensive IPR&D Assets" section in paragraphs 2.29–.33 for further discussion of defensive assets.)

- *Outlicensed.* If the reporting entity intends to outlicense an acquired intangible asset (or acquires an already outlicensed intangible asset) but plans to play an active role[3] in the development of the outlicensed asset (for example, under a *collaborative arrangement* with another party), the task force believes that such asset would be considered "used in R&D activities." This is because the reporting entity will use the acquired asset in its R&D activities jointly with another party.

  However, the task force believes that if the reporting entity intends to outlicense an acquired intangible asset and does not plan to be actively involved in its development, then such asset would not be considered "used in R&D activities." If such *outlicensing arrangement* was in place at the time of business combination, the outlicensed asset would not be considered "used in R&D activities;" it would be considered a contract-based intangible asset, provided it meets the recognition criteria described in the "Asset Recognition Criteria" section in paragraphs 2.06–.07. (See the "Outlicensing Arrangements" section in paragraphs 4.30–.31 for further discussion of these arrangements.)

- *Idled.* Even though both idled and defensive assets are not actively used by the reporting entity, idled assets are different from defensive assets. The difference between these two asset categories is the value, or lack thereof, resulting from the reporting entity's decision not to actively use the asset. Although the reporting entity derives value from defensive assets because they "defend" the value of its other assets, idled assets do not contribute to an increase (or maintenance) in the value of the reporting entity's other assets.

  Although FASB ASC 360, *Property, Plant, and Equipment*, is applicable to long-lived assets, the task force believes that it may be helpful to consider this guidance when assessing whether an acquired intangible asset will be used in R&D activities. With respect to acquired intangible assets that the reporting entity plans

---

[3] Paragraphs 8–9 of FASB ASC 808-10-15 provide the following guidance on what constitutes *active involvement*:

    15-8   Whether the parties in a collaborative arrangement are active participants will depend on the facts and circumstances specific to the arrangement. Examples of situations that may evidence active participation of the parties in a collaborative arrangement include, but are not limited to, the following:

        a.   Directing and carrying out the activities of the joint operating activity

        b.   Participating on a steering committee or other oversight or governance mechanism

        c.   Holding a contractual or other legal right to the underlying intellectual property

    15-9   An entity that solely provides financial resources to an endeavor is generally not an active participant in a collaborative arrangement within the scope of [FASB ASC 808, *Collaborative Arrangements*.]

to idle indefinitely, the task force believes that such assets would not be considered "used in R&D activities." The task force believes that this view is consistent with guidance on long-lived assets in FASB ASC 360-10-35-47, which states that "a long-lived asset to be abandoned is disposed of when it ceases to be used." See paragraph 2.35 for further discussion.

With respect to assets that the reporting entity plans to temporarily idle, the task force believes that such assets could be considered "used in R&D activities." Furthermore, the task force believes that this view is supportable by guidance in FASB ASC 350-30-35-17A, which states that "[c]onsistent with the guidance in paragraph 360-10-35-49, intangible assets acquired in business combination that have been temporarily idled shall not be accounted for as if abandoned."

R&D-Related Intangibles Not Used in R&D Activities

2.11 Acquired intangible assets that will not be "used in R&D activities" by the acquirer are not subject to guidance in FASB ASC 350-30-35-17A, which provides that intangible assets acquired in a business combination that are used in R&D activities (regardless of whether they have an alternative future use) are capitalized and classified as indefinite-lived until the completion or abandonment of the associated R&D efforts. Such assets should be accounted for in accordance with other applicable accounting principles generally accepted in the United States of America (GAAP). These assets would first need to be evaluated against the recognition criteria described in the "Asset Recognition Criteria" section in paragraphs 2.06–.07. For those assets that meet the recognition criteria, the reporting entity would need to determine their useful life in accordance with guidance in paragraphs 1–5 of FASB ASC 350-30-35. Please refer to FASB ASC 350-30 for further guidance because such assets are outside of the scope of this guide.

2.12 Once R&D activities produce an asset that is complete (for example, a software program released for sale), such asset represents an *asset resulting from R&D activities*. Once an IPR&D project has been completed, it also represents an asset resulting from R&D activities. An asset resulting from R&D activities can potentially be used in R&D activities in other ways, but the asset itself is complete, and there is no more substantive work to be performed to finish it.

2.13 In a business combination, it is important to distinguish acquired intangible assets *used in* R&D activities (that is, IPR&D assets) from acquired intangible assets *resulting from* R&D activities because assets resulting from R&D activities are generally evaluated as acquired intangible assets that, unlike IPR&D assets acquired in a business combination, are not defined by the authoritative literature to have an indefinite life. (See the "Completed Intangible Assets Used in R&D Activities" section in paragraphs 2.36–.37 for further discussion.)

Questions and Answers—Recognition of IPR&D Assets Acquired in a Business Combination

2.14 *Question 1:* Company A acquired Company T in a business combination. Prior to the date of the acquisition, Company T had entered into a licensing arrangement with Company L. Pursuant to the terms of the license,

Company T acquired rights related to a drug candidate that had been patented by Company L. At the time of Company T's license, the drug candidate had not yet been approved for marketing. Under the terms of the license, Company T acquired all of the rights to develop, manufacture, and sell the drug candidate. In exchange for these rights, Company T made a payment at the inception of the agreement and is obligated to make additional payments if certain substantive milestones are achieved (for example, initiation of phase III clinical trials), as well as royalties based on a percentage of sales of the drug if it is approved for marketing. Should the milestone and royalty payments be considered elements of the acquired contract-based intangible or a separate unit of account?

Answer: Provided that separation is not required by accounting literature, the milestone and royalty obligations may be considered elements of the acquired contract-based intangible, rather than a separate unit of account. In determining the fair value of this contract-based intangible asset, Company A will most likely use an income approach, such as a discounted cash flow method, that will consider all the anticipated cash flows associated with this contract that a market participant would consider. Accordingly, in addition to the anticipated development costs, revenues, cost of product, commercialization costs, and other cash flows, Company A would also consider the anticipated milestones and royalties and, if necessary, would adjust the cash flows to reflect market participant assumptions. The milestone and royalty obligations would, therefore, reduce the fair value of the licensed IPR&D asset.

2.15 *Question 2:* Company T acquired Company L in a business combination. At the acquisition date, Company L was developing a patented drug candidate, which Company T recorded as an IPR&D asset. The terms of the acquisition agreement required Company T to make a cash payment at the acquisition date, as well as additional cash payments to the former shareholders of Company L if certain substantive milestones were achieved in the future relating to the acquired drug candidate (for example, initiation of phase III clinical trials). Company T accounted for the contingent milestone payments as contingent consideration and, therefore, recorded a contingent consideration liability at fair value at the acquisition date. Company A subsequently acquired Company T in a business combination. At the time of the acquisition, none of the milestones had been achieved. Company A recorded the IPR&D asset relating to the patented drug candidate that was previously recorded by Company T at fair value at the acquisition date. When determining the fair value of the IPR&D asset, should Company A consider the preexisting contingent consideration arrangement as an element of the IPR&D asset or as a separate unit of account?

Answer: Because FASB ASC 805 requires contingent consideration arrangements of an acquiree that have been assumed by the acquirer in a business combination to be separately recognized, Company A should treat the preexisting contingent consideration arrangement as a separate unit of account. Thus, when determining the fair value of the IPR&D asset, Company A should not include the future milestone payments in the discounted cash flow analysis to avoid double-counting.

Attributes of an Acquired IPR&D Project

2.16 FASB concluded in FASB Statement No. 141(R), *Business Combinations,* that an acquired IPR&D project will generally satisfy the definition of an asset because the observable exchange at the acquisition date provides evidence that the parties to the exchange expect future economic benefits to result from that R&D.[4] Additionally, the task force believes that an acquired IPR&D project will commonly be identifiable.

2.17 In addition to satisfying the general recognition criteria applicable to each asset acquired in a business combination that is to be used in R&D activities, if the asset to be used in R&D activities is a specific IPR&D project, the task force believes that there should also be persuasive evidence that each of the acquired IPR&D projects has substance and is incomplete.

- *Substance*—For a specific IPR&D project of an acquired company to give rise initially to an asset, the acquired company must have performed R&D activities that constitute more than insignificant efforts and that

    — meet the definition of R&D under FASB ASC 730-10 and

    — result in the creation of value.

- *Incompleteness*—Incompleteness means there are remaining risks (for example, technological or engineering) or certain remaining regulatory approvals at the date of acquisition. Overcoming those risks or obtaining the approvals requires that additional R&D costs are expected to be incurred.

Unit of Account

2.18 The task force discussed at length the manner in which assets acquired in a business combination that are to be used in R&D activities are to be recognized (that is, how the unit of account to record those assets is to be determined). The task force does not believe that it would be appropriate to combine into a single unit of account tangible assets used in R&D activities with intangible assets used in R&D activities. Similarly, the task force does not believe that it would be appropriate to combine into a single unit of account a finite-lived intangible asset and an indefinite-lived intangible asset. As a result, the task force's views expressed in this section are limited to intangible assets acquired in a business combination that are to be used in R&D activities (that is, IPR&D assets) and whether it is appropriate to combine such assets into a single unit of account.

2.19 Although not referenced explicitly in FASB ASC 805, consistent with the manner in which other identifiable intangible assets are recognized, the task force believes that the definition of identifiable in the FASB ASC glossary should be considered when determining the unit of account for IPR&D assets. However, the task force believes that the application of the concept of identifiable should not result in a unit of account that is so disaggregated that the cost of recognizing, measuring, and maintaining assets at that level exceeds the benefits of such a disaggregated unit of account.

2.20 In practice, separately identifiable IPR&D assets that share similar characteristics are sometimes aggregated into a single unit of account because they are considered to be substantially the same. The determination of unit of

---

[4] FASB Statement No. 141(R), *Business Combinations*, was codified in FASB ASC 805, *Business Combinations*. This explanation is provided in paragraph B152 of FASB Statement No. 141(R), which was part of the "Basis for Conclusions" section, none of which was codified in FASB ASC. However, the task force believes that paragraph B152 provides helpful guidance and, therefore, decided to incorporate it into this guide.

account will depend on the relevant facts and circumstances of each acquisition. When making that determination, the task force believes that it may be helpful to consider the factors listed subsequently. None of those factors are individually determinative. The following list is not meant to be all inclusive; there may be other factors to consider:

- The phase of development of the related IPR&D project (see the "Specific IPR&D Projects—Life Cycle" section in paragraphs 2.44–.47 for further discussion on phases of development)
- The nature of the activities and costs necessary to further develop the related IPR&D project
- The risks associated with the further development of the related IPR&D project
- The amount and timing of benefits expected to be derived in the future from the developed asset(s)
- The expected economic life of the developed asset(s)
- Whether there is an intent to manage costs for the developed asset(s) separately or on a combined basis in areas such as strategy, manufacturing, advertising, selling, and so on
- Whether the asset, whether an incomplete IPR&D project or when ultimately completed, would be transferred by itself or with other separately identifiable assets

The task force notes that determining the appropriate unit of account requires considerable judgment.

Questions and Answers—Determining the Unit of Account

2.21 *Question 1:* Company A acquired Company T in a business combination. At the acquisition date, Company T was pursuing completion of an IPR&D project that, if successful, would result in a drug for which Company A would seek regulatory approval in the United States, Europe, and Japan. What is the appropriate unit of account for this IPR&D project?

Answer: It depends. With specific regard to the acquired incomplete IPR&D project, the task force believes that the decision to recognize one IPR&D asset (representing the compound) or three IPR&D assets (representing the compound in each of the jurisdictions the compound is expected to be sold in) requires considerable judgment because it is likely "separable" as a "global" or "jurisdictional" asset. As indicated previously, the determination of unit of account will depend on the relevant facts and circumstances of each acquisition and, more specifically, the evaluation of factors identified previously.

The following factors indicate that the recording of a single (global) IPR&D asset may be appropriate:

- The IPR&D project is still in the early development phase, at which point it may be less likely to have separate units of account for different jurisdictions than in later phases of development.
- The nature of the activities and costs necessary to further develop the IPR&D project are substantially the same (for example, the development of the project will occur centrally, and Company A only intends to incur a small portion of the total development costs to obtain approval within each regulatory jurisdiction towards the later stages of testing).

- Based on historical experience (or expectations), the risks associated with the further development of the IPR&D project are substantially the same (for example, Company A believes it will likely result in approval in all three jurisdictions or none of the jurisdictions, although the timing of approval may differ).

- The amount and timing of benefits expected to be derived in the future from the developed asset(s) and the expected economic life of the developed assets are substantially the same (for example, if approved, the patent is expected to have approximately the same life in all three jurisdictions).

- Company A intends to manage strategy, manufacturing, advertising, and selling costs from the perspective of the global brand, not the individual jurisdictions where the product will be sold.

- Based on historical experience and current intentions, once completed, the compound (if ever transferred) would be transferred in one worldwide arrangement.

The following factors indicate that the recording of three separate "jurisdictional" IPR&D assets could be appropriate:[5]

- The IPR&D project is in a later phase of development (for example, the product phase for the pharmaceutical industry), and development risks associated with different jurisdictions are known.

- The nature of the activities and costs necessary to further develop the IPR&D project are not substantially the same. For example, the development of the project will occur centrally for a portion of the process; however, the extent of separate regulatory approval costs is expected to be a significant portion of the overall development cost.

- The risks associated with the further development of the IPR&D project are not substantially the same. For example, Company A believes the risks of obtaining approval in each jurisdiction is different, and they do not believe approval in one jurisdiction has relevance to other jurisdictions.

- The amount and timing of benefits expected to be derived in the future from the developed asset(s) and the expected economic life of the developed asset(s) are not substantially the same. For example, if approved, the patent life is expected to be different for each of the three jurisdictions.

- Company A intends to manage strategy, manufacturing, advertising, and selling costs separately in each jurisdiction the compound is sold in.

- Based on historical experience and current intentions, once completed, the compound (if ever transferred) would not be transferred as a single asset.

---

[5] Although in this example the unit of account determination is based on different geographic locations, the same logic can be applied to different drug indications (for example, physical ailment, disease state, treatment regime.)

There may be situations when disaggregation[6] beyond that contemplated by this example may be appropriate. However, the task force does not believe that a unit of account that is aggregated beyond the individual project (compound) level would be appropriate.

2.22 *Question 2:* Assume the same facts as in preceding question 1, except that the project has received regulatory approval in the United States but not in Japan and Europe. How many assets (units of account) should Company A recognize relative to the acquired IPR&D project?

Answer: With specific regard to the incomplete IPR&D project, one *indefinite-lived IPR&D asset* may be recognized, which would represent the IPR&D project related to the compound that may be approved in Japan and Europe.

It may also be appropriate to record two indefinite-lived IPR&D assets in this example. Each asset would represent the IPR&D project related to the compound that may be approved in each of the two remaining jurisdictions: Japan and Europe.

However, if Company A views the global compound as a single unit of account and it expects to earn in the United States a significant portion of total revenue or cash flows expected to be generated by that compound, it may conclude that it did not acquire an incomplete IPR&D project because the project has received regulatory approval in the United States. In this case, Company A would recognize an asset resulting from R&D activities and determine its useful life in accordance with guidance in paragraphs 1–5 of FASB ASC 350-30-35. It should be noted that under the "global compound" view, the task force believes that Company A acquired a single finite-lived intangible asset (that is, an asset resulting from R&D activities), as opposed to a combination of a finite-lived intangible asset (completed R&D project in the United States) and indefinite-lived intangible asset(s) (incomplete IPR&D projects in Japan and Europe.) Please refer to the "Completion and Readiness for Its Intended Use" section in paragraphs 4.33–.36 for further guidance.

2.23 *Question 3:* In a business combination, Company A acquired the worldwide exploitation rights to Internet-based access technology. The rights supported an existing specific IPR&D project to develop a product for exploitation in the United States. Company A does not have the resources to exploit the potential product in foreign countries and, therefore, it reasonably expects that it will license the exclusive rights to exploitation in countries outside the United States. How should the non-U.S. rights be recognized?

Answer: The expected license of the non-U.S. rights is an intangible asset that is identifiable and should be recognized because it meets the separability criterion in FASB ASC 805. However, this intangible asset would not meet the "used in R&D activities" criteria (discussed in the "Used in R&D Activities Criteria" section in paragraphs 2.08–.10) because Company A plans to outlicense it and does not plan to be actively involved in its development. As a result, this intangible asset would not represent an IPR&D asset. Whether this intangible asset should be recognized as one asset (all non-U.S. jurisdictions) or more than one asset may, in large measure, depend on how Company A expects to transfer that asset. Assuming that the licensing arrangement will be treated as a sale for accounting purposes, it may also be appropriate for Company A

---

[6] However, it should be noted that there are certain valuation implications associated with disaggregated unit of account. See footnote 5 in paragraph 6.50 for further discussion.

to account for the asset(s) expected to be licensed as "held for sale" asset(s), as discussed further in the "Assets Held for Sale" section in paragraph 2.28. The specific IPR&D project, with respect to the development of a product for the U.S. market, would be accounted for as an IPR&D asset in accordance with the best practices described herein.

2.24 *Question 4:* Company A acquired Company T in a business combination. At the acquisition date, Company T was pursuing completion of two IPR&D projects. One of the projects relates to the potential development of software improvements to the service delivery engine, which allows telecommunication companies the ability to provide services to mobile device subscribers. The other IPR&D project relates to the potential development of software that adds incremental features to mobile devices. Given the specific needs of telecommunication companies with respect to software to deliver their services to subscribers, the IPR&D project related to the service delivery engine is considered riskier and more time-consuming than the development of software that adds incremental features to mobile devices. In addition, the expected life of the potential software improvements to the service delivery engine is expected to be at least twice the expected life of the potential software that adds incremental features to mobile devices. How many IPR&D assets (units of account) should Company A recognize relative to the two acquired IPR&D projects?

Answer: Given this fact pattern, two separate IPR&D assets would be recognized because it would be difficult to argue that the IPR&D projects are substantially the same. One of the IPR&D projects is considered riskier and more time consuming than the other, and the expected life of the potential software from each of the projects differs.

Core Technology

2.25 In light of the current guidance under which identifiable intangible assets acquired in a business combination that are to be used in R&D activities are no longer charged to expense at acquisition and are generally assigned an indefinite life at the time of the acquisition (see the "Completed Intangible Assets Used in R&D Activities" section in paragraphs 2.36–.37 for further discussion), the task force reconsidered the original practice aid's definition of core (or base) technology and its recommendation that an acquirer identify core technology as an asset to be recognized apart from IPR&D. The original practice aid defined *core* (or *base*) *technology* as "[t]hose technical processes, intellectual property, and the institutional understanding that exist within an organization with respect to products or processes that have been completed and that will aid in the development of future products, services, or processes that will be designed in a manner to incorporate similar technologies." The task force believes that the central element of that definition of core technology is that it represents "technical processes, intellectual property, and the institutional understanding that exist within an organization . . ." The task force also believes that "technical processes, intellectual property, [and] institutional understanding"[7] each generally meet the criteria of FASB ASC 805 for separate recognition. As a result, the task force believes that it is no longer necessary

---

[7] Although institutional understanding is not generally recognized as an asset on an entity's balance sheet, it would be reflected in items, such as unpatented processes and "know-how," that would typically meet FASB ASC 805 requirements for separate recognition.

to recommend that core (or base) technology be separately recognized as an intangible asset.

2.26 As long as acquired "technical processes, intellectual property, [and] institutional understanding" are recognized and measured in accordance with FASB ASC 805, the task force believes that going forward, for new transactions, there should be no additional intangible assets (value) that would otherwise have been attributed to core technology to recognize and measure. The task force does not necessarily believe that value historically attributed to core technology should be allocated to acquired IPR&D projects only (or any other specific identifiable intangible asset). Rather, entities should perform an asset identification process by applying the recognition and measurement criteria in FASB ASC 805, as described previously. As a result, the task force believes that going forward, as it applies to new transactions, the value historically attributed to core technology will be allocated to other identifiable intangible assets, including possibly IPR&D assets. The task force's current recommendations are intended to reflect the developments in the accounting standards, which resulted in an improved understanding of asset identification and valuation.

2.27 The task force acknowledges that practice generally recognized core or base technology in periods prior to the effective date of FASB Statement No. 141(R). With respect to such past transactions, the task force does not believe that it would be appropriate to reallocate value previously assigned to core (or base) technology to other identifiable intangible assets. Rather, the task force believes that the existing core (or base) technology assets should continue to be evaluated for impairment in accordance with the applicable guidance. The task force observes that, in practice, core (or base) technology assets had generally been determined to have a finite useful life and, as such, they would be evaluated for impairment in accordance with FASB ASC 360-10. Furthermore, in situations in which an entity has to perform step 2 of the goodwill impairment test, which involves valuing all the assets and liabilities of that reporting unit (including any unrecognized intangible assets) as if the reporting unit had been acquired in a business combination, no value would be assigned to core technology. Instead, the entity would assign value to other intangible assets that would encompass the value previously recognized as core technology. Also, please refer to paragraphs 6.51–.70, which discuss concepts of *enabling technology* and *technology migration* and the relationship between core (or base) technology and enabling technology.

Assets Held for Sale

2.28 As described in FASB ASC 360-10-45-12, an acquirer of a long-lived asset (or disposal group) may account for that asset (or disposal group) as "held for sale" if it is probable that the criteria in FASB ASC 360-10-45-9 will be met shortly after acquisition. A long-lived asset (or disposal group) that is newly acquired and classified as held for sale is measured at fair value less cost to sell at the acquisition date. As a consequence, it is an exception to general measurement principles within FASB ASC 805. However, as indicated in FASB ASC 820-10-15-1, measurements based on fair value, such as fair value less cost to sell, are within the scope of FASB ASC 820, *Fair Value Measurement*, and, therefore, subject to its measurement and disclosure requirements. It may be acceptable to account for an indefinite-lived intangible asset as held for sale, as long as the criteria in FASB ASC 360-10-45-9 are satisfied.

Defensive IPR&D Assets

2.29 Sometimes, an entity will acquire in a business combination an IPR&D asset that the acquirer intends to hold (or lock up) to prevent others from obtaining access to the asset in order to "defend" the value of other IPR&D assets or developed products.

2.30 Intangible assets that the acquirer does not intend to actively use but intends to hold (or lock up) to prevent others from obtaining access to the assets are generally described as being *defensive intangible assets*, the accounting for which is prescribed by paragraphs 5A–5B in FASB ASC 350-30-35. However, IPR&D assets are specifically scoped out from this guidance.

2.31 As discussed in paragraph 2.10, if the reporting entity intends to hold (or lock up) an acquired intangible asset to prevent others from obtaining access to the asset in order to "defend" the value of other intangible assets used in R&D activities, the task force believes that such asset would be considered "used in R&D activities." Therefore, in accordance with guidance in FASB ASC 350-30-35-17A, the task force recommends that such assets be assigned an indefinite life until the "defended" IPR&D project is completed or abandoned.

2.32 Acquired intangible assets that defend developed products would not be considered "used in R&D activities" because they will not be associated with R&D (see the "Used in R&D Activities Criteria" section in paragraphs 2.08–.10 for further discussion). As a result, these assets would be within the scope of guidance in FASB ASC 350-30-35-5A, which provides that "[a] defensive intangible asset shall be assigned a useful life that reflects the entity's consumption of the expected benefits related to that asset." As indicated in FASB ASC 350-30-35-5B, "[i]t would be rare for a defensive intangible asset to have an indefinite life because the fair value of the defensive intangible asset will generally diminish over time as a result of a lack of market exposure or as a result of competitive or other factors."

Questions and Answers—Defensive IPR&D Assets

2.33 *Question 1:* Company A acquires Company T. At the time of the acquisition, Company T owns patented technology and know-how that is in development and, if successfully completed, would compete with a technology under development by Company A. Company A does not intend to pursue further development of the patented technology and know-how of Company T. Rather, it will hold it to "protect" the value of the technology under development by Company A. What depreciable (accounting) life should Company A assign to the patented technology and know-how of Company T?

Answer: In such an instance, Company A may assign an indefinite life to the acquired patented technology and know-how at the time of acquisition. Company A would begin amortizing the acquired asset(s) once it had completed the development of its technology or, if the development efforts were abandoned, it would expense the carrying amount of the acquired technology in the period of abandonment unless the acquirer intended to develop the acquired technology in the event the development of the existing technology is unsuccessful. It should be noted that although Company A acquired and held the patented technology and know-how for defensive purposes, Company A would need to continue to evaluate the acquired asset(s) for impairment during the period it was developing its own patented technology and know-how.

Temporarily Idled or Abandoned Assets

2.34 There may also be situations in which an acquirer obtains control of a business that is pursuing numerous IPR&D projects or owns a great number of IPR&D assets (such as unpatented technology and know-how), or both, that the acquirer either does not need or does not intend to use further. The task force does not believe that it would be appropriate to write off the fair value of those assets through income on the acquisition date.

2.35 The task force observes that an entity may acquire an identifiable intangible asset that is attributable to an IPR&D project that it does not plan to pursue further development of, but which the acquirer may not expect to derive defensive value from, nor does it expect to subsequently sell, license, or rent the intangible asset. Intangible assets with these characteristics are not the primary asset acquired or a basis for the acquisition of the business. It may take a period of time for the acquirer to determine what it might ultimately do with these assets. In order to conclude that such an acquired intangible asset is not a defensive intangible asset, the task force notes that the acquirer would need to be able to conclude that continued ownership of the asset will not contribute to an increase (or maintenance) in the value of other assets owned by it. Assuming such a conclusion is appropriate, the task force believes that such an intangible asset would not meet the "used in R&D activities" criteria (discussed in the "Used in R&D Activities Criteria" section in paragraphs 2.08–.10). However, the acquirer would need to recognize such an asset and measure it at its fair value (which might be *de minimis*) using the assumptions of a market participant. Such assets will commonly not have a significant individual fair value, but, in the aggregate, may be material to the acquirer. The task force believes that such assets should be written off when the acquirer decides not to use them in any way and deems them abandoned (that is, it will not pursue further development of those assets, will not derive defensive value from them, and will not sell, license, or rent them).[8] The task force expects that it would be uncommon to expense such intangible assets immediately upon acquisition.

Completed Intangible Assets Used in R&D Activities

2.36 FASB ASC 350-30-35-17A provides that "[i]ntangible assets acquired in a business combination or an acquisition by a not-for-profit entity that are used in research and development activities (regardless of whether they have an alternative future use) shall be considered indefinite lived until the completion or abandonment of the associated research and development efforts." There may be situations in which individually completed intangible assets are used in R&D activities. In general, the task force believes that *incompleteness*, as further described in the "Specific IPR&D Projects—Incompleteness" section in paragraphs 2.54–.63, is an essential characteristic of IPR&D assets. Therefore, the task force believes that intangible assets used in R&D activities lacking that characteristic (that is, assets that are complete) that are being used the way they are intended to be used would not be considered IPR&D assets and should be accounted for in accordance with their nature, whereas intangible assets that are incomplete and used in R&D activities should be accounted for

---

[8] If such a decision is made close to the acquisition date, the task force recommends that the reporting entity reassesses market participant assumptions used to measure the asset's acquisition date fair value and considers whether those assumptions are still appropriate in light of the entity's decision not to use the asset. Also see question 3 in paragraph 2.67 for further discussion.

in accordance with FASB ASC 350-30-35-17A (that is, assigned an indefinite useful life upon acquisition). For example:

- Assume Company A acquires Company T. Company T owns a patent of intellectual property used in the production of integrated circuits based on 45 nanometer transistors. Company T uses that intellectual property in the production and sale of integrated circuits to its customers. Company T is also using that intellectual property in certain ongoing R&D activities. Company A expects to continue to use the intellectual property in identified *future R&D* activities. The task force believes that the acquired patent is not an IPR&D asset because it represents a completed asset that is being used the way it is intended to be used. The fact that the patent is also being used in certain ongoing R&D activities and will be used in identified future R&D activities does not necessarily mean the patent itself should be characterized as an IPR&D asset and automatically assigned an indefinite useful life. In this example, Company A would not assign the acquired patent an indefinite life upon acquisition because a patent has a finite legal life (also see paragraph 2.37 that discusses a situation in which a patent that is used exclusively in an IPR&D project may be encompassed within an indefinite-lived IPR&D asset.)

- Assume Company A, a pharmaceutical company, acquired Company T in a business combination. Company T's assets include a library of molecules for high-throughput screening of drug candidates. Company T is using portions of the library in its existing specific IPR&D projects, and it is reasonably expected that other portions will be used in currently identified future projects. The task force believes that the acquired library of molecules is not an IPR&D asset because the library is a tool that is completed and is being used the way it is intended to be used (that is, in R&D activities). In this example, Company A would not assign the acquired library of molecules an indefinite life upon acquisition because the library may be reasonably expected to produce economic benefits for a finite period of time (see paragraph 3.29 for an explanation about why the library would be assigned a finite useful life).

2.37   However, the task force believes that to the extent that individually completed intangible assets are solely and directly related to IPR&D projects that are still in development (for example, in the pharmaceutical industry, a patent on a compound that has not yet been approved), such assets may be aggregated with other intangible assets used in R&D activities. That is, an acquirer would recognize one asset for each IPR&D project, which would comprise all the intangible assets used exclusively in that project, and that asset would be assigned an indefinite useful life.

Tangible Assets Used in R&D Activities

2.38   Acquired tangible assets to be used in R&D activities (for example, computer-testing equipment used in an R&D department) should be recognized and measured at their fair value. After initial recognition, acquired tangible assets that are used in R&D activities are accounted for in accordance with their nature.

Explanatory Comments

Scope of R&D Activities

2.39 Paragraphs 3–5 of FASB ASC 730-10-15 set forth broad guidelines on the activities whose costs are and are not to be classified as R&D. Paragraphs 1–2 of FASB ASC 730-10-55 identify activities that are and are not within the FASB ASC definition of R&D activities. Although FASB ASC 730-10-15-4(f) explicitly excludes "research and development assets acquired in a business combination" from the scope of FASB ASC 730-10, the examples provided in FASB ASC 730-10-55 may be useful when determining whether an activity in a business combination is typically considered R&D. These paragraphs are reproduced as follows:

55-1. The following activities typically would be considered [R&D]...:

    a. Laboratory research aimed at discovery of new knowledge

    b. Searching for applications of new research findings or other knowledge

    c. Conceptual formulation and design of possible product or process alternatives

    d. Testing in search for or evaluation of product or process alternatives

    e. Modification of the formulation or design of a product or process

    f. Design, construction, and testing of preproduction prototypes and models

    g. Design of tools, jigs, molds, and dies involving new technology

    h. Design, construction, and operation of a pilot plant that is not of a scale economically feasible to the entity for commercial production

    i. Engineering activity required to advance the design of a product to the point that it meets specific functional and economic requirements and is ready for manufacture

    j. Design and development of tools used to facilitate research and development or components of a product or process that are undergoing research and development activities.

55-2. The following activities typically would not be considered [R&D]...:

    a. Engineering follow-through in an early phase of commercial production

    b. Quality control during commercial production including routine testing of products

    c. Trouble-shooting in connection with break-downs during commercial production

    d. Routine, ongoing efforts to refine, enrich, or otherwise improve upon the qualities of an existing product

    e. Adaptation of an existing capability to a particular requirement or customer's need as part of a continuing commercial activity

   f. Seasonal or other periodic design changes to existing products

   g. Routine design of tools, jigs, molds, and dies

   h. Activity, including design and construction engineering, related to the construction, relocation, rearrangement, or start-up of facilities or equipment other than the following:

      1. Pilot plants (see [h] in [FASB ASC 730-10-55-1])

      2. Facilities or equipment whose sole use is for a particular research and development project...

   i. Legal work in connection with patent applications or litigation, and the sale or licensing of patents.

2.40 However, it should be noted that, in a business combination, certain activities that may qualify as R&D activities based on the preceding guidance may not ultimately be classified as IPR&D assets. This is because an asset acquired in a business combination has to meet a number of criteria in order for it to be recognized as an IPR&D asset. See paragraphs 2.06–.15 for further discussion.

Questions and Answers — Scope of R&D Activities

2.41 *Question 1:* Company A acquired Company T in a business combination. Company T produces a personal financial management software package and currently is marketing Version 4.2 of that product. Company T provides periodic updates to its customers who have subscribed to postcontract customer support. At the acquisition date, development of Version 4.3 was underway and was approximately 60 percent complete. Version 4.3 will correct programming errors (bug fixes) and provide minor improvements that do not extend the life or improve significantly the marketability of the personal financial management software. Do the efforts to develop Version 4.3 meet the scope requirements of R&D activities?

Answer: No. FASB ASC 730-10-55-2 provides examples of activities that typically are excluded from its definition of R&D. When describing activities that are not typically R&D, FASB ASC 730-10-55-2(d) says that "routine, on-going efforts to refine, enrich, or otherwise improve upon the qualities of an existing product" do not meet the definition of R&D. The activities described with respect to the development of Version 4.3 fall within the type of activities described in FASB ASC 730-10-55-2(d) and, therefore, are not R&D activities. The fair value of Version 4.2 should reflect the improvements made through the efforts to develop Version 4.3 and would be recognized as an intangible asset, provided the asset meets the criteria of being identifiable as defined in the FASB ASC glossary for separate recognition apart from goodwill. In contrast, the task force believes that efforts to develop an upgrade or enhancement to an existing product that is intended to extend the life or improve significantly the marketability of the original product would generally meet the definition of R&D activities.

2.42 *Question 2:* Company A acquired Company T, a telecommunications company, in a business combination. At the acquisition date, Company T was developing new software to run its switches that are necessary for various telephone services (for example, voice mail and call forwarding) that it provides to its customers. Company T does not plan to sell, license, or otherwise market the software under development; rather, Company T plans to use the software internally to help provide the telephone services to its customers. Company A decided that the reporting entity would continue the development of the new software. Do the efforts to develop the new software meet the scope requirements of an IPR&D project?

Answer: No. To qualify as an IPR&D project, the activities and costs should be R&D, as described in FASB ASC 730-10. FASB ASC 350-40 provides that the costs related to the development of the new software that will be used internally are not R&D costs (unless it is a pilot project or the software will be used in a R&D project). In that case, the internal-use software project should be initially recognized and measured at fair value (provided the asset meets the criteria of being *identifiable* as defined in the FASB ASC glossary for separate recognition apart from goodwill) and subsequently accounted for in accordance with the provisions of FASB ASC 350-40. However, if Company T also was engaged in licensing software as an element of its switching equipment and had a substantive plan in existence or under development to externally market the new software under development and Company A intended to carry through on that plan, the activities and costs of the new software under development would qualify as R&D in accordance with FASB ASC 730-10, and the software development project would meet the scope requirements of an IPR&D project. Costs of that project incurred subsequent to the consummation of the business combination would be accounted for in accordance with the provisions of FASB ASC 985-20.

2.43 *Question 3:* Company A acquired Company T in a business combination. Company T produces a well-known cardiovascular product to treat hypertension. Company T has been working on a process change to increase its production yields and create more efficiency in its manufacturing process. The process change is significant and considered to be nonroutine. U.S. Food and Drug Administration (FDA) approval of the process change is required due to the nature of the expected change, and the approval had not been obtained at the acquisition date. Do the efforts to develop the process change meet the scope requirements of R&D activities?

Answer: Yes. FASB ASC 730-10-55-1 provides examples of activities that typically would be considered R&D activities. The task force believes that because FDA approval of the process change is required, the process modifications fall within the example in FASB ASC 730-10-55-1(e), which specifically addresses modification of the formulation or design of a product or process.

Specific IPR&D Projects—Life Cycle

2.44 R&D projects are managed in a variety of ways and, as a result, it is not always clear when a specific project has substance or whether it has been completed. One way to view an R&D project is to consider it as having a life cycle, which in a basic form, might consist of four phases, depicted as follows:

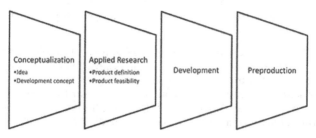

2.45 Within the earlier phases, the attribute of substance gradually evolves to the point at which it can be demonstrated; within the later phases, the project reaches a point at which it is no longer considered incomplete. Those four phases (more than one of which may be occurring simultaneously) are as follows:

- *a. Conceptualization.* This phase entails coming up with an idea, thought, new knowledge, or plan for a new product, service, or process, or for a significant improvement to an existing product, service, or process, or it may represent a decision by a company to focus its research activities within certain core competencies. Management might make an initial assessment of the potential market, cost, and technical issues for ideas, thoughts, or plans to determine whether the ideas can be developed to produce an economic benefit.

- *b. Applied Research.* This phase represents a planned search or critical investigation aimed at the discovery of additional knowledge in hopes that it will be useful in defining a new product, service, or process that will yield economic benefits, or significantly improve an existing product, service, or process that will yield economic benefits. In addition, work during this phase assesses the feasibility of successfully completing the project and the commercial viability of the resulting expected product, service, or process.

- *c. Development.* This phase represents the translation of research findings or other knowledge into a detailed plan or design for a new product, service, or process, or for a significant improvement to an existing product, service, or process, and carrying out development efforts pursuant to the plan.

- *d. Preproduction.* This phase represents the business activities necessary to commercialize the asset resulting from R&D activities for the entity's economic benefit.

2.46 Managers of the R&D project may require, at various points (or gates) during the life cycle, an evaluation of the probability of success and the potential economic results. At each of those points in time, a decision may be made about whether to continue funding the project. (See exhibit 2-1, "Phases of Development in the Pharmaceutical Industry," for a further description of phases that are particular to the pharmaceutical industry in the United States.)

2.47 The data (reflecting all of the relevant facts and circumstances) will influence the R&D project manager's decision to continue development efforts; that same data would be used when evaluating the R&D project for substance. A very low probability of success, combined with comparatively small expected positive net cash in-flows, may indicate that R&D project has not progressed to the level where it would have substance. Conversely, a high probability of success, combined with comparatively large expected positive net cash in-flows, very likely indicates substance. Facts and circumstances in between those extremes will present the greatest difficulty and will require the careful application of professional judgment. Factors influencing that judgment are discussed further in the next section.

Specific IPR&D Projects—Substance

2.48 A future product, service, or process is defined, and its potential economic benefits are identified at some point within the life cycle after the project's conceptualization. After the time that a future product, service, or process has been defined and its potential economic benefits have been identified, a specific IPR&D project begins to demonstrate substance. This generally occurs when more than insignificant R&D efforts have been expended after the characteristics of the future product, service, or process have been defined. In contrast, if the acquired company has only articulated a concept, this does not constitute substantive activities.

2.49 Factors that may demonstrate that a specific IPR&D project has substance include whether management has

- acquired the business to obtain the project, or the project constituted a significant part of the business acquired.

- considered the impact of potential competition and other factors (that is, existing patents that would block plans for further development and commercialization) on the potential economic benefits of the project.

- approved continued project funding.

- been able to make reasonably reliable estimates of the project's completion date.

- been able to make reasonably reliable estimates of costs to complete.

2.50 In many circumstances, there will be written evidence of the specific IPR&D project's economic and technical objectives (including identification of its technological, engineering, and regulatory risks) in the acquired company's records. In addition, there will be periodic contemporaneously prepared evidence of the progress being made as the specific IPR&D project evolves to completion. That data will aid in verifying that the acquired IPR&D project had substance at the acquisition date.

Questions and Answers—Substance

2.51 *Question 1:* Company A, a pharmaceutical company, acquired Company T, a biotechnology company engaged in cancer R&D, in a business combination. Company T is developing a small molecule compound that is thought to have a therapeutic application in the cancer market. The company has incurred R&D costs in (*a*) screening approximately 5,000 compounds, (*b*) identifying a lead compound, and (*c*) determining that the lead compound has the desired effect on the biological target (a part of the body, such as a protein, receptor, or gene, or something foreign to the body, such as a bacteria or virus, that appears to play an important role in causing certain diseases), whose function is understood and has been validated. (See exhibit 2-1 for a further description of phases that are particular to the pharmaceutical industry in the United States.) The lead compound is considered a potential drug development candidate, and Company T has gathered sufficient scientific data to decide to advance this compound to phase I clinical testing (that is, testing in humans). Based on Company T's understanding of the biological target's function and scientific data available in the public domain, Company T is able to make some general predictions on potential therapeutic benefits in treating several types of cancer and side effects of the compound, if successful. The activities already undertaken by Company T have resulted in its reporting R&D expenses. A multitumor cancer drug represents a significant market opportunity. Although no detailed market research has been conducted, market projections have been prepared based on patient population and cancer incidence rates. Patent searches have been completed with no findings of any patents that would block Company T's plans for further development and commercialization of the compound. In addition, Company T has filed for patent protection of this compound. Have sufficient R&D activities been undertaken for this small molecule program such that at the acquisition date, the acquired IPR&D project has substance?

Answer: Yes. The compound that may lead to a possible drug development candidate has progressed far enough through the R&D life cycle to have substance. Company T has selected a specific biological target whose function is understood and has been well validated. Company T has determined that the lead compound has the desired effect on the biological target and does not interact with other tissues in the body. Consequently, it is reasonable to anticipate that this compound may lead to a drug for treating cancer. Company T has gathered enough scientific data to decide to advance this compound to phase I clinical testing. Market potential can be reasonably estimated because incidence of cancer by tumor type is well documented and tracked by several reputable independent organizations. Market share for a particular compound can be estimated by reviewing data currently available in the public domain that tracks patented programs by biologic target from preclinical testing through market launch. Thus, Company T can determine the number of competitors conducting research on a particular biologic target and estimate the potential order of entry, given the competitors' stages of development. When evaluating whether the acquired IPR&D project has substance, Company T would also need to consider other factors enumerated in paragraph 2.49 and other relevant circumstances.

2.52 *Question 2:* Company A acquired Company T in a business combination. Company T designs and markets switches for sale to telecom companies, which use the switches to route telephone communications through their systems. Company T developed a routing technology for a switch that it believes will be pivotal in creating the next generation of switches to route Internet and video data over telephone systems (that is, it had completed the conceptualization and applied research phases of the project). Before the acquisition, Company T had surveyed several telecom companies to assist in designing the specifications of the proposed switch. In addition, Company T had a documented plan for development of the switches, which it expected would be complete in 18 months. As of the date of the acquisition, the development of the switches was underway. Have sufficient R&D activities been undertaken such that, at the date of acquisition, the specific IPR&D project has substance?

Answer: Yes. As of the date of the acquisition, Company T had completed the conceptualization and applied research phases of the project and was partially through development of the new switch. As a result, the project satisfied the attribute of substance.

2.53 *Question 3:* Company A acquired Company T in a business combination. Company T was an established contract manufacturer of electronic components. An important aspect of its manufacturing process involved the extrusion of copper wire into extremely fine strands. The R&D department of Company T had targeted improvements in this aspect of the manufacturing process as one of its top priorities. The basic objective of such a project would involve significant improvements to the current process that would further reduce the diameter of the copper strands without significantly increasing manufacturing costs (for example, through lower yields of acceptable material or increased consumption of energy and indirect materials). As of the date of the acquisition, Company T's R&D personnel had begun studying possible technological improvements to the extrusion process by researching relevant technical and academic material that was in the public domain. Company T's R&D personnel also had conducted an all-day brainstorming session in which a number of theoretical approaches were debated. As a result of that meeting, a consensus on the most promising approach had been identified, and a project plan was being drafted that would define expected timing, resource requirements, and key technical issues of the R&D project. Company T personnel were excited about the novel approach and believed that the project had a fairly high likelihood of ultimate success. Have sufficient R&D activities been undertaken such that, at the acquisition date, the specific IPR&D project has substance?

Answer: No. At the date of the acquisition, Company T's R&D project had only been conceptualized. Company T had not expended a more than insignificant effort in R&D activities to advance existing knowledge and technology toward the project objective. As a result, even though the project concept was promising, the project lacked substance at the acquisition date and would not qualify to be recognized as an asset.

Specific IPR&D Projects — Incompleteness

2.54 At some point before commercialization (that is, before earning revenue), and possibly before the end of the development or preproduction stages, the task force believes that the IPR&D project is no longer considered incomplete for accounting purposes (that is, ultimate completion of the project has occurred), and an asset resulting from R&D emerges from what was previously an asset used in R&D.

2.55 The attribute of incompleteness with respect to a specific IPR&D project acquired as part of a business combination suggests that there are remaining technological or engineering risks or regulatory approvals.

2.56 Both of the following factors would need to be considered when evaluating whether activities making up a specific R&D project are incomplete at the acquisition date:

a. Whether the reporting entity expects[9] to incur more than *de minimis* future costs related to the acquired project that would qualify as R&D costs under FASB ASC 730-10

b. Whether additional steps or milestones in a specific R&D project remain for the reporting entity, such as successfully overcoming the remaining risks or obtaining regulatory approvals related to the results of the R&D activities

2.57 Examples of circumstances, which are broken out by product type, that the task force believes demonstrate that a specific R&D project is incomplete as of the date of acquisition include the following:

---

[9] An entity may choose to evaluate its expectations, but is not required to do so, by employing a probability-weighted expected cash flow method. For example, an entity may believe that it is 50-percent likely that it will obtain regulatory approval for the product derived from its research and development (R&D) efforts; if such approval is obtained, the entity does not expect further cash outflows for additional R&D activities. The same entity believes that if regulatory approval is not obtained (also a 50-percent likely outcome) that it will incur $100 of additional R&D costs. In this simple example, the entity expects to spend $50 on future R&D costs. That amount may or may not be *de minimis.*

- *Tangible products that are not subject to governmental regulations.* The acquired company's project has not reached a level of completion such that "first customer acceptance" (or a similar demonstration of completion for those products not subject to first customer acceptance) of the product has occurred. The task force notes that obtaining customer acceptance for a new product often requires a demonstration of the product's performance in relation to planned operating measurements. Therefore, obtaining first customer acceptance evidences completion of the project. Upon achieving first customer acceptance (or a similar demonstration of completion for those products not subject to first customer acceptance), the reporting entity would not incur additional costs that qualify as R&D pursuant to FASB ASC 730-10 to further develop the product.

- *Software to be sold, licensed, or otherwise marketed.* The software product is not available for general release to customers. The task force notes that the risks of successful completion of a software project are sometimes greater than for a hardware project. When formulating the guidance for completion of a specific IPR&D project for the development of software, the task force looked to the requirements of FASB ASC 985-20-25-6, which indicates that completion of a software project is not necessarily tied to technological feasibility but, rather, to availability of the product for general release to customers. However, the task force believes that if a software product has established technological feasibility but requires only minor, routine modifications prior to general release to customers, which is imminent, that such software product would generally be viewed as a completed R&D project. (See question 2 in paragraph 2.61.)

- *Pharmaceutical products and processes related to right to market or use that are subject to governmental regulations.* The acquired company's product or process has not been approved for marketing or production by the appropriate regulatory body. Approval for marketing for this purpose includes only the approval of the product to be marketed. For example, in the United States, the task force believes that only FDA approval of a product is sufficient for a project to be complete (FDA approval of a product for marketing also includes approval of the manufacturing process). Approval of the label or, when applicable, the pricing, is not necessary for the project to be complete.

2.58 There may be circumstances in which a specific IPR&D project comprises a number of subprojects that, individually, could be used by the reporting entity in a manner that would create an anticipated economic benefit. (See the "Unit of Account" section in paragraphs 2.18–.24 for further discussion.) If any of those subprojects are complete and it is anticipated that the reporting entity will derive incremental economic benefit from the discrete exploitation of those subprojects, then the fair values of the completed subprojects would represent assets resulting from R&D activities. As a consequence, the fair values of those projects would be recognized and accounted for in accordance with the provisions of FASB ASC 350, *Intangibles—Goodwill and Other*, provided the assets meet the criteria in FASB ASC 805 for separate recognition apart from goodwill.

2.59 For example, the acquired company may be in the process of developing a variety of software products that can be marketed both individually and in combination as an integrated suite of products (the suite). The development effort for certain of the individual products is complete, and the development of the others is incomplete. Consequently, the development of the suite is incomplete. If it is anticipated that the reporting entity will market the discrete products individually and include the discrete products as part of the suite, the task force believes that the fair value of any of the individual products whose development is complete should be capitalized as an asset resulting from R&D activities, provided the asset meets the criteria in FASB ASC 805 for separate recognition apart from goodwill.

Questions and Answers — Incompleteness

2.60 *Question 1:* Company T was acquired in a business combination and had an IPR&D project to develop the next generation of its microchip. The project was estimated to be 70 percent complete in terms of costs incurred. Although time-consuming and expensive technological and engineering hurdles remain, they are not believed to be high-risk development issues and not considered particularly difficult to accomplish. In fact, in similar previous development efforts, Company T consistently demonstrated that it could accomplish the remaining tasks once it got to a similar stage of completion. However, the remaining tasks are of the type described as R&D activities in FASB ASC 730-10-55-1, rather than of the type of activities described in FASB ASC 730-10-55-2 that are not considered R&D activities. Is the project incomplete?

Answer: Yes, because first customer acceptance of the microchip has not occurred. Even though the likelihood of success in achieving first customer acceptance may seem high based on Company T's history, first customer acceptance has not occurred, and additional qualifying R&D costs will be incurred. Consequently, completion of the project has not occurred at the date of acquisition.

2.61 *Question 2:* Company A acquired Company T in a business combination. At the acquisition date, Company T had an IPR&D project in process to develop the next generation of its job scheduling software. Company T had delivered a working model of the software to several of its customers as part of the beta test stage. As of the acquisition date, engineers were working to incorporate improvements discovered as a result of the beta testing. Company A expects to complete the development and market any resulting product in a manner generally consistent with the plans of Company T that existed at the acquisition date. Is the project incomplete?

Answer: Yes. The task force notes that although the project may have reached technological feasibility as discussed in FASB ASC 985-20, in this fact pattern the project is still incomplete. As discussed in FASB ASC 985-20-25-2, "the technological feasibility of a computer software product is established when the entity has completed all planning, designing, coding, and testing activities that are necessary to establish that the product can be produced to meet its design specifications including functions, features, and technical performance requirements." Despite reaching technological feasibility, additional research or development, or both, may be required in order for the product to be available for general release to customers. Conversely, if after reaching technological feasibility, this project required only minor, routine modifications prior to general release to customers, and the general release was imminent, this project would generally be considered to be completed.

2.62 *Question 3:* Company A acquired Company T in a business combination. At the acquisition date, Company T had an application to market a new drug pending FDA approval. Both Company A and T believe that Company T had completed all necessary tasks related to the filing (including having obtained satisfactory test results), and they believe that they will ultimately obtain FDA approval. Is the project incomplete?

Answer: Yes. Industry experience shows that there are uncertainties about obtaining approval for a new drug upon filing with the FDA. FASB ASC 730-10 does not specifically address whether costs of obtaining FDA approval are R&D; however, the task force believes that such future expenditures satisfy the condition that, to be considered incomplete, additional R&D costs must be expected to be incurred by the reporting entity.

2.63 *Question 4:* Company T was acquired in a business combination and was involved in the design, manufacture, and marketing of consumer video communications devices. Company T had a successful product in the market and had been working on the next generation of the product, which involved significant improvements to features and functions. Given the target market of young retail consumers, Company T planned to debut the new product at an upcoming trade show, followed shortly after by a nationwide marketing campaign. For competitive reasons, Company T did not allow prototypes of the product outside of its facilities, although it did use focus groups representing its target market demographics for feedback on design and features, product and performance quality, and marketing approaches. As of the acquisition date, Company T had approved the design and specifications of the latest prototype of new product as being ready for commercial manufacture. As a result, Company T's production facilities were preparing to begin mass production of product intended for commercial sale. However, Company T had yet to finalize specifications of the product shell (for example, color, ergonomic design, and brand graphics), which were still being tested with focus groups. Commercial manufacturing had not yet begun, and no products had been sold. Is the project incomplete?

Answer: No. The R&D project related to the significant improvement of the existing product has been completed, and there are no remaining R&D costs to be incurred. The remaining tasks before commercial manufacture and product launch do not involve technological or engineering risks, and the associated costs would not qualify as R&D. Although first customer acceptance has not occurred, Company T has demonstrated an equivalent internal milestone based on its product development practices and life cycle.

Questions and Answers—Miscellaneous

2.64 In addition to the topics discussed previously, the task force identified the following questions related to the accounting for business combinations, which are intended to aid in the application of the best practices.

2.65 *Question 1: Measurement Period:* When recording a business combination, if information (such as a third-party valuation report) is not available to estimate fair value of assets acquired to be used in R&D activities in the period when the business combination closes, is a preliminary estimate of fair value required to be recorded for those assets?

Answer: Yes. FASB ASC 805-10-25-13 provides guidance on when an acquirer should recognize and measure assets acquired to be used in R&D activities in connection with recording the acquisition of a business:

> If the initial accounting for a business combination is incomplete by the end of the reporting period in which the combination occurs, the acquirer shall report in its financial statements provisional amounts for the items for which the accounting is incomplete. During the measurement period, the acquirer shall retrospectively adjust the provisional amounts recognized at the acquisition date to reflect new information obtained about facts and circumstances that existed as of the acquisition date that, if known, would have affected the measurement of the amounts recognized as of that date.

Further, FASB ASC 805-10-25-17 states

> During the measurement period, the acquirer shall recognize adjustments to the provisional amounts as if the accounting for the business combination had been completed at the acquisition date. Thus, the acquirer shall revise comparative information for prior periods presented in financial statements as needed, including making any change in depreciation, amortization, or other income effects recognized in completing the initial accounting. Paragraph 805-10-55-16 and Example 1 (see paragraph 805-10-55-27) provide additional guidance.

Best practices suggest that the acquirer often is able to estimate fair value of assets acquired to be used in R&D activities in the same accounting period that the business combination is consummated based on the due diligence it performs before or immediately after agreeing to the terms of the acquisition. Exceptions may be acquisitions of very large companies with significant R&D activities and hostile takeover situations. In those circumstances, the task force believes that best practice would be for the acquirer to (*a*) record its best estimate within the range of possible fair values of the assets acquired to be used in R&D activities for purposes of recording its provisional amount and (*b*) provide the disclosures as outlined in FASB ASC 805-10-50-6:

> If the initial accounting for a business combination is incomplete (see paragraphs 805-10-25-13 through 25-14) for particular assets, liabilities, noncontrolling interests, or items of consideration and the amounts recognized in the financial statements for the business combination thus have been determined only provisionally, the acquirer shall disclose the following information for each material business combination or in the aggregate for individually immaterial business combinations that are material collectively to meet the objective in preceding paragraph:
>
> a.   The reasons why the initial accounting is incomplete
>
> b.   The assets, liabilities, equity interests, or items of consideration for which the initial accounting is incomplete
>
> c.   The nature and amount of any measurement period adjustments recognized during the reporting period in accordance with paragraph 805-10-25-17.

2.66 *Question 2: Equity Method Investment:* How should an acquirer apply IPR&D accounting requirements to initial investments in common stock that are to be accounted for using the equity method? Would the acquirer be precluded from using the equity method of accounting in circumstances in which the acquirer's lack of control precludes access to reliable information on which to base a determination of the existence of IPR&D projects, estimate their fair value with reasonable reliability, or both? In this question, it is assumed that the investee meets the definition of a business in the FASB ASC glossary. Chapter 3, "Accounting for Assets Acquired in an Asset Acquisition That Are to Be Used in Research and Development Activities," addresses a similar situation in which the investee does not meet the FASB ASC glossary definition of a business (see question 3 in paragraph 3.31).

Answer: FASB ASC 323, *Investments—Equity Method and Joint Ventures*,[10] requires that the difference between the cost of an investment and the amount of underlying equity in net assets of an investee be accounted for as if the investee were a consolidated subsidiary. Accordingly, the task force believes the value related to the investor's proportionate interest in intangible assets acquired to be used in R&D activities would be recognized as an acquired IPR&D asset in the acquirer's pro forma analysis for determining equity method income or loss and subsequently accounted for like any IPR&D asset acquired in a business combination. In the subsequent accounting, however, the task force notes that FASB ASC 323-10-35-32A states that

> an equity method investor shall not separately test an investee's underlying asset(s) for impairment. However, an equity investor shall recognize its share of any impairment charge recorded by an investee in accordance with the guidance in paragraphs 323-10-35-13 and 323-10-45-1 and consider the effect, if any, of the impairment on the investor's basis difference in the assets giving rise to the investee's impairment charge.

FASB ASC 323-10-15-10 provides examples of indicators that an investor may be unable to exercise significant influence over the operating and financial policies of an investee. Item (d) provides the following indicator that the equity method may not be appropriate (in this question, it is assumed that other indicators listed in FASB ASC 323-10-15-10 are not present): "The investor needs or wants more financial information to apply the equity method than is available to the investee's other shareholders (for example, the investor wants quarterly financial information from an investee that publicly reports only annually), tries to obtain that information, and fails."

The task force believes that an investee's sensitivity to maintain confidentiality with respect to the nature of its IPR&D projects may result in a circumstance in which an investor cannot obtain needed information to estimate the fair value of the investee's IPR&D with reasonable reliability. This circumstance may indicate a lack of significant influence.

Consequently, although the task force believes that an acquirer's inability to determine the fair value of assets acquired to be used in R&D activities could

---

[10] FASB and the International Accounting Standards Board are currently working on a joint project, *Accounting for Financial Instruments*, which may affect the equity method of accounting. Specifically, as of the date of publication of this guide, FASB tentatively decided that an entity would be required to classify and measure equity investments, which would otherwise qualify for the equity method of accounting, at fair value, with changes in fair value included in net income if the investment is held for sale. The latest information on the status of this project is available at www.fasb.org/cs/ContentServer?c=FASBContent_C&pagename=FASB%2FFASBContent_C%2F ProjectUpdatePage&cid=1175801889654.

preclude the acquirer from assigning value to IPR&D in its pro forma analysis for determining equity method income or loss, that circumstance may not, in and of itself, preclude the use of the equity method of accounting. When determining whether the use of the equity method of accounting is appropriate, all indicators listed in FASB ASC 323-10-15-10 would need to be considered.

2.67 *Question 3: Impact of Decision to Abandon R&D Efforts on Recognition and Measurement of the Associated R&D Project:* Subsequent to a business combination, but before the end of the measurement period, the reporting entity abandons R&D efforts associated with an R&D project that existed at the acquisition date. Should this R&D project be recognized as an IPR&D asset in the final accounting for the acquisition? Should the initial measurement of this R&D project be adjusted in the final accounting for the business combination?

Answer: Regardless of whether an intangible asset is specifically associated with an IPR&D project, it may, nonetheless, satisfy the recognition criteria of FASB ASC 805-20-25 and, accordingly, should be recognized and measured consistent with the principles of FASB ASC 805-20 (that is, at fair value). In other words, not all acquired intangible assets are within the scope of FASB ASC 350-30-35-17A, but that does not otherwise affect the recognition and measurement of those assets at the date of acquisition.

As discussed in the "Used in R&D Activities Criteria" section in paragraphs 2.08–.10, the task force notes that at the date of acquisition, the acquirer would need to determine whether an acquired asset will be "used in R&D activities." That determination is entity-specific and based upon how the acquirer plans to use the acquired asset subsequent to the date of acquisition. The task force believes that whether an acquired asset should be considered to be "used in R&D activities" upon its acquisition is dependent, at least in part, upon the extent of information available to the acquirer.

Whether initial measurement should be adjusted during the measurement period for the business combination depends on the circumstances giving rise to the decision to abandon the associated R&D efforts. If the abandonment decision was based on circumstances that arose subsequent to the acquisition date (that is, circumstances analogous to a "nonrecognized subsequent event" as discussed in FASB ASC 855, *Subsequent Events*), the task force believes that the R&D project should be recognized as an IPR&D asset, and its initial measurement should not be adjusted in the measurement period of the business combination. An example of such circumstances is when the results of postacquisition testing are judged to not be promising and lead to the conclusion that the technological hurdles to successful completion cannot be realistically overcome. Another example is if, subsequent to the business combination, a competitor introduces a product with performance and pricing characteristics that are superior to those envisioned for the planned product. In these cases, the decision to abandon the associated R&D efforts would not be accounted as a part of a business combination but, rather, would be a part of subsequent accounting. The task force expects that such an outcome is the most likely outcome, particularly for the significant R&D activities of the acquired business. See the "Abandoning of the Associated R&D Efforts" section in paragraphs 4.24–.29 for more information.

Alternatively, if the abandonment decision was based on circumstances that existed at the acquisition date (that is, circumstances analogous to a "recognized subsequent event"), the task force believes that the abandoned R&D project would not meet the "used in R&D activities" criteria and, therefore, should not be recognized as an IPR&D asset in the final accounting for the business combination. However, this abandoned R&D project may still need to be recognized in the acquirer's financial statements if it meets the recognition criteria in FASB ASC 805 (see the "Temporarily Idled or Abandoned Assets" section in paragraphs 2.34–.35). An example of such circumstances might be if management of the acquirer had not had the opportunity to investigate the project as part of its due diligence before the business combination and, subsequent to the business combination and before significant additional R&D costs had been incurred, determines that the expected economic benefits and associated risks of completion do not warrant continued funding of the project.

2.68 *Question 4:* Impact of Receiving Results of Clinical or Other R&D Efforts Subsequent to the Acquisition Date but Before the End of the Measurement Period: Subsequent to a business combination, but before the end of the measurement period, the reporting entity receives the results of clinical or other R&D efforts that have begun prior to the acquisition date, but such results were not known, or could not have been known, as of the acquisition date. Should the initial measurement of this R&D project be adjusted in the final accounting for the business combination since the results would likely provide information about the facts and circumstances that existed as of the acquisition date?

Answer: No. The initial accounting for the R&D project would not be adjusted for any information concerning clinical or other R&D efforts in which that information was not known or could not have been known as of the acquisition date.

Exhibit 2-1: Phases of Development in the Pharmaceutical Industry[11]

DISCOVERY RESEARCH PHASE—TWO TO FOUR YEARS

This is the earliest phase of the new drug R&D process. In the discovery research phase, scientists attempt to identify, from the literally millions of molecules existing in the world, one that has a desired effect against a given disease or illness. This whole process begins with the identification of a biological "target" that appears to play an important role in causing the disease or illness in question. This target could be something that is a part of the body itself, such as a protein, receptor, or gene, or it could be something normally foreign to the body, such as a bacteria or virus. The process of identifying lead molecules (or leads) is a trial-and-error process in which tens of thousands of different molecules are tested or screened to see if they have a desirable impact on the target. For example, if the target is a particular bacteria that causes infection, those molecules that kill or inhibit the bacteria would be considered leads, and scientists would go on to the next phase of development. The probability of any one lead actually making it through the rest of the drug development process and becoming a product is extremely low.

EARLY DEVELOPMENT PHASE—FOUR TO SIX YEARS

The drug development phase is all about taking a lead molecule, refining it, learning how to manufacture it, and testing it for safety and efficacy. The initial testing takes place in animals and looks for toxicity and other potential safety issues that might preclude ever introducing the compound into humans. Standard predictive models are used to project these findings from animals into potential toxicity and dosing levels for humans. The first human tests (phase I) are conducted in a very small group of healthy volunteers to assess the safety and the potential dosing range. After a safe dose has been established, the drug is administered to a still relatively small population of sick patients (phase II) to look for initial signs of effectiveness in treating the targeted disease. In parallel to this animal and human testing, scientists are also developing a manufacturing process that will allow the molecule to be manufactured in a safe, efficient, and economical way. Long-term animal studies continue to test for potential toxicology issues. The early development phase is a very high-risk part of the overall process in which the vast majority of leads fail to move on to the next phase of the process. Those molecules that do show some initial signs of efficacy move on to the final phase of the R&D process known as the "product phase."

PRODUCT PHASE—THREE TO FIVE YEARS

Those molecules that move on to the product phase (phase III) have already demonstrated safety and preliminary efficacy and, therefore, have a much higher likelihood of success. The drug is now tested in much larger patient populations to prove efficacy in a more rigorous and statistically significant way. These trials are generally global in nature and are designed to generate all the data necessary for inclusion in the regulatory submission documents. Often, these studies will involve a comparison of the new drug with existing competitive therapies, with placebo, or both. All of the data is compiled and submitted to regulatory agencies around the world. Often, there will be several

---

[11] As mentioned in paragraphs 2.44–.45.

exchanges of questions and answers with the regulators, and then hopefully, the drug is approved for marketing.

POSTMARKETING SURVEILLANCE TRIALS

Additional clinical trials may be performed after a drug is approved for marketing by the regulatory agencies (phase IV). These include studies that are required of or agreed to by the sponsor and are conducted in accordance with the current approved labeling. Studies in this phase go beyond the prior demonstration of the drug's safety, efficacy, and dose definition and are important for optimizing the drug's use relative to the approved indication. The objectives of these studies may include (1) comparison of the drug with other drugs already in the market; (2) monitoring a drug's long-term effectiveness and impact on a patient's quality of life; and (3) determining the cost-effectiveness of a drug therapy relative to other traditional and new therapies. Phase IV studies can result in a drug being taken off the market, or restrictions of use could be placed on the product, depending on the findings in the study.

Chapter 3

Accounting for Assets Acquired in an Asset Acquisition That Are to Be Used in Research and Development Activities

Introduction

3.01 As set forth in chapter 2, "Definition of and Accounting for Assets Acquired in a Business Combination That Are to Be Used in Research and Development Activities," Financial Accounting Standards Board (FASB) *Accounting Standards Codification* (ASC) 805, *Business Combinations*, requires that an acquirer recognize and measure at fair value, separately from goodwill, the identifiable assets acquired in a business combination.[1] Identifiable assets acquired in a business combination that are to be used in research and development (R&D) activities are separately recognized and measured at fair value, regardless of whether those assets have an alternative future use. Separately identifiable assets include both tangible and intangible assets, including intangible assets representing specific in-process R&D (IPR&D) projects to be pursued by the reporting entity. After initial recognition, tangible assets acquired in a business combination that are used in R&D activities are accounted for in accordance with their nature. After initial recognition, intangible assets acquired in a business combination that are used in R&D activities are accounted for in accordance with FASB ASC 350-30.

3.02 Consistent with FASB ASC 730-10-25-2, tangible and intangible assets that are purchased from others for use in R&D activities in a transaction other than a business combination (subsequently referred to as an *asset acquisition*) are capitalized only if they have alternative future uses. Otherwise, such assets are expensed. In addition to the "alternative future use criteria," the acquired asset must also meet the definition of an asset in FASB Concepts Statement No. 6, *Elements of Financial Statements*, at the acquisition date.

3.03 While deliberating FASB Statement No. 141(R), *Business Combinations*, FASB acknowledged the difference in treatment of assets used in R&D activities acquired in a business combination and those acquired in a transaction outside the scope of FASB ASC 805. However, in the interest of time, FASB decided to move forward with guidance on business combinations and separately reconsider the accounting for assets acquired in an asset acquisition for use in R&D activities.[2]

---

[1] See footnote 2 in paragraph .01 of the introduction for the definitions of business combination and business. This guide does not provide guidance on how to distinguish an asset acquisition from a business combination. The determination of whether acquired assets constitute a business depends on specific facts and circumstances and is subject to professional judgment.

[2] Financial Accounting Standards Board (FASB) Statement No. 141(R), *Business Combinations*, was codified in FASB *Accounting Standards Codification* (ASC) 805, *Business Combinations*. This explanation is provided in paragraphs B154–B155 of FASB Statement No. 141(R), which were part of the "Basis for Conclusions" section, none of which was codified in FASB ASC. However, the IPR&D Task Force (task force) believes that paragraphs B154–B155 provide helpful guidance and, therefore, decided to incorporate them in this guide.

3.04 Emerging Issues Task Force (EITF) Issue No. 09-2, "Research and Development Assets Acquired and Contingent Consideration Issued in an Asset Acquisition," which was added to the EITF agenda in January 2009, was intended to address the inconsistencies between the accounting for assets acquired in a business combination to be used in R&D activities and the accounting for those assets acquired in other types of transactions. In September 2009, FASB issued an exposure draft of a proposed FASB Accounting Standards Update (ASU), *Research and Development (Topic 730): Research and Development Assets Acquired and Contingent Consideration Issued in an Asset Acquisition (A Consensus of the FASB Emerging Issues Task Force)*, which, among other things, recommended that all tangible and intangible assets acquired in an asset acquisition for use in R&D activities be capitalized, regardless of whether those assets have an alternative future use. However, the proposed ASU was never finalized, and the project was ultimately removed from the EITF agenda.

3.05 As a result, assets used in R&D activities acquired in a business combination and those acquired in an asset acquisition are still subject to different accounting treatment.

3.06 This chapter sets forth what the IPR&D Task Force (task force) believes are best practices in the accounting for assets acquired in an asset acquisition that are to be used in R&D activities. Additionally, this chapter highlights differences in accounting for assets used in R&D activities acquired in business combinations and those acquired in asset acquisitions. This chapter should be read in connection with chapter 2, which provides guidance on identifying and accounting for assets acquired in a business combination that are to be used in R&D activities. Specifically, chapter 2 discusses scope of R&D activities, recognition criteria applicable to specific IPR&D projects, "used in R&D activities" criteria, unit of account, core technology, assets held for sale, and other topics.

3.07 This chapter's "Introduction" and "Key Concepts" sections are supplemented by the "Explanatory Comments" section, which expands on the discussion and sets forth the task force's support for the determination of best practices. In addition, this chapter includes questions and the task force's answers, which are intended to aid in the application of the best practices.

3.08 In this guide, an R&D project that has not yet been completed is referred to as an *IPR&D project* (see chapter 2 for more information regarding projects). Intangible assets that are to be used or are used in R&D activities, including specific IPR&D projects, are referred to as *IPR&D assets*. References to *assets acquired for use (or, to be used) in R&D activities* encompass both tangible and intangible assets, unless indicated otherwise. In this chapter, unless indicated otherwise, references to *IPR&D assets* and *assets acquired for use (or, to be used) in R&D activities* refer to assets acquired in an asset acquisition.

3.09 The following diagram illustrates a thought process for evaluating transactions that involve acquisition of assets for use in R&D activities to determine the appropriate accounting for such assets.

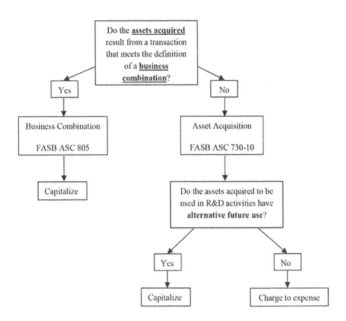

Key Concepts

Key Differences in the Accounting for Asset Acquisitions and Business Combinations

3.10 The list that follows briefly describes some of the key differences in the accounting for asset acquisitions and business combinations. This list is not all-inclusive, and there are other differences in the accounting for asset acquisitions and business combinations that are not discussed here because they do not have a direct impact on accounting for assets acquired for use in R&D activities. Readers should refer to FASB ASC 730-10 and FASB ASC 805 for further guidance on accounting for asset acquisitions and business combinations.

    a. Initial recognition of assets acquired for use in R&D activities. Assets acquired in a business combination that are used in R&D activities are capitalized and measured at fair value. However, in an asset acquisition, assets that were acquired for use in R&D activities are capitalized only if they have alternative future use. Furthermore, assets acquired in asset acquisitions for use in R&D activities are measured at cost allocated based on their relative fair values. For further guidance, refer to the "Alternative Future Use" section and related questions and answers in paragraphs 3.13–.27.

    b. Useful lives of acquired IPR&D assets. IPR&D assets acquired in a business combination are considered indefinite-lived until the completion or abandonment of the associated R&D efforts. IPR&D assets acquired in an asset acquisition may be either finite- or indefinite-lived or, if no alternative future use is identified, expensed immediately. When determining useful life of an IPR&D asset acquired in an asset acquisition that is capitalized, readers

AAG-RDA 3.10

should refer to paragraphs 1–5 of FASB ASC 350-30-35, which provide guidance on determining useful life of an intangible asset. For further discussion, refer to question 1 in paragraph 3.29 and the "Additional Considerations for Asset Acquisitions" section in paragraphs 4.83–.86.

c. *Goodwill.* Based on guidance in FASB ASC 805-50-30-3, no goodwill is created in an asset acquisition. However, goodwill may be recognized in a business combination.

d. *Transaction costs.* Based on guidance in FASB ASC 805-50-30-2, transaction costs in asset acquisitions are capitalized; however, with respect to business combinations, FASB ASC 805-10-25-23 requires that transaction costs be expensed in the periods in which the costs are incurred. In asset acquisitions, when the acquired IPR&D asset does not have an alternative future use and the IPR&D asset was the only asset acquired, the transaction costs would form part of the basis in the IPR&D asset, which would be expensed.

e. *Contingencies.* Contingencies acquired in an asset acquisition would be accounted for in accordance with FASB ASC 450, *Contingencies,* whereas contingencies acquired in a business combination should be recognized at fair value at the acquisition date to the extent determinable in accordance with FASB ASC 805-20-25 and, if not determinable, in accordance with FASB ASC 450. Specifically, FASB ASC 805-20-25-19 provides that "[i]f the acquisition-date fair value of the asset or liability arising from a contingency can be determined during the measurement period, that asset or liability shall be recognized at the acquisition date." However, if the acquisition-date fair value cannot be determined during the measurement period, consistent with FASB ASC 805-20-25-20, "an asset or a liability shall be recognized at the acquisition date if both of the following criteria are met: (a) Information available before the end of the measurement period indicates that it is probable that an asset existed or that a liability had been incurred at the acquisition date...and (b) The amount of the asset or liability can be reasonably estimated."

f. *Contingent consideration.* In an asset acquisition, contingent consideration is accounted for in accordance with applicable accounting principles generally accepted in the United States of America (GAAP). For example, if a contingent consideration meets the definition of a derivative, FASB ASC 815, *Derivatives and Hedging,* requires that it be recognized at fair value. In addition, FASB ASC 450 may require recognition of the contingent consideration if it is probable that a liability has been incurred, and the amount of that liability can be reasonably estimated. As discussed in paragraphs 5–7 of FASB ASC 450-20-05, the measurement objective in FASB ASC 450 is inconsistent with the fair value measurement objective. Specifically, FASB ASC 450-20-30-1 states that "[i]f some amount within a range of loss appears at the time to be a better estimate than any other amount within the range, that amount shall be accrued. When no amount within the range is a better estimate than any other amount, however, the minimum amount in the range shall be accrued." Therefore, contingent consideration in an asset acquisition may not be measured at fair value.

In a business combination, FASB ASC 805-30-25-5 requires that a contingent consideration be recognized at its acquisition-date fair value as part of the consideration transferred in exchange for the acquiree. Contingent consideration may be classified as equity, a liability, or an asset. Subsequently, FASB ASC 805-30-35-1 requires that contingent consideration classified as equity not be remeasured and that its subsequent settlement be accounted for within equity. FASB ASC 805-30-35-1 also requires that contingent consideration classified as an asset or a liability be remeasured to fair value at each reporting date until the contingency is resolved and that the changes in fair value be recognized in earnings unless the arrangement is a hedging instrument for which FASB ASC 815 requires the changes to be initially recognized in other comprehensive income.

Relevant Accounting Guidance

3.11 FASB ASC 805-50 contains guidance on the accounting and reporting for transactions that have certain characteristics that are similar to business combinations but do not meet the requirements to be accounted for as business combinations because the assets acquired and liabilities assumed do not constitute a business. Specifically, this subtopic contains the following guidance on acquisition of assets rather than a business:

Acquisition Date Recognition of Consideration Exchanged

FASB ASC 805-50-25-1. Assets commonly are acquired in exchange transactions that trigger the initial recognition of the assets acquired and any liabilities assumed. If the consideration given in exchange for the assets (or net assets) acquired is in the form of assets surrendered (such as cash), the assets surrendered shall be derecognized at the date of acquisition. If the consideration given is in the form of liabilities incurred or equity interests issued, the liabilities incurred and equity interests issued shall be initially recognized at the date of acquisition.

Determining Cost

FASB ASC 805-50-30-1. Assets are recognized based on their cost to the acquiring entity, which generally includes the transaction costs of the asset acquisition, and no gain or loss is recognized unless the fair value of noncash assets given as consideration differs from the assets' carrying amounts on the acquiring entity's books.

FASB ASC 805-50-30-2. Asset acquisitions in which the consideration given is cash are measured by the amount of cash paid, which generally includes the transaction costs of the asset acquisition. However, if the consideration given is not in the form of cash (that is, in the form of noncash assets, liabilities incurred, or equity interests issued), measurement is based on either the cost which shall be measured based on the fair value of the consideration given or the fair value of the assets (or net assets) acquired, whichever is more clearly evident and, thus, more reliably measurable.

Allocating Cost

FASB ASC 805-50-30-3. Acquiring assets in groups requires not only ascertaining the cost of the asset (or net asset) group but also allocating that cost to the individual assets (or individual assets and liabilities) that make up the group. The cost of such a group is determined using the concepts described in the preceding two paragraphs. The cost of a group of assets acquired in an asset acquisition shall be allocated to the individual assets acquired or liabilities assumed based on their relative fair values and shall not give rise to goodwill. The allocated cost of an asset that the entity does not intend to use or intends to use in a way that is not its highest and best use, such as a brand name, shall be determined based on its relative fair value.

Accounting After Acquisition

FASB ASC 805-50-35-1. After the acquisition, the acquiring entity accounts for the asset or liability in accordance with the appropriate generally accepted accounting principles (GAAP). The basis for measuring the asset acquired or liability assumed has no effect on the subsequent accounting for the asset or liability.

3.12 FASB ASC 730-10 establishes standards of financial accounting and reporting for R&D costs. It sets forth broad guidelines regarding what constitutes R&D activities, indicates the elements of costs to be identified with R&D activities, and specifies the accounting and disclosures for R&D costs. Specifically, items (a) and (c) of FASB ASC 730-10-25-2 contain the following guidance:

a. *Materials, equipment, and facilities.* The costs of materials (whether from the entity's normal inventory or acquired specially for research and development activities) and equipment or facilities that are acquired or constructed for research and development activities and that have alternative future uses (in research and development projects or otherwise) shall be capitalized as tangible assets when acquired or constructed. The cost of such materials consumed in research and development activities and the depreciation of such equipment or facilities used in those activities are research and development costs. However, the costs of materials, equipment, or facilities that are acquired or constructed for a particular research and development project and that have no alternative future uses (in other research and development projects or otherwise) and therefore no separate economic values are research and development costs at the time the costs are incurred ....

c. *Intangible assets purchased from others.* The costs of intangible assets that are purchased from others for use in research and development activities and that have alternative future uses (in research and development projects or otherwise) shall be accounted for in accordance with Topic 350. The amortization of those intangible assets used in research and development activities is a research and development cost. However, the costs of intangibles that are purchased from others for a particular research and development project and that have no alternative future uses (in other research and development projects or otherwise) and therefore no separate economic values are research and development costs at the time the costs are incurred.

Explanatory Comments

Alternative Future Use

3.13 As discussed previously, the concept of alternative future use is not relevant in the accounting for assets acquired in a business combination to be used in R&D activities. However, based on guidance in FASB ASC 730-10-25-2, the concept is still relevant for an asset acquisition when determining whether the allocated cost of these assets should be capitalized or immediately charged to expense.

3.14 For an asset acquired in an asset acquisition for use in R&D activities to have an alternative future use, the task force believes that (*a*) it is reasonably expected[3] that the reporting entity will use the asset acquired in the alternative manner and anticipates economic benefit from that alternative use, and (*b*) the reporting entity's use of the asset acquired is not contingent on further development of the asset subsequent to the acquisition date (that is, the asset can be used in the alternative manner in the condition in which it existed at the acquisition date).

3.15 If the use of the acquired asset is only in one or more other R&D projects of the reporting entity that have commenced[4] at the acquisition date, the task force believes that use represents a present (as opposed to a future) R&D activity, and the cost of that asset should be immediately charged to expense. If the asset will also be used in an R&D project to be commenced at a future date, the task force believes that such use is an alternative future use and that the cost of that asset should be capitalized.

3.16 Furthermore, the task force believes that an alternative future use that would require capitalization is one that is capable of using the assets acquired as those assets exist at the acquisition date. Consider a circumstance in which successful completion of an IPR&D project might give rise to additional R&D projects designed to significantly improve the just-completed product. Because those subsequent projects are contingent on the successful completion of the current project and would use the current R&D project in its future completed condition, the task force believes that they do not constitute an alternative future use at the acquisition date.

3.17 The task force believes that the determination of whether an alternative future use exists for an asset is based on specific facts and circumstances. However, for an acquired tangible asset to be used in R&D activities (for example, computer testing equipment used in an R&D department), the task force believes that there is a rebuttable presumption that such asset has an alternative future use because that asset generally has separate economic value (other than scrap or insignificant value) independent of the successful completion and commercialization of the IPR&D project. This presumption would be overcome, for example, if it were reasonably expected that the reporting entity will use

---

[3] For purposes of this guide, *reasonably expected* is used in the context of its meaning as provided in footnote 18 of paragraph 25 of FASB Concepts Statement No. 6, *Elements of Financial Statements* (that is, believed on the basis of available evidence or logic but is neither certain nor proved). The task force believes that *reasonably expected* connotes a slightly greater than 50-percent chance of occurring.

[4] A research and development (R&D) project is considered to have commenced when more than insignificant costs that qualify as R&D costs in accordance with FASB ASC 730-10 have been incurred.

that asset only in a specific IPR&D project that had commenced before the acquisition date.

3.18 Whether an acquired intangible asset to be used in R&D activities (that is, an IPR&D asset) has an alternative future use depends on specific facts and circumstances. Facts and circumstances that suggest the presence of an alternative future use include when it is reasonably expected that the reporting entity will use the intangible asset being acquired in its current condition in another currently identifiable R&D project to be commenced at a future date.

3.19 Facts and circumstances that suggest the absence of an alternative future use include intangible assets that represent incomplete specific IPR&D projects that are narrow in focus and for which the technology involved has the likely potential of being obsolete if the acquired specific IPR&D project fails or is terminated. Those circumstances suggest that if the specific IPR&D project were to be unsuccessful, management of the reporting entity would abandon the specific IPR&D project and direct its future R&D spending to areas using a different technology. Therefore, the specific IPR&D project, as it existed at the date of acquisition, would not have an alternative future use.

3.20 Another example of the absence of an alternative future use is when an entity acquires an intangible asset that is to be used in R&D activities for the sole purpose of holding (locking up) that asset to prevent others from obtaining access to it. Based on the criteria discussed in paragraph 2.10, if an acquired intangible asset will be defending a developed product, the acquired asset would not be considered an IPR&D asset but would be viewed as a defensive intangible asset and would be accounted for in accordance with guidance in paragraphs 5A–5B in FASB ASC 350-30-35. However, if the acquired asset will be defending the value of other intangible assets used in R&D activities, the acquired asset would be considered an IPR&D asset and, in accordance with FASB ASC 805-50-30-3, the entity would be required to allocate cost to such asset based on its relative fair value. However, because such asset is deemed not to have an alternative future use, the entity would expense the allocated cost of this asset.

Questions and Answers—Alternative Future Use

3.21 *Question 1:* Company A acquired two specific IPR&D projects from Company T. Project 1 is a word processing package to be used in hand-held computing devices, and project 2 is an advanced version of that project that incorporates significant additional features and functionality. Project 2 is dependent on the successful completion of project 1. Is project 2 an alternative future use for project 1?

Answer: No. Because project 2 builds off project 1 and is, therefore, contingent upon successful completion of project 1, the task force believes that it is not an alternative future use for project 1 because project 2 will only use the completed project 1 and, thus, project 2 would not have used project 1 as it existed at the acquisition date.

3.22 *Question 2:* Company A acquired a license that gives it the exclusive right to develop and market a certain compound for the treatment of various diseases. At the time of the acquisition, the compound was in early stage clinical trials as a drug for treating certain cancers. The project met the definition of an asset in FASB Concepts Statement No. 6 and the additional recognition criteria applicable to specific IPR&D projects because it is incomplete and presumed to have substance because it was the only asset acquired (see chapter 2 for an in-depth discussion of the "used in R&D activities" criteria and recognition criteria applicable to specific IPR&D projects). It is believed the same compound also might be effective in treating a type of cardiovascular disease. The cancer treatment projects were in early stage testing, and human studies for toxicity (safety) of the compound were not yet completed. If the results of those studies are negative, the project will be abandoned, and the compound would not be considered for use in a development project to address cardiovascular disease. Should the potential use of the license rights to the compound for a project addressing cardiovascular disease represent an alternative future use?

Answer: No. The task force believes that studies for toxicity represent a contingency that must be resolved before an alternative future use is reasonably expected to occur. Unless the compound successfully completes the toxicity studies for the indication for cancers, it will not be considered for use in treating any other disease.

3.23 *Question 3:* Company A acquired from custom software Company T certain custom-designed software packages based on specifications provided by Company T's customers. As part of this acquisition, Company A also received the rights to a specific custom software package Company T recently had designed for one of its customers with the intent of externally marketing that software. The custom software package had been programmed to run on a proprietary operating system with interfaces to the customer's legacy systems. Company T intended to modify the software so that it would be integrated into a widely used enterprise resource planning (ERP) package marketed by Company B. Company A planned to pursue a project after the acquisition to modify the Company T software so that it could be integrated into its own ERP software that competes with that of Company B. However, Company A did not plan to pursue modification of the Company T software to work with Company B's package. Is the Company B modification of the software package an alternative future use for the acquired software?

Answer: No. The task force believes that an alternative future use is one that is reasonably expected to occur based on entity specific considerations. Because Company A did not have the intent to pursue the Company B modification of the software package, that potential use, which was the intended use by Company T, is not an alternative future use. Company A would still need to evaluate, however, whether any of the technology represented by the custom version of the software project (*a*) met the definition of an asset in FASB Concepts Statement No. 6, and (*b*) had another alternative future use.

3.24 *Question 4:* In an asset acquisition, Company A acquired from Company T Drug 1, Drug 2, and the development and commercialization rights to a delivery mechanism for the delivery of those drugs. The delivery mechanism has been approved by the U.S. Food and Drug Administration (FDA) for the delivery of Drug 1, and Company T has been selling that product for two years. In addition, prior to the asset acquisition, Company T has commenced clinical trials for delivery of Drug 2 via the delivery mechanism in anticipation of applying to the FDA for approval for such use. It is expected that significant R&D costs will be incurred to customize the delivery mechanism technology to accommodate the unique characteristics of Drug 2 before obtaining FDA approval for delivery of Drug 2. Those actions are underway and are approximately 50-percent complete, but the FDA has not approved delivery of Drug 2. In evaluating whether Drug 2's delivery mechanism has alternative future use, does the marketing of the delivery mechanism for delivery of Drug 1 while the project to obtain FDA approval for delivery of Drug 2 is underway constitute an alternative future use for the delivery mechanism?

Answer: No. Drug 1, along with its delivery mechanism and related "know-how," is complete and, presumably, recognizable. The remainder of this response is limited to the considerations related to Drug 2 and its delivery mechanism. The characteristics of Drugs 1 and 2 are different, and the design of a delivery mechanism for each drug must reflect those different characteristics. Therefore, the delivery mechanism for Drug 2 will not use the design of the delivery mechanism for Drug 1 as it existed at the transaction date. Company A would still need to evaluate, however, whether Drug 2's delivery mechanism (*a*) met the definition of an asset in FASB Concepts Statement No. 6 and (*b*) had another alternative future use, including other possible drug applications.

3.25 *Question 5:* Company A licensed from Company T a compound for a new drug with multiple indications. Company A expects that its only use for the compound will be in four currently active IPR&D projects for other indications in addition to the lead indication. Do the four currently active IPR&D projects constitute alternative future uses for the compound?

Answer: No. The licensed compound is expected to be used only in currently active IPR&D projects and not in future IPR&D projects. Therefore, the task force believes that Company A should immediately charge to expense the cost of the license.

3.26 *Question 6:* Company A licensed from Company T a patented technology that will be used for screening of novel biologic targets to generate potential biologic therapies or diagnostics for multiple projects, including current projects, as well as planned future projects that Company A reasonably expects to occur. The technology has been used successfully in the past by Company T and does not need to be further developed for use by Company A. Does the licensed technology have alternative future use?

Answer: Yes. The licensed technology will be used in future IPR&D projects that are not currently being developed, and the technology can be used in the alternative manner in the condition in which it existed at the acquisition date. Thus, the task force believes the technology would have an alternative future use, and the cost of the technology would be capitalized.

3.27 *Question 7:* Company A acquired a unique piece of medical testing equipment and reasonably expects that it will use the equipment only in the specific IPR&D project. How should Company A account for the cost of the medical testing equipment?

Answer: Based on guidance in FASB ASC 730-10-25-2 (a), the task force believes that Company A should immediately expense the cost, less salvage value, of the medical testing equipment because the equipment does not have an alternative future use.

Questions and Answers — Miscellaneous

3.28 In addition to the alternative future use topic discussed previously, the task force identified the following questions related to the accounting for asset acquisitions, which are intended to aid in the application of the best practices.

3.29 *Question 1: Useful Life and Amortization:* In an asset acquisition, Company A, a pharmaceutical company, acquired from Company T a library of molecules for high-throughput screening of drug candidates. Company A determined that the library of molecules has alternative future uses because Company A will use portions of the library in its existing specific IPR&D projects, and it is expected that other portions will be used in currently identified future projects. As a result, Company A capitalizes the allocated cost of this library. What life should Company A assign to this library, and when should it begin amortizing the library?

Answer: When determining the useful life of an intangible asset acquired in an asset acquisition for use in R&D activities that has alternative future uses, the reporting entity would need to consider guidance in paragraphs 1–5 of FASB ASC 350-30-35, which discuss determining useful life of an intangible asset. In this fact pattern, because the library is a tool that is completed and being used the way it is intended to be used (that is, in R&D activities), the task force believes that Company A would treat the library as a finite-lived intangible asset and would begin amortizing it immediately. (Please also refer to paragraph 4.86 for further discussion of useful lives.)

3.30 *Question 2: "Used in R&D Activities" Criteria and Asset Held for Sale:* Company A acquired the worldwide exploitation rights to Internet-based access technology. The rights supported an existing specific IPR&D project to develop a product for exploitation in the United States. Company A does not have the resources to exploit the potential product in foreign countries and, therefore, it reasonably expects that it will license the exclusive rights to exploitation in countries outside the United States. Assuming that non-U.S. exclusive rights for exploitation meet the recognition criteria, should the allocated cost of the non-U.S. exclusive exploitation rights be capitalized?

Answer: Yes. The expected license of the non-U.S. exclusive rights for exploitation in foreign countries is an intangible asset because it meets the separability criterion in FASB ASC 805. However, this intangible asset would not meet the "used in R&D activities" criteria (discussed in the "Used in R&D Activities Criteria" section in paragraphs 2.08–.10) because Company A plans to outlicense it and does not plan to be actively involved in its development. As a result, this intangible asset would not represent an asset to be used in R&D activities, and the alternative future use criteria would not be applicable in this case. This asset would be recognized as an intangible asset and could potentially be accounted for as an asset held for sale (as discussed further in the "Assets Held for Sale" section in paragraph 2.28). The specific IPR&D project with respect to the development of a product for the U.S. market would also be capitalized, provided it had an alternative future use.

3.31 *Question 3: Equity Method Investment:* How should an acquirer apply IPR&D accounting requirements to initial investments in common stock that are to be accounted for using the equity method? In this question, it is assumed that the investee does not meet the FASB ASC glossary definition of a business. Chapter 2 of this guide addresses a similar situation in which the investee does meet the FASB ASC glossary definition of a business (see question 2 in paragraph 2.66).

Answer: FASB ASC 323, *Investments—Equity Method and Joint Ventures*, requires that the difference between the cost of an investment and the amount of underlying equity in net assets of an investee be accounted for as if the investee were a consolidated subsidiary. Therefore, the task force believes that if the equity method investee does not meet the definition of a business and a portion of the equity investor's acquisition price paid in excess of the underlying equity in net assets is attributable to IPR&D of the investee, the cost allocated to acquired intangible assets to be used in R&D activities would need to be expensed unless the assets have an alternative future use.

Chapter 4

Subsequent Accounting for Acquired Intangible Assets That Are to Be Used in Research and Development Activities

Introduction

4.01 This chapter provides guidance on subsequent accounting for acquired intangible assets that are used in research and development (R&D) activities (subsequently referred to as *in-process R&D [IPR&D] assets*). This chapter primarily focuses on subsequent accounting for IPR&D assets acquired in a business combination. Subsequent accounting for IPR&D assets acquired in an asset acquisition is discussed in the "Additional Considerations for Asset Acquisitions" section in paragraphs 4.83–.86.

Business Combinations

4.02 In a business combination, acquired IPR&D assets are initially recognized at fair value using market participant assumptions and classified as indefinite-lived intangible assets until the completion or abandonment of the associated R&D efforts. In this chapter, these indefinite-lived intangible assets are subsequently referred to as *indefinite-lived IPR&D assets*.

4.03 Following the business combination and before indefinite-lived IPR&D assets are ready for their intended use, they should be tested for impairment under Financial Accounting Standards Board (FASB) *Accounting Standards Codification* (ASC) 350-30 annually and more frequently if events or changes in circumstances indicate that it is more likely than not that the assets are impaired.

4.04 In addition, in periods subsequent to the business combination, management may (*a*) continue internal R&D efforts associated with the assets or collaborate with another party in R&D efforts, (*b*) dispose of the assets through sale, (*c*) outlicense the assets, (*d*) decide to temporarily postpone further development, or (*e*) abandon R&D efforts. These assets may be subject to different subsequent accounting treatment depending on the course of action chosen by management with respect to those assets. Readers should refer to applicable accounting literature when determining the appropriate accounting in each situation.

4.05 R&D expenditures related to the acquired indefinite-lived IPR&D assets and incurred subsequent to the business combination or outside a business combination are generally expensed as incurred unless they represent costs of materials, equipment, or facilities that have alternative future uses.

4.06 After the completion of an IPR&D project, the reporting entity would need to determine the useful life of the asset resulting from R&D activities. Such assets would generally have a finite useful life. However, prior to changing their life from indefinite to finite, these assets should be tested for impairment under FASB ASC 350-30 as if they were still indefinite-lived. Once the classification of these assets is changed from indefinite- to finite-lived, these assets should be amortized over their estimated useful lives. Thereafter, assets resulting from R&D activities will be tested for impairment under FASB ASC 360, *Property, Plant, and Equipment*, only when events or changes in circumstances indicate that the carrying amount of the assets may not be recoverable.

4.07 The following table highlights some differences in the accounting for indefinite-lived IPR&D assets and assets resulting from R&D activities acquired in a business combination:

	Indefinite-Lived IPR&D Asset	*Asset Resulting From R&D Activities*
Amortization period	N/A	Period over which the asset is expected to contribute directly or indirectly to the future cash flows of the entity.
Method of amortization	N/A	Reflects the pattern in which economic benefits of the intangible asset are consumed or otherwise used up. If that pattern cannot be reliably determined, a straight-line amortization method should be used.
Model and timing for impairment testing	Test for impairment in accordance with paragraphs 18–19 of FASB ASC 350-30-35.	Test for impairment in accordance with paragraphs 17–35 of FASB ASC 360-10-35.
	Testing required annually and more frequently if events or changes in circumstances indicate that it is more likely than not that the asset is impaired. Testing for impairment once the associated R&D efforts are completed or abandoned and, therefore, the indefinite-lived IPR&D asset is determined to have a finite life.	Testing required whenever events or changes in circumstances indicate that the carrying amount of an asset resulting from R&D activities (asset group) may not be recoverable.
	An entity may first perform a qualitative assessment to determine whether it is necessary to perform the quantitative impairment test. Impairment loss is recognized if the carrying amount of the asset exceeds its fair value.	Impairment loss is recognized if the carrying amount of the asset (asset group) is not recoverable and exceeds its fair value.

4.08 Several important accounting considerations exist related to indefinite-lived IPR&D assets and assets resulting from R&D activities. They include (*a*) when to test for impairment, (*b*) which impairment model to follow, (*c*) disposal of assets other than by sale, (*d*) attribution, and (*e*) tax considerations.

4.09 This chapter discusses some of the accounting considerations that result from management's decision to continue internal R&D efforts associated with the asset or collaborate with another party in R&D efforts, dispose of the asset through sale, outlicense the asset, temporarily postpone further development, or abandon R&D efforts associated with the project.

Accounting for Indefinite-Lived IPR&D Assets

Impairment Testing of Indefinite-Lived IPR&D Assets

4.10 Certain developments and events after a business combination may result in a decrease in the value of indefinite-lived IPR&D assets, potentially leading to impairment. Depending on the affected assets and the circumstances, accounting principles generally accepted in the United States of America (GAAP) provide guidance on when to test for impairment, how to determine whether impairment should be recognized, and how to measure and record such impairment in the financial statements. The IPR&D Task Force (task force) also would not generally expect impairment of acquired indefinite-lived IPR&D assets immediately after the acquisition.

When to Test Indefinite-Lived IPR&D Assets for Impairment

4.11 Indefinite-lived IPR&D assets should be tested for impairment as indefinite-lived intangible assets under guidance in paragraphs 18–19 of FASB ASC 350-30-35 annually and more frequently if events or changes in circumstances indicate that it is more likely than not that the assets are impaired. Although FASB ASC does not explicitly require it, entities with indefinite-lived IPR&D assets generally select a recurring date for impairment testing purposes. Also, as further discussed in paragraph 4.14, indefinite-lived IPR&D assets would generally need to be tested for impairment upon completion or abandonment of the associated R&D efforts.

4.12 *Changes in facts and circumstances.* FASB ASC 350-30-35-18B provides that

> [i]n assessing whether it is more likely than not that an indefinite-lived intangible asset is impaired, an entity shall assess all relevant events and circumstances that could affect the significant inputs used to determine the fair value of the indefinite-lived intangible asset. Examples of such events and circumstances include the following:
>
> a. Cost factors such as increases in raw materials, labor, or other costs that have a negative effect on future expected earnings and cash flows that could affect significant inputs used to determine the fair value of the indefinite-lived intangible asset
>
> b. Financial performance such as negative or declining cash flows or a decline in actual or planned revenue or earnings compared with actual and projected results of relevant prior periods that could affect significant inputs used to

determine the fair value of the indefinite-lived intangible asset

c. Legal, regulatory, contractual, political, business, or other factors, including asset-specific factors that could affect significant inputs used to determine the fair value of the indefinite-lived intangible asset

d. Other relevant entity-specific events such as changes in management, key personnel, strategy, or customers; contemplation of bankruptcy; or litigation that could affect significant inputs used to determine the fair value of the indefinite-lived intangible asset

e. Industry and market considerations such as a deterioration in the environment in which an entity operates, an increased competitive environment, a decline in market-dependent multiples or metrics (in both absolute terms and relative to peers), or a change in the market for an entity's products or services due to the effects of obsolescence, demand, competition, or other economic factors (such as the stability of the industry, known technological advances, legislative action that results in an uncertain or changing business environment, and expected changes in distribution channels) that could affect significant inputs used to determine the fair value of the indefinite-lived intangible asset

f. Macroeconomic conditions such as deterioration in general economic conditions, limitations on accessing capital, fluctuations in foreign exchange rates, or other developments in equity and credit markets that could affect significant inputs used to determine the fair value of the indefinite-lived intangible asset.

4.13   FASB ASC 350-30-35-18C indicates that the examples included in the preceding paragraph are not all-inclusive, and an entity should consider other relevant events and circumstances that could affect the significant inputs used to determine the fair value of the indefinite-lived intangible asset. Therefore, in addition to considering those examples, the task force recommends that management consider the following factors specific to their industry:

- Development of a competing drug (generic or branded), product, or technology
- Changes in the legal framework covering patents, rights, or licenses
- Change in the economic lives of similar assets
- Decision to postpone or delay the development of the IPR&D project
- Regulatory or other developments that could cause either delays in getting the developed product to market or significant additional costs to be incurred (for example, in the case of the pharmaceutical and life sciences industry, a requirement to conduct additional clinical trials)
- An increase in the projected technological risk of completion for the IPR&D project

- A decrease in the projected technological contribution of the IPR&D project to the overall future product, if the IPR&D project is a component of it

- A decrease in the projected market size for the developed product, reflected by a downward revision to the projected revenue or operating margin for the developed product (for example, in the case of the pharmaceutical and life sciences industry, indications that the potential patient population may be significantly smaller than originally anticipated)

- In the case of the pharmaceutical and life sciences industry, failure of the drug's efficacy after a mutation in the disease that it is supposed to treat

- In the case of the pharmaceutical and life sciences industry, advances in medicine or technology, or both, that affect the medical treatments

- In the case of the pharmaceutical and life sciences industry, changes in anticipated pricing or third-party payer reimbursement that cause a significant change to expected revenues

- In the case of the software and electronic device industry, an overall change in the road map for existing, in-process, and future products

4.14 *Completion or abandonment of the associated R&D efforts.* Based on guidance in FASB ASC 350-30-35-17A, completion or abandonment of the associated R&D efforts would generally cause the indefinite-lived IPR&D asset to become a finite-lived asset (that is, asset resulting from R&D activities). Consistent with FASB ASC 350-30-35-17, prior to commencing amortization of this asset, the entity should test it for impairment as an indefinite-lived intangible asset. The asset should then be amortized over its estimated useful life and accounted for in the same manner as other intangible assets subject to amortization (including applying the impairment provisions of FASB ASC 360).

The Impairment Model for Indefinite-Lived IPR&D Assets

4.15 *Qualitative assessment.* For indefinite-lived IPR&D assets, an entity may first perform a qualitative assessment, as described in paragraphs 18A–18F of FASB ASC 350-30-35, to determine whether it is necessary to perform the quantitative impairment test as described in FASB ASC 350-30-35-19. An entity has an unconditional option to bypass the qualitative assessment for any indefinite-lived intangible asset in any period and proceed directly to performing the quantitative impairment test as described in FASB ASC 350-30-35-19. An entity may resume performing the qualitative assessment in any subsequent period. If an entity elects to perform a qualitative assessment, it first should assess qualitative factors to determine whether it is more likely than not (that is, a likelihood of more than 50 percent) that an indefinite-lived IPR&D asset is impaired.

4.16 It should be noted that paragraph BC12[1] of FASB Accounting Standards Update (ASU) No. 2012-02, *Intangibles—Goodwill and Other (Topic*

---

[1] Paragraph BC12 was part of the "Basis for Conclusions" section of Financial Accounting Standards Board (FASB) Accounting Standards Update No. 2012-02, *Intangibles—Goodwill and Other (Topic 350): Testing Indefinite-Lived Intangible Assets for Impairment*, none of which was codified

(continued)

350): Testing Indefinite-Lived Intangible Assets for Impairment, acknowledges that fair value of certain indefinite-lived intangible assets, such as IPR&D assets, involves significant uncertainties related to characteristics specific to the indefinite-lived intangible asset. FASB acknowledges the difficulty in applying qualitative factors to evaluate such assets; however, it decided not to explicitly exclude any types of indefinite-lived intangible assets from the qualitative assessment because the assessment is optional, and there may be circumstances in which it would be appropriate to use the qualitative assessment for those types of assets. FASB also acknowledges that an entity should assess the reliability of the factors evaluated during the qualitative assessment of such assets and, if it would not be possible for the entity to make a positive assertion that it is not more likely than not that the indefinite-lived intangible asset is impaired, the entity should perform a quantitative impairment test that involves calculation of the fair value.

4.17   The task force believes that, for IPR&D assets, the qualitative assessment may be used with greater frequency for situations in which an IPR&D project is nearing successful completion or is completed successfully and tested one last time as an indefinite-lived intangible asset (provided there has been no deterioration in other relevant events and circumstances that could affect the significant inputs used to determine the fair value of the asset).

4.18   *Quantitative impairment test.* If after performing the qualitative assessment an entity determines that it is more likely than not that the indefinite-lived IPR&D asset is impaired, or if an entity elects to skip the qualitative assessment and proceed directly to the quantitative impairment test, the entity should calculate the fair value of the asset and perform the quantitative impairment test. The quantitative impairment test for an indefinite-lived IPR&D asset consists of a comparison of the fair value of the asset with its carrying amount. If the carrying amount of the asset exceeds its fair value, an entity should recognize an impairment loss in an amount equal to that excess. The carrying amount of the indefinite-lived IPR&D asset is reduced by the impairment loss, and the adjusted amount becomes the asset's new basis. As indicated in FASB ASC 350-30-35-19, subsequent reversal of a previously recognized impairment loss is prohibited.

4.19   *Determining the fair value portion of the impairment calculation.* For purposes of impairment testing, the fair value of the indefinite-lived IPR&D asset should be determined under the framework of FASB ASC 820, *Fair Value Measurement.* The task force also recommends following the guidance outlined in chapter 6, "Valuation of In-Process Research and Development Assets." When determining the fair value of an indefinite-lived IPR&D asset, it is important to revisit all assumptions used in measuring the indefinite-lived IPR&D asset at the time of acquisition (such as likely market participants, prospective financial information [PFI], discount rates, and so forth), as well as evaluate and consider new and updated data and information available. For example, if after the acquisition there is a significant decline in the anticipated cash flows associated with an IPR&D asset, it may indicate that the asset is impaired. Such decline may not always be associated with negative developments discussed in paragraphs 4.12–.13. Consider the following example: As part

---

(footnote continued)

in the FASB *Accounting Standards Codification* (ASC); however, the IPR&D Task Force (task force) believes that it provides helpful guidance and, therefore, decided to incorporate it in this guide.

of a business combination, a company acquired an outlicensing arrangement, which qualifies to be recognized as an indefinite-lived IPR&D asset (because the acquirer plans to play an active role in the development of the outlicensed project [see paragraph 2.10]). At acquisition, the anticipated milestone and royalty payments associated with the outlicensed project were considered in the valuation and, therefore, increased the fair value of the outlicensed IPR&D asset. If, subsequent to the business combination but before the impairment testing date, the acquirer receives a significant milestone payment associated with this project and, assuming there are no other developments that could mitigate the resulting decline in the anticipated cash inflows (such as a reduction in anticipated cash outflows; increase in the project's probability of success, which would lead to an increase in the present value of future outcomes; and so on), the fair value of the outlicensed IPR&D asset could decline. In this situation, the fair value of the outlicensed IPR&D asset may end up being below the asset's carrying amount, which would lead to an impairment loss.

4.20   In most circumstances, the valuation methodology used to measure the indefinite-lived IPR&D asset at the time of acquisition is also used for purposes of estimating the fair value for impairment testing. However, it is important to consider any recent information and developments that may result in another valuation methodology being more appropriate given the circumstances.

4.21   For example, the multiperiod excess earnings method may have been used to estimate the fair value of the indefinite-lived IPR&D asset at the time of acquisition. Since then, a similar technology with comparable economic rights has been introduced and licensed in the marketplace for which royalty information is available. Under these circumstances, it is important to consider whether a change in valuation methodology may be warranted.

4.22   If assets are combined for impairment testing, it might be helpful to follow guidance in chapter 6 for such valuation matters as PFI, *expected cash flows*, and discount rate determination. However, the task force believes that, in practice, situations in which separate IPR&D assets are combined for impairment testing purposes would be rare.

4.23   *Classifying an impairment loss related to indefinite-lived IPR&D assets.* FASB ASC 350-30-45-2 provides that an impairment loss that an entity recognizes for an indefinite-lived intangible asset should be reported as a component of income from continuing operations. The impairment loss is included in the subtotal "income from operations" if presented.

Abandoning of the Associated R&D Efforts

4.24   This section does not address defensive IPR&D assets, which are discussed in chapter 2, "Definition of and Accounting for Assets Acquired in a Business Combination That Are to Be Used in Research and Development Activities." FASB ASC 350-30-35-17A provides that intangible assets acquired in a business combination that are used in R&D activities (regardless of whether they have an alternative future use) should be considered indefinite-lived until the completion or abandonment of the associated R&D efforts. Although FASB ASC 360 is applicable to finite-lived assets, the task force believes that this topic provides useful guidance that may be helpful to consider when assessing whether R&D efforts are either abandoned or temporarily idled. FASB ASC 360-10-35-47 provides that "a long-lived asset to be abandoned is disposed of when it ceases to be used." Further, FASB ASC 350-30-35-17A indicates that consistent with the guidance in FASB ASC 360-10-35-49, intangible assets acquired in a business combination that have been temporarily idled should not be accounted for as if abandoned.

4.25 The task force believes that determination of whether R&D efforts are abandoned or temporarily idled is a matter of judgment and depends on specific facts and circumstances. When making that determination, the task force believes the following factors may indicate that R&D efforts are abandoned. Existence of any one of these factors may not be determinative. The following list is not meant to be all inclusive; there may be other factors to consider:

- Management ceases maintaining or using the indefinite-lived IPR&D asset.

- Management makes a permanent decision to stop funding the project (internally or through external sources).

- Management does not have an intention to sell the indefinite-lived IPR&D asset.

4.26 The task force believes that writing off an indefinite-lived IPR&D asset immediately after a business combination would generally be rare. As time progresses and circumstances and events change, value associated with indefinite-lived IPR&D assets that management does not intend to use may diminish. However, it should be noted that the provisional value of an IPR&D asset could be adjusted to zero during the measurement period due to facts and circumstances that existed at the acquisition date (see question 3, "Impact of Decision to Abandon R&D Efforts on Recognition and Measurement of the Associated R&D Project," in paragraph 2.67 for further discussion).

4.27 If an entity has ceased using an indefinite-lived IPR&D asset (that is, it has ceased R&D efforts associated with the asset and does not plan to sell or license the asset or derive defensive value from the asset), then the asset will be considered abandoned, and the guidance in FASB ASC 360-10-35-47 would need to be followed by analogy. Based on such guidance, the asset would be written off (that is, disposed of) when the IPR&D asset ceases to be used by the entity.

4.28 FASB ASC 360-10-45-15 requires that long-lived assets to be disposed of other than by sale (for example, by abandonment) continue to be classified as held and used until disposal.

4.29 Chapter 2 includes an example that addresses the impact of the decision to abandon R&D efforts on recognition and measurement of the associated R&D project (see question 3 in paragraph 2.67.)

Outlicensing Arrangements

4.30 A transferor, such as a pharmaceutical company, may subsequently enter into an arrangement whereby it transfers (outlicenses) its rights to a previously identified and measured indefinite-lived IPR&D asset to a third party (transferee). The intangible asset transferred is commonly known as the *outlicensed asset*. Often, such arrangements involve the transferee making an initial nonrefundable payment and committing to make future (contingent) payments based upon achieving substantive development milestones and royalties based on future sales of the product that is expected to utilize the outlicensed asset. In the event that the development efforts of the transferee are unsuccessful, the rights initially transferred commonly revert to the transferor.

4.31   Commonly, the amount of the initial fixed nonrefundable payment is less than the carrying amount (and current fair value) of the outlicensed asset. Assuming the carrying amount of the outlicensed asset is derecognized because the outlicensing arrangement is determined to constitute a sale under GAAP, the task force has considered whether it would be appropriate for the transferor to recognize a loss in circumstances in which the total amount of noncontingent consideration is less than the carrying amount of the outlicensed asset. The task force has discussed this issue at length and ultimately decided not to provide specific guidance in this guide. However, this issue is expected to be addressed in the joint revenue recognition project.[2] Readers should be alert to further developments on this issue.

Accounting for Assets Resulting From R&D Activities

Overview

4.32   Once management determines that an R&D project acquired in a business combination is completed and the related IPR&D asset is ready for its intended use, the asset is no longer considered an IPR&D asset; it now represents an asset resulting from R&D activities for which management would need to determine its useful life. Such assets would generally have a finite useful life. Before commencing amortization of these assets, they should be tested for impairment as indefinite-lived assets in accordance with FASB ASC 350-30. Then, they should be amortized prospectively over their estimated useful life and accounted for similar to other intangible assets that are subject to amortization.

Completion and Readiness for Its Intended Use

4.33   Determining when an R&D project is completed and the resulting asset is ready for its intended use depends on the industry and the specific facts and circumstances. Chapter 2 of this guide discusses the concept of incompleteness, which would be viewed as the opposite of completeness. Paragraph 2.17 states that "[i]ncompleteness means there are remaining risks (for example, technological or engineering) or certain remaining regulatory approvals at the date of acquisition. Overcoming those risks or obtaining the approvals requires that additional R&D costs are expected to be incurred." Therefore, generally, an R&D project would be viewed as completed when there are no remaining technological or engineering risks.

4.34   Also, when determining whether an R&D project is completed, entities should consider if there are any regulatory or other requirements that are necessary to consider the resulting asset ready for its intended use. For example, pharmaceutical companies operate in a regulated environment and may conclude that the R&D project is no longer in-process at the point when regulatory approval of the drug is obtained. Given that pharmaceutical companies

---

[2] FASB and the International Accounting Standards Board are currently working on a joint revenue recognition project. An exposure draft of the proposed revenue recognition standard was originally issued in June 2010. However, the proposed standard was reexposed in November 2011 to provide interested parties with an opportunity to comment on revisions that have been made since the publication of the exposure draft in June 2010. With respect to the issue of outlicensing arrangements discussed previously, the 2011 reexposure draft included a question for respondents regarding variable consideration. The issue of intellectual property will also be considered as part of the project's outreach.

The latest information on the status of this joint project is available at www.fasb.org/cs/ContentServer?c=FASBContent_C&pagename=FASB%2FFASBContent_C%2FProjectUpdatePage&cid=900000011146.

are unique in that they require regulatory approval in a respective territory, the task force believes that entities should consider the unit of account when making a determination of when the R&D project is completed and the resulting asset is ready for its intended use. (See the "Unit of Account" section in paragraphs 2.18–.24.) The task force believes that if the unit of account is the global compound, the asset is considered to be ready for its intended use upon receiving an approval in one or more jurisdictions, which, individually or combined, are expected to generate a significant portion of the total revenue or cash flows expected to be earned for that compound.

4.35 When determining whether the R&D project is completed, entities may find it helpful to consider guidance in the "Specific IPR&D Projects—Incompleteness" section in paragraphs 2.54–.63, specifically factors listed in paragraph 2.56.

4.36 Also, FASB ASC 730-10-55-1 provides examples of activities that would typically be considered R&D, whereas FASB ASC 730-10-55-2 provides examples of activities that would not be considered R&D. This guidance may also be helpful to consider when determining whether the project is completed.

Useful Life of Assets Resulting From R&D Activities

4.37 Determining the appropriate useful life and method of amortization for assets resulting from R&D activities requires judgment and understanding the nature of these assets. FASB ASC 350-30-35-1 states that "[t]he accounting for a recognized intangible asset is based on its useful life to the reporting entity." Therefore, estimating the useful life is based on management's expectations, not market participant's expectations; however, these considerations may overlap because the entity is part of the market. This is further clarified in FASB ASC 350-30-55-1C, which states the following:

> For a recognized intangible asset, there might continue to be a difference between the useful life of the asset and the period of expected cash flows used to measure the fair value of the asset. However, that difference likely will be limited to situations in which the entity's own assumptions about the period over which the asset is expected to contribute directly and indirectly to the future cash flows of the entity are different from the assumptions market participants would use in pricing the asset. In those situations, it is appropriate for the entity to use its own assumptions because amortization of a recognized intangible asset should reflect the period over which the asset will contribute both directly and indirectly to the expected future cash flows of the entity.

4.38 FASB ASC 350-30-35-2 states that "[t]he useful life of an intangible asset to an entity is the period over which the asset is expected to contribute directly or indirectly to the future cash flows of that entity." Consistent with FASB ASC 350-30-35-9, the remaining useful life of an asset resulting from R&D activities should be evaluated each reporting period to determine whether events and circumstances warrant a revision to the remaining period of amortization. If the estimate of the remaining useful life is changed, the remaining carrying amount of the asset resulting from R&D activities should be amortized prospectively over that revised remaining useful life.

4.39 For purposes of evaluating the amortization period, FASB ASC 350-30-35 is silent regarding whether the reporting period is an annual period, an interim period, or both. The task force believes that consistent with other requirements in FASB ASC 350-30, it is reasonable to interpret the reference to reporting period to mean annual reporting periods. Therefore, absent some triggering event, such as a change in intended use, the task force believes that it would be appropriate to evaluate the useful lives of assets resulting from R&D activities at least annually.

4.40 When determining the useful life of an asset resulting from R&D activities, an entity should consider all pertinent factors, including the following factors discussed in FASB ASC 350-30-35-3:

- The expected use of the asset by the entity
- The expected useful life of another asset, or a group of assets, to which the useful life of the intangible asset may relate
- Any legal, regulatory, or contractual provisions that may limit the useful life
- The effects of obsolescence, demand, competition, and other economic factors (such as the stability of the industry, known technological advances, legislative action that results in an uncertain or changing regulatory environment, and expected changes in distribution channels)

4.41 Management should also consider other factors relevant to the entity's industry when determining the useful life of an asset resulting from R&D activities. For example, in addition to the factors listed previously, it may be helpful to consider the following factors:

- Duration of the patent right or license of the product
- Redundancy of the product because of changes in market preferences or development of a similar product
- Impact of bad publicity on the product
- Unfavorable court decisions on claims from product users
- Regulatory decisions over licenses
- Environmental changes that make the product ineffective or obsolete
- Changes, or anticipated changes, in how the reporting entity gets compensated for the product
- Changes in government policies

4.42 Please refer to the example in paragraphs 6.66–.70, which, among other things, discusses determining the useful life of an asset resulting from R&D activities.

Amortization of Assets Resulting From R&D Activities

Amortization Method

4.43 After estimating the useful life of an asset resulting from R&D activities, an entity needs to determine the appropriate method of amortization. FASB ASC 350-30-35-6 provides that the method of amortization should reflect the pattern in which the economic benefits of the intangible asset are consumed or otherwise used up. If that pattern cannot be reliably determined, a straight-line amortization method should be used.

4.44   The entity would need to consider the nature of the asset resulting from R&D activities and its expected use when evaluating if a pattern of consumption can be reliably determined or if the straight-line method of amortization should be used.

4.45   As was explained in paragraph B54 of FASB Statement No. 142, *Goodwill and Other Intangible Assets*,[3] when considering the methods of amortization, FASB noted that Accounting Principles Board Opinion No. 17, *Intangible Assets* (which was superseded by FASB Statement No. 142), required that a straight-line method be used to amortize intangible assets unless another method was demonstrated to be more appropriate. However, FASB also noted that circumstances may exist in which another method may be more appropriate, such as in the case of a license that entitles the holder to produce a finite quantity of product. FASB, therefore, concluded that the amortization method adopted should reflect the pattern in which the asset is consumed if that pattern can be reliably determined, with the straight-line method being used as a default.

4.46   Although the example of a license that permits production of a finite quantity of product provided in paragraph B54 of FASB Statement No. 142 may illustrate a reliably determinable pattern of consumption, other situations may not be as clear. For instance, if the license instead allowed for unlimited production over a finite period, it is not clear whether the asset should be viewed as consumed on the basis of the estimate of production or on the basis of a lapse in time (because the holder of the right has unlimited access throughout the license period).

4.47   Therefore, when determining the appropriate method of amortization, entities would need to evaluate specific facts and circumstances and consider whether the assets are consumed over time or as units are produced. The task force observes that in situations in which there is a significant level of uncertainty involved in determining the pattern in which the economic benefits of an asset resulting from R&D activities are consumed, the straight-line method is often used in practice to amortize such assets. For an example of a situation in which an accelerated method of amortization may be more appropriate, please refer to paragraphs 6.66–.70.

4.48   For example, pharmaceutical companies generally determine that the straight-line method of amortization best reflects the pattern in which assets resulting from R&D activities are consumed because their intangible assets are time based. Pharmaceutical companies generally derive most value from their products over the patent life, not as units are produced. Said differently, the value of an asset resulting from R&D activities does not diminish as one unit is produced. The value of the asset resulting from R&D activities diminishes as time passes and the branded drug draws closer to patent expiry and exposure to generic competition.

4.49   Electronic devices and software companies also typically attribute the decrease in value of assets resulting from R&D activities to time passage and the technology itself becoming outdated. As a result, these industries also

---

[3] This explanation is based on paragraph B54 of FASB Statement No. 142, *Goodwill and Other Intangible Assets*. Paragraph B54 of FASB Statement No. 142 was not codified in FASB ASC; however, the task force believes that it provides helpful guidance and, therefore, decided to incorporate it in this guide.

generally use the straight-line method of amortization for assets resulting from R&D activities.

Changes in Amortization Methods

4.50 Consistent with guidance in paragraph 18–19 of FASB ASC 250-10-45, a change from one amortization method to another may be made only if the new method is justifiable on the basis that it is preferable. Such change reflects a change in accounting estimate that is effected by a change in accounting principle. For SEC registrants, Section 4230.2(c)(4) of the SEC's *Financial Reporting Manual* indicates that such change does not require a preferability letter.

Impairment Testing of Assets Resulting From R&D Activities

4.51 Assets resulting from R&D activities should be tested for impairment as long-lived assets in accordance with guidance in FASB ASC 360-10. There are two impairment models under FASB ASC 360-10: (1) for assets classified as "held and used" and (2) for assets classified as "held for sale." As provided in FASB ASC 360-10-45-15, an asset to be abandoned should continue to be classified as held and used until it is disposed of, and the guidance on long-lived assets to be held and used should apply while the asset is classified as such. FASB ASC 360-10-35-47 provides that "a long-lived asset to be abandoned is disposed of when it ceases to be used." Therefore, assets to be abandoned should be tested for impairment as held and used assets until they cease to be used.

4.52 If management has not reached a final decision on the sale or the criteria described in FASB ASC 360-10-45-9 for classification as held for sale have not been otherwise met, the asset should be classified as held and used. For instance, management may be exploring a number of potential alternatives, including continuing to use the asset, abandoning the asset, exclusively outlicensing the asset, or disposing of the asset through sale.

4.53 The following chart depicts the impairment models based on the type and intended use of the assets:

Held and Used	*Held for Sale*
Event-driven test at asset (asset group) level	Lower of carrying amount or fair value less cost to sell the asset (disposal group)

Impairment Testing of Held and Used Assets Resulting From R&D Activities

4.54 Assets resulting from R&D activities that an entity plans to hold and use should be reviewed for impairment in accordance with guidance in paragraphs 17–35 of FASB ASC 360-10-35. Consistent with guidance in FASB ASC 360-10-35, assets resulting from R&D activities should be tested for recoverability at the asset (asset group) level whenever events or changes in circumstances indicate that their carrying amounts may not be recoverable.

4.55 First, the entity tests the asset (asset group) for recoverability by comparing its carrying amount with the sum of undiscounted cash flows expected to result from the use and eventual disposition of the asset (asset group). If the sum of undiscounted cash flows exceeds the carrying amount of the asset (asset group), the asset (asset group) is not impaired. If the sum of undiscounted cash flows is less than the carrying amount of the asset (asset group), then the fair value of the asset (asset group) is compared to its carrying amount. The excess of the carrying amount of the asset (asset group) over its fair value, if any, would be recognized as an impairment loss. With respect to an asset group, based on guidance in FASB ASC 360-10-35-28, the impairment loss should be allocated to the long-lived assets of the group on a pro rata basis using the relative carrying amounts of those assets, except that the loss allocated to an individual long-lived asset of the group should not reduce the carrying amount of that asset below its fair value whenever that fair value is determinable without undue cost and effort.

4.56 *When to test for impairment held and used assets resulting from R&D activities.* An asset resulting from R&D activities or asset group that is held and used should be tested for recoverability whenever events or changes in circumstances indicate that its carrying amount may not be recoverable. FASB ASC 360-10-35-21 provides examples of such events or changes in circumstances that may indicate the carrying amounts may not be recoverable. In addition to considering those examples, the task force recommends that management consider industry-specific indicators, such as the ones described in paragraph 4.13.

4.57 Consistent with FASB ASC 360-10-35-22, when the asset (asset group) is tested for recoverability, it also may be necessary to review amortization estimates and method as required by FASB ASC 250, *Accounting Changes and Error Corrections*, or the amortization period as required by FASB ASC 350, *Intangibles—Goodwill and Other*. Any revision to the remaining useful life of the asset resulting from that review also should be considered when developing estimates of future cash flows used to test the asset (asset group) for recoverability. However, any change in the accounting method for the asset resulting from that review should be made only after performing the impairment test.

4.58 *Asset grouping of held and used assets resulting from R&D activities.* Consistent with FASB ASC 360-10-35-23, for purposes of recognition and measurement of an impairment loss, a held and used asset resulting from R&D activities should be grouped with other assets and liabilities at the lowest level for which identifiable cash flows are largely independent of the cash flows of other assets and liabilities. The determination of an entity's asset groups involves significant judgment, and all relevant facts and circumstances should be considered. When making this determination, a number of entity-specific operating characteristics may need to be assessed, including the interdependency of revenue between asset groups.

4.59 The existence of a shared cost structure may also be a factor in the determination of the appropriate level at which to group assets. If cash flows from a particular asset group result from significant shared operations, it may be necessary to group assets at a higher level. However, the existence of shared service activities alone would not necessarily require grouping assets at a higher level because, in many instances, these types of services may not be considered significant.

4.60 *Estimating future cash flows used in the recoverability test of held and used assets resulting from R&D activities.* Consistent with FASB ASC 360-10-35-30, estimates of future cash flows used to test the recoverability of a held and used asset resulting from R&D activities (asset group) should incorporate the entity's own assumptions about its use of the asset (asset group) and should consider all available evidence. Therefore, the recoverability test is based on undiscounted cash flows expected to result from the entity's use and eventual disposition of the asset or asset group, rather than on market participant assumptions that would be used in measuring the asset's fair value. As a result, cash flows used in the recoverability test may be different from the cash flows used in measuring the fair value.

4.61   For example, if an income approach is used to measure the fair value of an asset resulting from R&D activities that is held and used, the cash flows would be based on market participant assumptions, rather than an entity's own assumptions about how it intends to use the asset.

4.62   FASB ASC 360-10-35-30 provides that "[e]stimates of future cash flows ... shall be reasonable in relation to the assumptions used in developing other information used by the entity for comparable periods, such as internal budgets and projections, accruals related to incentive compensation plans, or information communicated to others." Additionally, the task force recommends considering expected changes in market conditions when developing assumptions about price and volume levels.

4.63   FASB ASC 360-10-35-31 provides that estimates of future cash flows used to test the recoverability of the asset (asset group) should be made for the remaining useful life of the asset (asset group) to the entity. The remaining useful life of an asset group should be based on the remaining useful life of the primary asset of the group. The primary asset is the principal long-lived tangible asset being depreciated or intangible asset being amortized that is the most significant component asset from which the asset group derives its cash flow-generating capacity. The primary asset of an asset group, therefore, cannot be land or an indefinite-lived intangible asset.

4.64   Estimates of future cash flows include the following:

- All cash inflows expected from the use of the asset resulting from R&D activities (or, asset group) over the remaining useful life of the asset (or, the "primary asset" of the asset group), based on its existing service potential at the date of the recoverability test (for example, taking into account the asset's cash flow-generating capacity and physical output capacity, but excluding future capital improvements and other expenditures that would increase the service potential of the asset). For example, cash inflows may include, but are not limited to, revenues from sale of products or services associated with assets resulting from R&D activities or from the licensing of those assets.

- Any cash outflows necessary to obtain those cash inflows, including future expenditures to maintain the asset. For example, cash outflows may include, but are not limited to, cost of goods sold, sales and marketing expenses, and maintenance R&D.

- Cash flows associated with the eventual disposition, including selling costs and the salvage value of those assets. If the asset group constitutes a business, the proceeds from eventual disposition may include the terminal value of the business (although such terminal value may be less than that used for business valuation purposes because it would reflect only the value associated with maintaining the existing service potential of the business).

4.65 Consistent with FASB ASC 360-10-35-32, factors that an entity generally should consider in determining whether an asset resulting from R&D activities is the primary asset of an asset group include the following:

a. Whether other assets of the group would have been acquired by the entity without the asset.

b. The level of investment that would be required to replace the asset.

c. The remaining useful life of the asset relative to other assets of the group. If the primary asset is not the asset of the group with the longest remaining useful life, estimates of future cash flows for the group should assume the sale of the group at the end of the remaining useful life of the primary asset.

4.66 FASB ASC 360-10-35-33 provides that cash flow estimates should include cash flows associated with future expenditures necessary to maintain the existing service potential of the asset or asset group, including those that replace the service potential of component parts of the asset and component assets other than the primary asset of an asset group.

4.67 Consistent with FASB ASC 360-10-35-30, if alternative courses of action to recover the carrying amount of an asset resulting from R&D activities or asset group are under consideration, or if a range is estimated for the amount of possible future cash flows associated with the likely course of action, the likelihood of those possible outcomes should be considered. Therefore, a probability-weighted approach may be useful in considering the likelihood of those possible outcomes. See example 2 in FASB ASC 360-10-55-23 for an illustration of this guidance.

4.68 Whichever method of estimating cash flows is used, it would need to be applied consistently to asset groups with similar uncertainties and cash flow streams. FASB ASC 360-10-35 is silent about whether estimates of expected future net cash flows for the recoverability test should include or exclude income tax effects. Ordinarily, such calculations are performed on a pretax basis. However, there may be unusual situations in which incremental tax effects directly attributable to a specific asset would be considered when assessing an asset's recoverability. Such tax attributes would be included in the recoverability test if tax effects are important to the assets' economics.

4.69 *Classifying an impairment loss related to held and used assets resulting from R&D activities.* Based on FASB ASC 360-10-45-4, if an impairment loss is recognized, that loss should be included in income from continuing operations before income taxes and within income from operations, if such an amount is presented.

4.70 Consistent with FASB ASC 350-30-35-14, after recognition of an impairment loss, the adjusted carrying amount of an asset resulting from R&D activities becomes that asset's new accounting basis. FASB ASC 350-30-35-14 also states that "[s]ubsequent reversal of a previously recorded impairment loss is prohibited." Consistent with FASB ASC 360-10-35-20, the adjusted carrying amount of the asset resulting from R&D activities should be amortized over the asset's remaining useful life.

4.71 *Order of impairment testing for held and used assets resulting from R&D activities.* If assets resulting from R&D activities are tested for impairment at the same time with other assets of a reporting unit, including goodwill that is being tested for impairment, consistent with FASB ASC 360-10-35-27, the impairment testing should be performed in the following order:

- Adjust the carrying amounts of any assets (such as accounts receivable and inventory) and liabilities (such as accounts payable, long-term debt, and asset retirement obligations) not covered by FASB ASC 360-10 that are included in an asset group in accordance with other applicable GAAP.

- Test for impairment and adjust carrying amounts of indefinite-lived intangible asset(s) that are included in an asset group under FASB ASC 350-30.

- Test long-lived assets (asset group) and amortizable intangible assets, including assets resulting from R&D activities, under FASB ASC 360-10.

- Test goodwill of a reporting unit that includes the aforementioned assets under FASB ASC 350-20.

4.72 The carrying amounts are adjusted, if necessary, for the result of each test prior to performing the next test. This order differs from the held-for-sale approach (which is discussed in paragraphs 4.77–.79), which prescribes that goodwill be tested for impairment prior to the disposal group. The order of assessment may affect the recorded amount of goodwill impairment loss.

4.73 *Allocating impairment loss for held and used assets resulting from R&D activities*. Consistent with FASB ASC 360-10-35-28, an impairment loss for an asset group should reduce only the carrying amounts of an asset resulting from R&D activities or assets of the group. The loss should be allocated to the long-lived assets of the group on a pro rata basis using the relative carrying amounts of those assets, except that the loss allocated to an individual long-lived asset of the group should not reduce the carrying amount of that asset below its fair value whenever that fair value is determinable without undue cost and effort. See example 1 in FASB ASC 360-10-55-20 for an illustration of this guidance.

Impairment Testing of Held for Sale Assets Resulting From R&D Activities

4.74 *Criteria for classifying assets resulting from R&D activities or disposal groups as held for sale*. Consistent with FASB ASC 360-10-45-9, an asset resulting from R&D activities (disposal group) to be sold should be classified as held for sale in the period in which all of the following criteria are met:

a. Management, having the authority to approve the action, commits to a plan to sell the asset (disposal group).

b. The asset (disposal group) is available for immediate sale in its present condition subject only to terms that are usual and customary for sales of such assets (disposal groups). In other words, there is no operational requirement to use the asset.

c. An active program to locate a buyer and other actions required to complete the plan to sell the asset (disposal group) have been initiated.

d. The sale of the asset (disposal group) is probable (the term *probable* refers to a future sale that is likely to occur), and transfer of the asset (disposal group) is expected to qualify for recognition as a completed sale within one year, except as permitted by FASB ASC 360-10-45-11.

   e. The asset (disposal group) is being actively marketed for sale at a price that is reasonable in relation to its current fair value.

   f. Actions required to complete the plan indicate that it is unlikely that significant changes to the plan will be made or that the plan will be withdrawn.

4.75 If an entity meets all of the preceding criteria, the asset resulting from R&D activities or the related disposal group should be classified as held for sale. Consistent with FASB ASC 360-10-35-43, such asset should not be amortized while it is classified as held for sale.

4.76 *Impairment model for held for sale assets resulting from R&D activities.* Consistent with FASB ASC 360-10-35-43, an asset resulting from R&D activities (disposal group) classified as held for sale should be measured at the lower of its carrying amount or fair value less cost to sell.[4] Consistent with FASB ASC 360-10-35-40, an impairment loss should be recognized for any initial or subsequent write-down of the asset or disposal group to its fair value less cost to sell. A gain should be recognized for any subsequent increase in fair value less cost to sell of an asset resulting from R&D activities or disposal group, but not in excess of the cumulative loss previously recognized. That is, the asset resulting from R&D activities or disposal group should not be written up above its carrying amount as of its classification as held for sale.

4.77 *Order of impairment testing for held for sale assets resulting from R&D activities.* In accordance with FASB ASC 360-10-35-39, the carrying amounts of any assets not covered by this FASB ASC subtopic, including indefinite-lived intangible assets and goodwill, that are included in a disposal group classified as held for sale should be adjusted in accordance with other applicable GAAP prior to measuring the fair value less cost to sell of the disposal group. An entity should perform impairment testing in the following order:

- Adjust the carrying amounts of any other assets (such as accounts receivable and inventory) and liabilities (such as accounts payable, long-term debt, and asset retirement obligations) that are included in a disposal group in accordance with other applicable GAAP. Test for impairment and adjust carrying amounts of indefinite-lived intangible asset(s) that are included in the disposal group under FASB ASC 350-30.

- Test goodwill for impairment under FASB ASC 350-20 if it is included in a disposal group. (Paragraphs 1–7 of FASB ASC 350-20-40 provide guidance for allocating goodwill to a lower-level asset group to be disposed of that is part of a reporting unit and that constitutes a business. Goodwill is not included in a lower-level asset group to be disposed of that is part of a reporting unit if it does not constitute a business.)

---

[4] It should be noted that FASB ASC 820-10-15-1 indicates that measurements based on fair value, such as fair value less cost to sell, are within the scope of FASB ASC 820, *Fair Value Measurement*, and, therefore, subject to its measurement and disclosure requirements. Specifically, FASB ASC 820-10-50-2 uses an asset held for sale that is measured at fair value less costs to sell as an example of a nonrecurring fair value measurement. Paragraphs 1–2 of FASB ASC 820-10-50 contain a number of disclosure requirements for nonrecurring fair value measurements, and FASB ASC 820-10-55-100 provides a disclosure example that includes, among other things, disclosures related to nonrecurring fair value measurements.

- Test the disposal group for impairment under FASB ASC 360-10.

4.78 The carrying amounts are adjusted, if necessary, for the result of each test prior to performing the next test. This order is different from that applied for assets to be held and used as discussed in paragraphs 4.71–.72. The order of assessment may affect the amount of goodwill impairment loss.

4.79 According to FASB ASC 360-10-35-40, the expected disposal loss or gain should adjust only the carrying amount of a long-lived asset, whether classified as held for sale individually or as part of a disposal group.

Income Tax Considerations

Valuation Allowance Assessments

4.80 In situations in which a deferred tax liability related to an indefinite-lived IPR&D asset is recorded, it is important to consider when performing a valuation allowance assessment whether the deferred tax liability should be used as a source of income to realize a benefit from deferred tax assets. Deferred tax liabilities related to indefinite-lived assets typically cannot be used as a source of income to support realization of deferred tax assets in jurisdictions where tax attributes expire (such as in jurisdictions where net operating loss carryforwards expire) unless the deferred tax liability is expected to reverse prior to the expiration date of the tax attribute. When evaluating the need for a valuation allowance on deferred tax assets, a reporting entity would need to consider whether the deferred tax liabilities related to indefinite-lived IPR&D assets are expected to reverse in a period that would allow realization of the deferred tax assets. It should be noted that indefinite-lived IPR&D assets may be different than other indefinite-lived intangible assets because in certain circumstances an entity may be able to reliably estimate when it will cease to be an indefinite-lived intangible asset. Absent such ability, the task force believes it would not be appropriate to differentiate an indefinite-lived IPR&D asset from other indefinite-lived intangible assets for purposes of evaluating the recoverability of deferred tax assets.

Questions and Answers—Valuation Allowance Assessments

4.81 *Question 1:* Company A acquires Company T in a nontaxable business combination on January 1. As part of acquisition accounting, Company A capitalizes an acquired indefinite-lived IPR&D asset for $100 and records an associated deferred tax liability of $40. Company A plans to file a consolidated tax return with Company T. Company A had a preexisting deferred tax asset of $30 for net operating loss that will expire in 10 years (for simplicity, assume this is Company A's only deferred tax asset). Prior to the acquisition, Company A had a valuation allowance against the deferred tax asset. Can the future reversal of the taxable temporary difference associated with the indefinite-lived IPR&D asset be considered when determining whether the valuation allowance is required?

Answer: To determine whether the future reversal of the taxable temporary difference associated with the indefinite-lived IPR&D asset can be considered when determining whether the valuation allowance is required, Company A would need to assess how long it would take to complete the IPR&D project and the expected useful life of the asset resulting from R&D activities that will be produced by this project once the project is complete. If Company A expects the project to be completed within two years and expects the useful life of the asset resulting from R&D activities to be three years, then the deferred tax liability would be used as a source of realization for the deferred tax asset because the deferred tax liability is expected to reverse over years three to five, which is well before the expiration of the net operating loss carryforward. If Company A reverses all or a portion of its valuation allowance as a result of this analysis, the benefit would be recorded outside acquisition accounting in income from continuing operations.

Alternatively, if Company A has limited or no visibility into how long the IPR&D project may last or the useful life of the asset resulting from R&D activities that will be produced by this IPR&D project, or both, then the reversal of the taxable temporary difference might not provide a source of taxable income for tax attributes with expiration periods.

Identifying the Applicable Tax Rate to Calculate Deferred Tax Assets and Liabilities

4.82 When determining deferred taxes, the identification of the applicable tax rate for each jurisdiction (and sometimes for each individual type of temporary difference) is important. When determining the applicable tax rate, it is necessary to consider the effects of the business combination. The applicable rate is determined based on enacted tax rates, even if the parties included apparent or expected changes in tax rates in their negotiations. FASB ASC 740-10-25-47 requires that rate changes be reflected in the period when enacted. Further, a change in enacted rates subsequent to the acquisition date may result in an immediate positive or negative impact on the tax provision in the postcombination period. Reporting entities that file financial statements with the SEC may be required to apply push-down accounting, whereby the parent's basis in the investment is pushed down to the legal entities acquired. Regardless of whether push-down accounting is applied, the applicable tax rate(s) used to measure deferred taxes would be determined based on the relevant rate(s) in the jurisdictions where the acquired assets are recovered and the assumed liabilities are settled.

Additional Considerations for Asset Acquisitions

4.83 Chapter 3, "Accounting for Assets Acquired in an Asset Acquisition That Are to Be Used in Research and Development Activities," sets forth what the task force believes are best practices in the accounting for assets acquired in an asset acquisition that are to be used in R&D activities. Additionally, that chapter highlights differences in accounting for assets used in R&D activities acquired in business combinations and those acquired in asset acquisitions.

4.84 With respect to subsequent accounting for assets acquired and liabilities assumed in asset acquisitions, FASB ASC 805-50-35-1 provides that "[a]fter the acquisition, the acquiring entity accounts for the asset or liability in accordance with the appropriate generally accepted accounting principles (GAAP). The basis for measuring the asset acquired or liability assumed has no effect on the subsequent accounting for the asset or liability."

4.85 Subsequent accounting for an IPR&D asset acquired in an asset acquisition will depend on the conclusion reached regarding the alternative future use of the asset. If no alternative future use is identified for an asset acquired in an asset acquisition, the asset is expensed immediately, and there is no further accounting. If however, an alternative future use is identified for the asset acquired in an asset acquisition, then the asset would be capitalized as an IPR&D asset.

4.86 Once capitalized, the entity needs to determine useful life of an IPR&D asset acquired in an asset acquisition in accordance with paragraphs 1– 5 of FASB ASC 350-30-35, which provide guidance on determining useful life of an intangible asset. As a result, IPR&D assets acquired in an asset acquisition may be either finite- or indefinite-lived. However, given the nature of IPR&D assets acquired in asset acquisitions that meet the capitalization criteria, the task force believes that situations in which a capitalized IPR&D asset would be assigned an indefinite life would occur infrequently. This is because in order for an asset used in R&D activities to be capitalized in an asset acquisition, it has to satisfy the alternative future use criterion. Assets that generally meet this criterion are tools used in R&D activities that are completed, being used the way they are intended to be used (that is, in R&D activities), and expected to produce economic benefits for a finite period of time. A typical example of such tools in the pharmaceutical industry would be platform technology, which will allow an entity to develop molecules more quickly or identify them more efficiently. Accounting for finite-lived IPR&D assets acquired in an asset acquisition would be similar to accounting for finite-lived assets resulting from R&D activities, which is discussed in the "Business Combinations" section of this chapter. However, with respect to amortization, if an IPR&D asset represents a project, it would not be amortized until the R&D project is completed and, if an IPR&D asset represents a tool used in multiple projects, amortization would begin once the asset is completed and ready for its intended use (see the answer to question 1 in paragraph 3.29 for further discussion of an IPR&D asset that represents a tool). Indefinite-lived IPR&D assets acquired in an asset acquisition would be accounted for in accordance with general guidance in FASB 350-30 for indefinite-lived intangible assets. Accounting for these assets would differ from accounting for indefinite-lived IPR&D assets acquired in a business combination which, in accordance with FASB ASC 350-30-35-17A, are automatically presumed to have an indefinite life until completion or abandonment of the associated R&D efforts. In accordance with FASB ASC 350-30-35-16, the remaining useful life of indefinite-lived IPR&D assets acquired in an asset acquisition would need to be evaluated each reporting period to determine whether events and circumstances continue to support their indefinite useful life. Once these assets are determined to have a finite useful life, the accounting for them would be similar to accounting for assets resulting from R&D activities discussed in the "Business Combinations" section of this chapter; however, they would not be amortized until the R&D project is completed.

Chapter 5

Disclosures of Assets Acquired That Are to Be Used in Research and Development Activities

Business Combinations

5.01 When considering best practices for disclosures related to assets acquired in a business combination to be used in research and development (R&D) activities, the IPR&D Task Force (task force) observed that the disclosures required by accounting principles generally accepted in the United States of America (GAAP) and, for SEC registrants, Regulations S-K and S-X are somewhat limited. For example, Financial Accounting Standards Board (FASB) *Accounting Standards Codification* (ASC) 805-10-50-1(c) requires that for business combinations that occur during the reporting period, entities disclose the "amounts recognized as of the acquisition date for each major class of assets acquired and liabilities assumed."

5.02 The task force also observes that FASB ASC 805, *Business Combinations*, does not require disclosure of valuation methods and assumptions or qualitative information about assets acquired. The required disclosures for a business combination are addressed in FASB ASC 805-10-50, 805-20-50, 805-30-50, and 805-40-50.

5.03 When determining whether reporting entities should provide additional disclosures about in-process R&D (IPR&D), the task force identified the following general considerations:

- Financial statement disclosures need to be provided only about items that are qualitatively or quantitatively material—individually or in the aggregate.

- Disclosures about IPR&D should be considered in the context of the financial statements as a whole. The extent of disclosures about IPR&D should not give undue emphasis to IPR&D when R&D is a relatively minor aspect of the overall financial activities of the company.

- To the extent that contemplated disclosures about IPR&D include forward-looking information, a public company should consider the legal implications of including those disclosures in the financial statements, rather than outside the financial statements, such as in management's discussion and analysis (MD&A). The task force noted that the safe harbor for forward-looking information adopted in the Private Securities Litigation Reform Act of 1995 does not extend to financial statement disclosures.

- Nonpublic companies should consider making the disclosures that a comparable public company would make.

5.04 The task force developed the following sample footnote disclosures as an illustration of the disclosure requirements of FASB ASC 805-20-50-1(c) as it relates to a significant acquisition involving assets to be used in R&D activities. (FASB ASC 805-10-55 provides illustrations of some of its disclosure requirements.) Note that this sample disclosure is not intended to be inclusive

AAG-RDA 5.04

of all the disclosure requirements set forth in FASB ASC 805. In addition, this example is not intended to represent the necessary disclosures for all business combinations involving acquisition of assets to be used in R&D activities because an entity's disclosures are based upon the facts and circumstances, as well as the materiality of each acquisition.

    a. NOTE WW. SIGNIFICANT ACCOUNTING POLICIES—RESEARCH AND DEVELOPMENT (*Example not specific to any industry*)

> IPR&D assets represent capitalized incomplete research projects that Company A acquired through business combinations. Such assets are initially measured at their acquisition date fair values. For transactions that closed prior to 2009, the fair value of such projects was expensed upon acquisition unless they had an alternative future use. For transactions that close after January 1, 2009,[1] the fair value of the research projects is recorded as intangible assets on the consolidated balance sheet, rather than expensed, regardless of whether these assets have an alternative future use.
>
> The amounts capitalized are being accounted for as indefinite-lived intangible assets, subject to impairment testing, until completion or abandonment of R&D efforts associated with the projects. An IPR&D asset is considered abandoned when it ceases to be used (that is, R&D efforts associated with the asset have ceased, and there are no plans to sell or license the asset or derive defensive value from the asset). At that point, the asset is considered to be disposed of and is written off. Upon successful completion of each project, Company A will make a determination about the then remaining useful life of the intangible asset and begin amortization. Company A tests its indefinite-lived intangibles, including IPR&D assets, for impairment annually and more frequently if events or changes in circumstances indicate that it is more likely than not that the asset is impaired. When testing indefinite-lived intangibles for impairment, Company A may assess qualitative factors for some or all of its indefinite-lived intangibles to determine whether it is more likely than not (that is, a likelihood of more than 50 percent) that the asset is impaired. Alternatively, Company A may bypass this qualitative assessment for some or all of its indefinite-lived intangibles and perform the quantitative impairment test that compares the fair value of the indefinite-lived intangible asset with the asset's carrying amount.
>
> IPR&D projects acquired as part of an asset acquisition are expensed as incurred unless they have an alternative future use.

---

[1] Financial Accounting Standards Board (FASB) Statement No. 141(R), *Business Combinations* (codified in FASB *Accounting Standards Codification* 805, *Business Combinations*), was required to be applied prospectively to business combinations for which the acquisition date was on or after the beginning of the first annual reporting period beginning on or after December 15, 2008. Earlier application was prohibited. Therefore, for calendar year companies, FASB Statement No. 141(R) became effective for transactions that closed on or after January 1, 2009. The company in this example is assumed to be a calendar year company.

R&D costs are expensed as incurred. These expenses include the costs of our proprietary R&D efforts, as well as costs of IPR&D projects acquired as part of an asset acquisition that have no alternative future use.

b. NOTE XX. ACQUISITIONS (*Technology company example*)

On October 5, 2009, Company A acquired all of the outstanding shares of Company T in a transaction accounted for as a business combination. Company T was engaged in licensing, implementing, and supporting business network software systems and had a well-established global service and support team. As a result of this acquisition, Company A is expected to become the largest provider of business network software systems in North America.

The total consideration transferred of $1 billion for Company T's equity consisted of approximately $400 million in cash and the issuance of four million shares of Company A's common stock with a fair value of $600 million. In addition, $20 million of acquisition-related costs were included in selling, general, and administrative expenses for year ended December 31, 2009. The goodwill of $785 million recognized by Company A because of the acquisition is due primarily to synergies of the combination of Company A and Company T. Short-term liabilities with a fair value of $300 million and long-term liabilities with a fair value of $700 million were assumed by Company A. The results of operations of Company T and the fair value of the assets acquired and liabilities assumed are included in Company A's financial statements from the date of acquisition.

The following table summarizes the amounts of assets acquired and liabilities assumed that were recognized at the acquisition date:

Assets Acquired & Liabilities Assumed
as of the Acquisition Date

Inventory	$100
Property, plant, and equipment	650
Identifiable intangible assets:	
Developed technology	175
Customer list	25
Trade names	40
IPR&D	200
Other assets	25
Short-term liabilities	(300)
Long-term liabilities	(700)
Total identifiable net assets	$215
Goodwill	785
	$1,000

$200 million of the consideration paid represents the fair value of acquired IPR&D projects that are considered identifiable assets as of the acquisition date. Those assets are considered indefinite lived until R&D efforts associated with the projects are completed or abandoned. The major acquired technology IPR&D projects include project A and project B.

[Note: Required pro forma disclosures have been omitted.]

c. NOTE YY: GOODWILL AND OTHER INTANGIBLE ASSETS—IN-PROCESS RESEARCH AND DEVELOPMENT (*Pharmaceutical company example*)

IPR&D assets represent IPR&D projects that have not yet received regulatory approval and are required to be classified as indefinite-lived assets until the successful completion or the abandonment of the associated R&D efforts. Accordingly, during the development period after the date of acquisition, these assets will not be amortized until approval is obtained in one or more jurisdictions which, individually or combined, are expected to generate a significant portion of the total revenue expected to be earned by an IPR&D project. At that time, we will determine the useful life of the asset, reclassify the asset out of IPR&D, and begin amortization. In 2009, project A received regulatory approval in a jurisdiction that is expected to generate a significant portion of the total revenue expected to be earned by that project and, as a result, we reclassified the asset from IPR&D to Developed Technology and began to amortize the asset.

If the associated R&D effort is abandoned, the related IPR&D assets will likely be written off.

All of these IPR&D assets were acquired in connection with our acquisition of Company T. The significant components of IPR&D assets are project A and projects for the treatment of Alzheimer's disease, cancer, and leukemia, among others.

5.05 *MD&A.* The task force notes that the objectives and requirements of MD&A, as stated in the instructions in Regulation S-K, include the following:

- The purpose of MD&A is to provide to investors and other users information relevant to an assessment of the financial condition and results of operations of the registrant as determined by evaluating the amounts and certainty of cash flows from operations and outside sources. The information provided need only include that which does not clearly appear in the registrant's financial statements.

- MD&A should focus specifically on material events and uncertainties known to management that would cause reported financial information not to be necessarily indicative of future operating results or future financial condition. This would include descriptions and amounts of

    — matters that would have an impact on future operations and have not had an impact in the past and

— matters that have had an impact on reported operations and are not expected to have an impact upon future operations.

5.06 Registrants are encouraged, but not required, to supply forward-looking information. This is to be distinguished from presently known data that will affect future operating results, such as known future increases in costs. This latter data may be required to be disclosed. Any forward-looking information supplied is expressly covered by the safe harbor rule for projections.

5.07 The task force also notes the following considerations that could influence management's consideration of disclosures to be included in MD&A regarding IPR&D:

- Acquired IPR&D projects represent a known event that may produce uncertainty that could reasonably be expected to materially affect future operating results due to additional R&D expenses expected to be incurred to complete the projects and changes in revenue and profitability from changes in the product sales mix.

- Acquired IPR&D projects may represent a material demand on liquid resources to fund completion of the projects.

- Qualitative information about management's objectives in material acquisitions of businesses and intangibles may be helpful in understanding the financial statements "through the eyes of management."

- The nature of certain businesses may be high risk and require investment in a large number of projects for achieving a successful portfolio of approved products. As such, many of the early-stage acquired IPR&D projects could become impaired and be written off at some time in the future.

Additional Considerations for Asset Acquisitions

5.08 The task force observed that the disclosures required by GAAP in FASB ASC 730, *Research and Development*, are limited to the total R&D costs charged to expense in each period for which an income statement is presented. In addition, FASB ASC 350-30-50-1(c) requires disclosing the amount of IPR&D assets acquired in an asset acquisition and written off in the period, and the line item in the income statement in which the amounts written off are aggregated.

5.09 When determining whether entities should provide additional disclosures about IPR&D assets, the task force believes the same general considerations should be made for asset acquisitions as identified previously for IPR&D assets acquired in a business combination.

5.10 The task force developed the following sample footnote disclosures as an illustration of best practices for a significant asset acquisition involving IPR&D assets. Note that this sample disclosure is not intended to be applicable for all fact patterns; an entity's disclosures are based on the facts and circumstances, as well as the materiality of each acquisition.

a. NOTE X: SIGNIFICANT ACCOUNTING POLICIES—RESEARCH AND DEVELOPMENT

R&D costs are expensed as incurred. These expenses include the costs of our proprietary R&D efforts, as well as costs of IPR&D projects acquired as part of an asset acquisition that have no alternative future use. Upfront and milestone payments due to third parties in connection with R&D collaborations prior to regulatory approval are expensed as incurred. Milestone payments due to third parties upon, or subsequent to, regulatory approval are capitalized and amortized over the shorter of the remaining license or product patent life. Nonrefundable advance payments for goods and services that will be used in future R&D activities are expensed when the activity has been performed or when the goods have been received, rather than when the payment is made.

Company A incurred R&D expenses of $X, $Y, and $Z million in 2009, 2008, and 2007, respectively, including IPR&D of $200 million that was acquired in an asset acquisition in 2009 and had no alternative future use. The value of acquired IPR&D that was expensed was determined by identifying those acquired specific IPR&D projects that would be continued and which (a) were incomplete and (b) had no alternative future use.

b. NOTE XX. ASSET ACQUISITION

On October 5, 2009, Company A acquired a library of molecules for high-throughput screening of drug candidates and certain potential drug candidates for $300 million in cash. We allocated the consideration paid based on relative fair value, and $100 million was attributable to the intellectual property related to the library of molecules that had an alternative future use and, as a result, was recognized as an identifiable intangible asset with an estimated remaining useful life of five years. The remaining $200 million was recorded as R&D expense because the potential drug candidates do not have an alternative future use.

Questions and Answers—Asset Acquisitions

5.11 The task force identified the following question related to situations in which the reporting for asset acquisitions in financial statements has historically reflected diversity in practice.

5.12 *Question 1:* How should an acquiring entity classify in its statement of cash flows an R&D charge associated with the costs of IPR&D projects acquired as part of an asset acquisition that have no alternative future use?

Answer: Best practices suggest that an acquiring entity should report its cash acquisition of assets to be used in R&D activities as an investing outflow in its statement of cash flows. In this regard, an acquiring entity should treat assets acquired to be used in R&D activities similar to how it reports other acquired assets in the statement of cash flows. Although acquired IPR&D may lack an alternative future use and, therefore, would be expensed immediately, it is still an asset for cash flow statement purposes.

When arriving at cash flows from operating activities under the indirect method of reporting cash flows, best practices suggest that an acquiring entity should add back to net income the costs of assets acquired to be used in R&D activities that are charged to expense. That adjustment is necessary to eliminate from operating cash flows those cash outflows of assets acquired to be used in R&D activities that are reflected in investing activities.

Chapter 6

Valuation of In-Process Research and Development Assets[1]

Introduction

6.01 This chapter describes best practices related to measuring the fair value of the intangible assets used in research and development (R&D) activities, including specific in-process R&D (IPR&D) projects (subsequently referred to as *IPR&D assets*) for financial reporting purposes. Although this guide and this chapter focus mostly on IPR&D assets, methodologies described in this chapter can also be utilized for estimating fair value of assets resulting from R&D activities. This chapter discusses relevant considerations related to Financial Accounting Standards Board (FASB) *Accounting Standards Codification* (ASC) 820, *Fair Value Measurement*, identification of the appropriate valuation methodologies, use of prospective financial information (PFI), specific considerations for the various methodologies a reporting entity would use to value IPR&D assets and valuation report considerations and includes a comprehensive example that demonstrates application of concepts discussed.

6.02 It should be noted that the acquisition of IPR&D assets often involves an element of contingent consideration. Although the valuation of contingent consideration is beyond the scope of this guide, this chapter contains several references to contingent consideration to remind valuation specialists that assumptions used in valuing IPR&D assets and related contingent consideration in a business combination would need to be consistent or reconcilable. For example, discount rates used in measuring the contingent consideration would need to be compared and contrasted with the discount rates used for valuing IPR&D assets, which may contain similar, but not identical, conditional aspects. For instance, a payout of contingent consideration will often have a shorter duration than the IPR&D project and resulting product to which it is linked because it may be associated with a specific milestone or a series of milestones. Conversely, if there is a contingent consideration associated with the IPR&D asset being valued and the asset and liability correspond to each other (for example, in terms of cash flows, risk characteristics, and so on), the IPR&D Task Force (task force) recommends that a valuation specialist consider the appropriateness of synchronizing methodologies and inputs employed to value the IPR&D asset and the corresponding liability. However, in situations in which IPR&D assets are valued using conditional value (*discount rate adjustment techniques*), while liabilities such as those associated with contingent consideration are valued using *expected present value techniques*, discount rates used to value IPR&D assets and related contingent consideration in a business combination would likely be different and, thus, would need to be reconciled.

---

[1] This chapter includes a number of examples that demonstrate concepts discussed in this and preceding chapters of this guide and are not intended to establish requirements. Furthermore, the assumptions and inputs used in these examples are illustrative only and are not intended to serve as guidelines. Facts and circumstances of each individual situation should be considered when performing an actual valuation.

Considerations Related to FASB ASC 820

Overview

6.03 As noted previously, FASB ASC 805, *Business Combination*, requires that identifiable assets acquired and liabilities assumed in a business combination be recognized at their fair values (provided they meet the definitions of assets and liabilities in FASB Concepts Statement No. 6, *Elements of Financial Statements*, at the acquisition date.) In asset acquisitions, consistent with FASB ASC 730-10-25-2(c), intangible assets that are purchased from others for use in R&D activities are capitalized only if they have alternative future uses. Furthermore, IPR&D assets acquired in asset acquisitions are measured at cost allocated based on their relative fair values. Subsequent to a business combination or an asset acquisition, capitalized IPR&D assets and assets resulting from R&D activities would need to be measured at fair value for impairment testing purposes (see chapter 4, "Subsequent Accounting for Acquired Intangible Assets That Are to Be Used in Research and Development Activities," for a detailed discussion regarding impairment testing.) FASB ASC 820 provides the framework for measuring these fair values. Although this guide does not provide an in-depth discussion of FASB ASC 820, the following sections focus on those aspects of FASB ASC 820 that affect the assumptions and methods or techniques used in the valuation of IPR&D assets.

6.04 FASB ASC 820 codifies a number of fair value concepts, representing the framework for fair value measurement in financial reporting. These concepts include the following:

- *Fair value definition.* Under FASB ASC 820, *fair value* is defined as the price that would be received to sell an asset or paid to transfer a liability in an orderly transaction between market participants at the measurement date. It is important to note that under this definition, fair value is an exit price from a market participant perspective.

- *Principal (or most advantageous) market.* FASB ASC 820-10-35-5 states that a fair value measurement assumes that the transaction to sell the asset or transfer the liability takes place either in the *principal market* (defined as the market with the greatest volume and level of activity for the asset or liability) for the asset or liability or, in the absence of a principal market, in the *most advantageous market* (defined as the market that maximizes the amount that would be received to sell the asset or minimizes the amount that would be paid to transfer the liability, after taking into account transaction costs and transportation costs) for the asset or liability.

- *Highest and best use for nonfinancial assets.* Defined as the use of a nonfinancial asset by market participants that would maximize the value of the asset or the group of assets and liabilities (for example, a business) within which the asset would be used. FASB ASC 820-10-35-10E indicates that the highest and best use of a nonfinancial asset establishes the valuation premise used to measure the fair value of the asset, as follows: (*a*) in combination with other assets or with other assets and liabilities, and (*b*) on a standalone basis. Refer to the "Highest and Best Use for

Nonfinancial Assets" section in paragraphs 6.15–.18 for a more detailed discussion.

- *Market participants.* FASB ASC 820-10-35-9 provides that a reporting entity should measure the fair value of an asset or a liability using the assumptions that market participants would use in pricing the asset or liability, assuming that market participants act in their economic best interest. Refer to the "Identification of Market Participants" section in paragraphs 6.06–.14 for a more detailed discussion.

- *Valuation techniques.* FASB ASC 820-10-35-24A provides that three widely used valuation techniques are the market approach, cost approach, and income approach. The main aspects of those approaches are summarized in paragraphs 3A–3G of FASB ASC 820-10-55. An entity should use valuation techniques consistent with one or more of those approaches to measure fair value.

- *Fair value hierarchy.* FASB ASC 820-10 establishes a fair value hierarchy that categorizes into three levels (level 1, level 2, and level 3) the inputs to valuation techniques used to measure fair value. The fair value hierarchy gives the highest priority to quoted prices (unadjusted) in *active markets* for identical assets or liabilities (level 1 inputs) and the lowest priority to *unobservable inputs* (level 3 inputs). However, when valuing IPR&D assets, unobservable inputs are often used due to lack of relevant observable data.

6.05 Key considerations from FASB ASC 820 that affect fair value measurement of IPR&D assets include market participants and the highest and best use (in combination with other assets or with other assets and liabilities or on a standalone basis). The following are brief discussions of these concepts and some examples that illustrate them.

Identification of Market Participants

6.06 FASB ASC 820 defines *fair value* as the price that would be received to sell an asset or paid to transfer a liability in an orderly transaction between market participants at the measurement date. Therefore, before the appropriate valuation method or key assumptions can be selected for a given IPR&D asset, it is necessary to identify the characteristics of the appropriate market participants.

6.07 According to the FASB ASC glossary, *market participants* are

[b]uyers and sellers in the principal (or most advantageous) market for the asset or liability that have all of the following characteristics:

a. They are independent of each other, that is, they are not related parties, although the price in a related-party transaction may be used as an input to a fair value measurement if the reporting entity has evidence that the transaction was entered into at market terms

b. They are knowledgeable, having a reasonable understanding about the asset or liability and the transaction using all available information, including information that might be obtained through due diligence efforts that are usual and customary

  c. They are able to enter into a transaction for the asset or liability

  d. They are willing to enter into a transaction for the asset or liability, that is, they are motivated but not forced or otherwise compelled to do so.

6.08 As indicated in paragraph 6.04, when valuing IPR&D assets, unobservable inputs are often used due to lack of relevant observable data. FASB ASC 820-10-35-54A states that

> [a] reporting entity shall develop unobservable inputs using the best information available in the circumstances, which might include the reporting entity's own data. In developing unobservable inputs, a reporting entity may begin with its own data, but it shall adjust those data if reasonably available information indicates that other market participants would use different data or there is something particular to the reporting entity that is not available to other market participants (for example, an entity-specific synergy). A reporting entity need not undertake exhaustive efforts to obtain information about market participant assumptions. However, a reporting entity shall take into account all information about market participant assumptions that is reasonably available. Unobservable inputs developed in the manner described above are considered market participant assumptions and meet the objective of a fair value measurement.

Thus, the task force believes that the reporting entity is not precluded from being a market participant as long as the transaction entered into is arm's length in nature. However, the task force believes that it is incumbent upon the reporting entity to ensure that its own assumptions are consistent with those of market participants. See paragraphs 6.42–.47 for further discussion about ensuring that the reporting entity's assumptions are consistent with those of market participants.

6.09 FASB ASC 820-10-35-9 states that "the reporting entity need not identify specific market participants. Rather, the reporting entity shall identify characteristics that distinguish market participants generally." The identification of market participant characteristics is an important aspect of the valuation process, particularly when considering how an asset or liability will be used. However, the identification of market participant characteristics is subjective and dependent on specific facts and circumstances. Helpful sources of information to consider when performing this identification include the following:

- In the case of a business combination or an asset acquisition (subsequently collectively referred to as a *transaction*): press releases, prior bids, board of director presentations, due diligence documents, transaction models, a list of all known bidders in the transaction and those who did not participate in the bidding process (if the transaction was subject to competitive bids), a list of comparable companies, and so forth

- In the absence of a transaction: management's discussion and analysis of the reporting entity and its competitors; industry, market, and government studies; merger and acquisition activity surrounding private equity, venture capital, and hedge funds

6.10 Also, when identifying market participant characteristics, it may be helpful to consider the following factors:

- Current industry trends (for example, consolidation), as well as motivations of key competitors and potential bidders for entities and assets and whether market transactions align with those trends and motivations. For example, a shortage of raw materials or decline in demand for certain industries could be an indication for future industry consolidation. As another example, consolidation would generally be anticipated in the pharmaceutical industry if pharmaceutical companies face dwindling drug pipelines, coupled with increasing R&D costs.

- In the case of a transaction, the subject entity's growth and profitability prospects on a standalone basis and in conjunction with the operations and perspectives of the potential market participants (that is, the actual and potential bidders). This analysis would take into account the subject entity's expected performance within the context of key competitors' performance, industry performance, and the overall economy.

- In the case of a transaction, strategic intent of the acquirer versus the intent of the potential market participants to determine the rationale for the transaction.

- In the case of a transaction, nature of any preexisting relationship between acquirer and subject, if any. Assumptions regarding whether the acquirer could be a key supplier, a key customer, or a key competitor of the target (present or potential) should be evaluated.

- Geographic location of the reporting entity's operations or markets served, or both, which could affect highest and best use of assets being valued, existence and extent of *synergies*, and so forth.

- The general economy and capital market condition, which could affect the ability of companies to successfully bid for similar businesses, the volume of acquisitions entered into by strategic buyers versus financial buyers, and so forth. For instance, during periods of economic turmoil, acquisitions by private equity firms decline significantly because such buyers are generally unable to access debt capital levels or terms that are available to them during times of economic strength and growth.

6.11 If there are numerous potential market participants for a particular business or asset, the most likely market participant may be considered to be the one who would most highly value the business or asset as of the acquisition date. As a result, the acquirer in the subject transaction may be presumed to have been willing to pay the highest price for the acquired assets and, therefore, could be indicative of the characteristics of likely market participants. However, for situations in which there was no bidding process, the seller was under distress, entity-specific synergies affected the transaction, or pricing errors were made, this may not be an appropriate assumption.

6.12 In addition, reporting entities and valuation specialists need to be aware that there may be a difference between the market participants for a particular business and those for a specific asset or collection of assets. In most circumstances, the highest price is paid for a collection of assets or the business as a whole. Therefore, determining the likely market participants may prove to be challenging at the individual asset level. From a practical perspective, however, due to the lack of transaction activity for specific assets or collection of assets, the set of likely market participants may be identical for the overall entity, as well as for the specific asset or collection of assets. However, there could be exceptions, such as a defensive asset situation in which market participants would continue with the development of the asset.

6.13 When identifying market participants, a reporting entity should consider both strategic and financial buyers. *Strategic buyers* engage in the same or related businesses and are likely peer companies or competitors of the subject entity or the reporting entity. Other buyers, including those that may not have investments in similar businesses or operations of the subject entity or the reporting entity, may also be considered market participants. These buyers, commonly referred to as *financial buyers*, may include individual investors, private equity and venture capital investors, and institutional investors. Private equity buyers, who have traditionally been considered financial buyers, have recently often been viewed as strategic buyers as well, based on their deep technical expertise in certain industries or through potential synergies that may be obtained in combination with other portfolio companies. Strategic buyers may also invest in businesses or operations unrelated to their business for diversification purposes.

6.14 FASB ASC 820 requires that fair value be measured using the assumptions that market participants would use when pricing an asset or a liability. Therefore, the distinction between financial and strategic buyers becomes significant when considering the cash flows and returns these assets and liabilities would be expected to generate in the postacquisition period. For example, consideration of operating synergies would be quite different between the two sets of potential buyers. Although strategic buyers will often expect to realize cost-saving synergies resulting from eliminating redundant administrative and other personnel functions or revenue synergies resulting from introduction to new markets or customers or the cross-selling of complementary products, or both, financial buyers will be unlikely to expect such synergies. The identification of the appropriate market participants and fact patterns will, therefore, influence whether the effects of such synergies should be included or excluded from the analysis.

Highest and Best Use for Nonfinancial Assets

6.15 In addition to the requirement to identify the characteristics of market participants for a given asset or liability, for nonfinancial assets, FASB ASC 820 also requires an entity to identify the asset's highest and best use. The FASB ASC glossary defines *highest and best use* as the use of a nonfinancial asset by market participants that would maximize the value of the asset or the group of assets and liabilities (for example, a business) within which the asset would be used. According to FASB ASC 820-10-35-10B, the highest and best use of a nonfinancial asset takes into account the use of the asset that is physically possible, legally permissible, and financially feasible. FASB ASC 820-10-35-10E provides that the highest and best use of a nonfinancial asset establishes the valuation premise used to measure the fair value of the asset. The valuation premise assumes that the asset would be used either (*a*) in combination with other assets as a group (as installed or otherwise configured for use) or in combination with other assets and liabilities (for example, a business) or (*b*) on a standalone basis.

6.16 Most IPR&D assets will provide maximum value through their use in combination with other assets or other assets and liabilities. Situations may arise, however, in which IPR&D assets will provide maximum value on a standalone basis. For example, if market participant buyers of a technology asset would likely choose to maximize value by outlicensing the IPR&D asset, the highest and best use of that asset would be on a standalone basis, and the valuation should be based on that premise. (See "Case A: Asset Group" in paragraphs 26–29 of FASB ASC 820-10-55, which demonstrates the asset grouping concept.)

6.17 As discussed in FASB ASC 805-20-30-6, the highest and best use by a market participant may differ from that of the reporting entity. For example, although the reporting entity might choose to discontinue the use of certain IPR&D assets, if market participants would maximize value by utilizing the asset for an extended period, this longer useful life would be used in the valuation analysis. (However, according to FASB ASC 350-30-35-1, "[t]he accounting for a recognized intangible asset is based on its useful life to the reporting entity." Therefore, the useful life for accounting purposes is based on management's expectations, not market participant's assumptions. For more information, see the "Useful Life of Assets Resulting From R&D Activities" section in paragraphs 4.37–.42.) Other operating assumptions are similarly affected by the highest and best use valuation premise.

6.18 The identification of market participants and their highest and best use of a given nonfinancial asset are often of the utmost importance when dealing with assets used in R&D activities that may become monetized through various methods. Specifically, in the pharmaceutical and biotechnology industries, larger companies with developed infrastructure and expertise will often research, develop, manufacture, market, and distribute products independently. Smaller companies in these industries, however, will typically partner with a third party once their products reach a certain level of development and effectively outsource a number of the research and operational functions in exchange for profit-sharing arrangements. Because the cash flows and risks of these two business models vary significantly, the determination of how market participants would choose to monetize their investment in IPR&D assets has a substantial impact on the prospective cash flows from these assets and the valuation method or technique used to measure their fair value. See "Case C: In-Process Research and Development Project" in FASB ASC 820-10-55-32, which discusses how to determine the highest and best use for an IPR&D project, which the reporting entity does not intend to complete.

Questions and Answers—Market Participants; Highest and Best Use; Defensive IPR&D Assets; and IPR&D Assets That Will Continue to Be Pursued

Electronic Devices Industry

6.19 *Question 1:* Company A acquired Company T in a business combination. Both Company A and Company T design, manufacture, and market networking products used in the IT and telecommunications markets. Based on an assessment of Company T and the networking products industry, Company A's management believes that industry participants, such as Company A, represent the most likely buyers of Company T's assets. Therefore, Company

A's management believes that strategic buyers reflect the market participants for the acquisition of Company T. Company A has an ongoing IPR&D project, project A, the goal of which is to develop a product for optimizing the performance of in-home wireless computing, which is believed to represent a significant market opportunity. At the time of the business combination, Company T also had an ongoing IPR&D project, project T, related to the design of a product that would compete directly against the product developed by project A. In evaluating Company T's IPR&D project, Company A's management determined that it would not continue project T due to the greater potential of Company A's project A, but that other market participants would likely choose to continue investing in project T because such a decision would maximize the value of the group of assets in which project T would be used. Assuming recognition is appropriate for accounting purposes (which is discussed in chapter 2, "Definition of and Accounting for Assets Acquired in a Business Combination That Are to Be Used in Research and Development Activities"), what valuation premise should company A use to value project T?

Answer: Company A's decision to discontinue project T reflects entity-specific factors that are unique to Company A and, therefore, do not represent market participant assumptions. Due to the determination that other market participants would likely continue investing in project T, the highest and best use of project T would be assessed considering its continued pursuit by market participants. (The outcome in this example is similar to outcome (a) in "Case C: In-Process Research and Development Project" in FASB ASC 820-10-55-32.)

6.20 *Question 2:* Assuming the same fact pattern as in question 1, how should this asset be valued, and from what sources should data be gathered?

Answer: Company A should consider using appropriate valuation techniques and potentially consider data sources primarily from Company T's management and other market participants because they would represent parties that would continue developing project T. See chapter 1, "Valuation Techniques Used to Measure Fair Value of In-Process Research and Development Assets," for discussion of valuation techniques commonly used to value IPR&D assets. See paragraphs 6.28–.47 (Steps 1–3) for a discussion of sources of data to be used in valuing IPR&D assets, including those that would be considered when preparing and evaluating PFI. The quality and quantity of data available, along with the characteristics of an IPR&D asset, may influence the selection of valuation techniques used to value that IPR&D asset.

6.21 *Question 3:* Assume the same facts as in question 1. However, in evaluating Company T's IPR&D project, Company A's management determined that other market participants either have already launched competing products or had their own IPR&D projects nearing completion. As a result, Company A's management determined that other market participants would also likely choose to discontinue investing in project T. However, due to the fact that idling project T removes a potential competing product from the market, the decision to idle project T improves the outlook for competing IPR&D projects, such as project A, and existing products. Assuming recognition is appropriate for accounting purposes (which is discussed in chapter 2), what valuation premise should Company A use to value project T?

Answer: Company A should value project T at fair value based on market participant assumptions, which in this circumstance, would reflect its use as a defensive asset. In this example, project T is an asset that Company A does not intend to use directly, but it is likely contributing to an increase in the fair value of Company A's assets related to project A. (The outcome in this example is similar to outcome (b) in "Case C: In-Process Research and Development Project" in FASB ASC 820-10-55-32.)

6.22 *Question 4:* Assuming the same fact pattern as in question 3, how should this asset be valued, and from what sources should data be gathered?

Answer: Methods that recognize the incremental revenue, decreased costs, decreased risks, and so forth, to a market participant (for example, using the "with and without" method) might be more appropriate for use in situations such as this. Data would be gathered primarily from Company A's management as long as their use of the asset is consistent with market participant assumptions.

Pharmaceutical Industry

6.23 *Question 5:* Company A, a biopharmaceutical company engaged in drug development, acquired 100 percent of the equity of Company T, also a biopharmaceutical company engaged in drug development. Company T was acquired primarily for its two IPR&D assets, compound T-1 and compound T-2 (the compounds). The compounds, currently in phase II of clinical trials, were acquired largely to be combined with Company A's own existing compound, compound A-3. Company A's management believes either of the compounds could be combined with compound A-3 as part of an overall drug portfolio to be sold in the market as a comprehensive treatment of a specific medical condition. As part of this assumption, Company A has projected significant revenue synergies resulting from this acquisition. Further, Company A's management indicated the incremental cost associated with selling one of the compounds in conjunction with another existing product was minimal, resulting in significant increases in profitability. Several other biopharmaceutical companies were part of the bidding process for Company T; as such, they are assumed to be market participants. These fellow bidders also own and are developing similar compounds to compound A-3, and these bidders would have similar intentions for combining their similar compounds with the compounds of Company T. Therefore, the assumptions Company A's management made in the PFI surrounding the revenue synergies resulting from the acquisition were considered to be consistent with other market participants. What is the highest and best use for compounds T-1 and T-2, including whether they should be valued on a standalone basis or in combination with other assets or with other assets and liabilities?

Answer: Facts described in question 5 suggest that from a market participant perspective, the highest and best use of either compound T-1 or compound T-2 will be in combination with compound A-3. It is uncertain which of these two compounds will eventually produce the successful product. Also, the facts suggest that only one compound will ultimately be used, and R&D efforts associated with the other one will be abandoned. Therefore, the highest and best use for the two acquired compounds is in combination with compound A-3, and the valuation would be based on the single product that would result from the combination of compound A-3 with either compound T-1 or T-2. (Please note that question 5 only addresses the highest and best use considerations for purposes of valuing the asset(s) and does not address the unit of account from an accounting perspective. For an in-depth discussion of unit of account considerations, please refer to chapter 2.)

6.24 *Question 6:* Assume the same facts as in question 5. Also, compound T-1 was considered the lead compound, whereas compound T-2 was considered a secondary asset, which would be developed if compound T-1 fails in clinical trials. Any strategic buyer of Company T would expect to achieve the highest sales synergies through developing compound T-1. Based on the phase I trial results, Company A's management believes compound T-1 is a superior compound. Compound T-2 was deemed less potent, has a lesser effect, and faced potential formulation challenges when compared with compound T-1, based on the latest clinical trial results. Therefore, Company A's management believes any market participant would pursue development of compound T-2 only if compound T-1 fails clinical trials. What is the highest and best use for compounds T-1 and T-2, including whether they should be valued on a standalone basis or in combination with other assets or with other assets and liabilities?

Answer: In this case, the highest and best use would likely be to measure the fair value of compound T-1 and T-2 on a combined basis because the value of compound T-2 is contingent on the success or failure of compound T-1, from the perspective of the market participant. As in question 5, the revenue and cost synergies available to Company A would have to be evaluated from the perspective of the market participants.

6.25 *Question 7:* Assume the same facts as in question 5. Also, Company T has developed compound T-4 for the treatment of a medical condition that is different from the medical condition that will be treated by compounds T-1, T-2, and A-3. Because Company A does not have a development platform for this different medical condition, Company A does not intend to develop compound T-4 further. However, other market participants with these development platforms may perceive compound T-4 to be valuable. What is the highest and best use for compound T-4, including whether it should be valued on a standalone basis or in combination with other assets or with other assets and liabilities?

Answer: In this case, compound T-4's fair value would best be measured on a standalone basis. The fair value of compound T-4 would be measured based on the highest and best use from a market participant perspective, which in this case, would differ from Company A's expected usage.

Use of Prospective Financial Information

Overview

6.26 As noted in chapter 1, valuation approaches may be classified broadly as cost, market, or income approaches. IPR&D assets are most typically valued using the income approach, which requires the use of PFI. This section addresses steps to derive, prepare, and analyze the PFI for IPR&D assets.

6.27 The application of the valuation methods or techniques that fall under the income approach (such as the multiperiod excess earnings, relief from royalty, decision tree, and real option techniques) generally begin with the following steps related to the overall PFI for the subject entity:

- Step 1: In the case of a transaction, select the PFI that best reflects the assumptions made by the parties in determining the final purchase price. Alternatively, consider subject company's budgets, business plans, forecasts, and projections.[2]

- Step 2: Evaluate and document the key assumptions relating to the PFI.

- Step 3: Ensure that the assumptions made in the development of the PFI are consistent with those of market participants.

- Step 4: Isolate the PFI related to the IPR&D assets.

- Step 5: Compare the PFI attributable to the IPR&D assets to the PFI for the overall entity.

Steps

Step 1: In the Case of a Transaction, Select the PFI That Best Reflects the Assumptions Made by the Parties in Determining the Final Purchase Price. Alternatively, Consider Subject Company's Budgets, Business Plans, Forecasts, and Projections

6.28 PFI can potentially come from a number of different sources, each of which may require certain modifications and considerations in order to be used in the valuation of IPR&D assets. The following is a list of some sources from which PFI can be derived:

- Acquisition models prepared by the acquirer or its advisers to perform due diligence on the subject company or determine a bidding price

- Internal budgets and forecasts prepared by the subject company

- Projections prepared by the subject company or its advisers in connection with efforts to market the business to potential acquirers (for example, offering memoranda)

- Board of director presentations prepared by the acquirer or the subject company

- Product road maps, project snapshots, or other similar detail of the subject company's expected evolution from current products and technologies to future products and technologies

- Forecasts prepared for lenders

- Outlooks prepared by equity or industry analysts, government agencies, market experts, or other third parties who forecast operational trends for the subject company or its peers and competitors

6.29 Although not all of these data sources will be available in a given transaction, the task force believes that, at a minimum, the valuation specialist should collect data that would have been considered by potential acquirers in performing their due diligence. For instance, interviews with management and other informed parties can reveal additional information that was known or

---

[2] The terms *forecast* and *projection*, as used in this guide, refer to any process by which available evidence is accumulated and evaluated for purposes of measuring fair value of acquired in-process research and development (IPR&D) assets. Judgment is necessary to determine how detailed or formalized that evaluation process should be. This guide does not imply the need to prepare either a *financial forecast* or a *financial projection* within the meaning of those terms in AT section 301, *Financial Forecasts and Projections* (AICPA, *Professional Standards*).

knowable as of the date of the business combination but not contained in any of the documentation listed in the preceding paragraph. The valuation specialist also would need to consider significant changes in performance expectations that may have occurred between the date when the acquiring and subject companies came to final terms and the actual date of the business combination.

6.30 The task force believes that the valuation specialist should gain an understanding of the PFI that best represents the expectations that were used in negotiating the final purchase price and how this PFI reconciles with market participant assumptions. Typically, PFI considered by the acquiring company may be the most readily available data to the valuation specialist. However, this data may not accurately represent the expectations of market participants or the highest and best use of the assets (as discussed further in paragraphs 6.42–.47). As such, this PFI may not be the most appropriate for use in valuing the acquired assets and liabilities, and the task force believes that the PFI should be challenged and, when appropriate, adjusted to reflect market participant assumptions.

6.31 The valuation specialist should develop an understanding of the process by which the PFI was prepared in order to support various inputs and assumptions and evaluate their suitability for use in the valuation analysis.

6.32 When evaluating a potential target, various PFI alternatives may be prepared. The PFI may encompass various alternatives, including optimistic, base case, pessimistic scenarios, or all three. All PFI produced by parties to the transaction (as well as by their advisers) would need to be evaluated by the valuation specialist to understand the underlying assumptions and the differences between the sets of assumptions. Ultimately, however, the source PFI would need to be adjusted, when appropriate, to reflect the PFI expected by market participants.

Step 2: Evaluate and Document the Key Assumptions Relating to the PFI

6.33 The task force believes that management of the reporting entity should take responsibility for the completeness and accuracy of the PFI selected for use in the valuation analysis. Management would be expected to represent to the valuation specialist that the PFI represents management's best estimate of the economic benefits resulting from the assets being valued. Although the PFI may be documented only at an aggregate entity level, the aggregate PFI may need to be split into relevant components, which may include current and future products, IPR&D projects, geography, and so forth. Ultimately, management also would be expected to provide the valuation specialist with data supporting the key assumptions used in the preparation of the PFI, including identification of any expected synergies. Accordingly, the task force believes that the valuation specialist should not simply accept PFI from management without investigating its suitability for use in the valuation analysis. Instead, the valuation specialist is responsible for evaluating the assumptions used by management when preparing the PFI and concluding whether the PFI appears appropriate for use in valuing the IPR&D assets. In cases in which management does not have an appropriate set of PFI, the valuation specialist may assist management in the identification of such assumptions based on reasonable industry research and due diligence. However, management of the reporting entity is ultimately responsible for the PFI.

6.34 Historical financial data of the subject company is generally used as a starting point for evaluating the assumptions underlying the PFI to support the expectations for revenue and expense items, such as cost of sales, sales and marketing expenses, other operating expenses, R&D expenses, tax expenses, required levels of working capital and tangible assets, and so forth. Industry data, data from public filings of competitors, and reports generated by market research firms and industry analysts would also need to be considered as sources of objective evidence to support the assumptions in PFI.

6.35 The following is a brief discussion of specific elements of the PFI that generally would need to be evaluated by the valuation specialist, along with potential sources of objective evidence that may support each material assumption underlying the specific elements of PFI:

- *Revenue*. The valuation specialist's assessment of PFI begins with an analysis of the key assumptions related to revenue from current products and revenue that is expected to result from both specific IPR&D projects and R&D projects not yet commenced, including, when available, estimated number of units expected to be sold, estimated selling prices throughout the selling period, estimated market penetration, and estimated market share. The valuation specialist would need to evaluate year-over-year unit growth (or decline) rates over the product(s) life cycle(s) (that is, the period of years over which revenue is expected to be received for a given technology or related product offering) and the reasonableness of average per-unit selling prices during the period, taking into consideration expected competitors' reactions, anticipated technological developments, and historical trends. Also, in some cases, it may be appropriate to evaluate milestone payments as part of the revenue or cash flow streams. See question 1 in paragraph 2.14.

- *Costs of sales*. Valuation specialists would need to understand the difference between company-wide costs of sales and specific product-by-product costs of sales because costs of sales may change over a product's life cycle and likely will differ from product to product. It is important for valuation specialists to query management about past experience with prior product offerings and compare the trend of costs of sales for prior product offerings with those contained in the PFI.

- *R&D expense*. Historical financial data of the subject company and industry data would need to be analyzed to support R&D expense assumptions in the PFI for currently developed, in-process, and future projects. Valuation specialists would need to consider the maintenance R&D expenses for developed products and after the in-process and future projects launch, as well as the costs to complete for the in-process and future projects.

- *Sales and marketing expense*. Product launch costs would need to be included in PFI if product development activities are expected to lead to the introduction of new product offerings. Product launch costs commonly are incurred during the introduction of new product offerings and can differ dramatically from routine sales and marketing expense. Objective evidence may be gathered from the reporting entity or subject company's prior experience with previously launched product offerings or from industry and competitors' data.

- *Other operating expense.* Historical financial data of the subject company and industry data would need to be analyzed to support assumptions in the PFI related to general and administrative, technical support, and other operating expenses.

- *Required levels of net working capital and tangible assets.* PFI may include expectations regarding working capital and tangible asset needs for the subject company. Historical levels of working capital and tangible assets, combined with industry experience available from the public filings of competitors, typically serve as the best evidence of required levels of assets. Such levels will further serve as an input to the calculation of future contributory asset charges in the valuation analysis. See paragraphs 6.82–.98 for guidance on contributory asset charges.

- *Required levels of intangible assets.* PFI typically does not include expectations regarding the need to acquire additional intangible assets for the business in the aggregate because companies often do not budget purchases of intangible assets. Expenses related to the internal development of new intangible assets or maintenance of existing intangible assets, however, are typically included in PFI. Examples of such expenses include marketing or R&D expenses associated with the internal development or enhancement, or both, of brands and technology. Thus, such types of expenses would need to be considered and included within the PFI. Additionally, levels of other intangible assets calculated as a result of the fair value measurement process, combined with industry experience available from the competitors' public filings, typically serve as the best evidence of required levels of intangible assets. Such levels will further serve as an input to the calculation of contributory asset charges in the valuation analysis. See paragraphs 6.82–.98 for guidance on contributory asset charges.

6.36 When evaluating the assumptions used by management to develop the PFI, it is recommended that the valuation specialist also request (or gather through third party sources, when appropriate) some or all of the following information:

- Government, regulatory, or industry publications; market surveys; and engineering studies
- General economic indicators and industry statistics
- Historical financial statements of the subject company for an appropriate period of time (for example, the most recent three to five years for established companies)
- Transaction documents, press releases, board of directors' presentations, or other disclosures of the transaction
- Reports of analysts, market experts, governmental agencies, or other third parties, that relate to the transaction
- Technical analysis that relates to the subject company's products or technologies
- Sales or marketing materials used to sell the subject company's products and services

- Data on patents held by the subject company
- Subject company's analysis of its specific IPR&D projects, including analysis supporting management's approval of the projects and periodic status reports
- Description of the subject company's R&D function and how it is organized; R&D projects tracking system by stage of development; and availability of project financial snapshots
- Historical R&D expenditures and the subject company's R&D budget
- Product road map or other similar detail of the subject company's expected evolution from current products and technologies to future products and technologies
- Licensing agreements that exist for either the development of technologies or ultimate marketing of product manifestations
- Trends and patterns developed from the subject company's operating history (for example, life cycles of prior generations of products and rate of changes in average selling prices)
- Any other relevant information when available, as appropriate

6.37 In the case of a transaction, the overall purchase price is most often based on unconditional or expected cash flows (discussed in greater detail in paragraphs 6.99–.121). If the IPR&D cash flows are *conditional cash flows* or assume commercial success, these cash flows would need to be adjusted for the probability of success or weighted with downside cash flows that reflect potential development failure. Thus, it should be noted that the assumptions used to value the overall entity would not always be identical to the assumptions used to value an IPR&D asset. However, valuation specialists would need to understand how and why they differ and ensure that, although different, they are not contradictory or inconsistent. For example, if the PFI that is used to value the overall entity is based on expected cash flows, while the PFI that is used to value an IPR&D asset is based on conditional cash flows, those cash flows may not be identical. As a result, because cash flows themselves could be different, it may be appropriate to apply different discount rates to those cash flows. The task force recommends comparing and contrasting the assumptions used to value the individual asset to those used to value the overall entity to make sure they are consistent or can be reconciled.

6.38 Some of the factors to consider when assessing probability factors and their impact include the following:

- *Industry segment.* Higher risk may be associated with industries or subsegments within an industry with certain characteristics, such as rapid technological or competitive change.
- *Length of time to complete the project.* The longer the development horizon (as measured by the stage of completion, milestones achieved, and so forth), the greater the risk that the expected market for the new product, service, or process will change.
- *History of the company bringing products to commercial success.* The more experience the reporting entity, the subject company, and others in the marketplace have had with successfully completing development of products of this nature and bringing

those products to market, the greater the likelihood of commercial success.

- *Competitive position.* If the IPR&D project is expected to introduce a product that will be the first to market, then expectations about commercial success may be higher than a project that will result in a follow-on product. Conversely, the technological feasibility of first-to-market products may be lower (and, therefore, with a lower probability of success) than that of follow-on projects.

- *Regulatory environment.* The nature of the regulatory approval process that the IPR&D project will be subject to prior to commercialization would need to be taken into account.

- *External factors.* When the IPR&D project is affected by external events, such as the completion of complementary technology, the successful development of a competing technology, and so forth, these matters would need to be taken into account when assessing the probability of reaching technological feasibility.

- *Other factors.* Any other factors that would affect the probability of reaching technological feasibility would need to be considered.

Economic Cash Flows

6.39 It is important to ensure that the overall entity PFI is developed on a cash flow basis. Ultimately, the prospective cash flows would need to reflect economic cash flows, which may differ from budget data based on accounting principles generally accepted in the United States of America (GAAP). Consistent with guidance in paragraph 2.2.07 of the Appraisal Foundation document setting forth best practices for *The Identification of Contributory Assets and the Calculation of Economic Rents* (the Appraisal Foundation document), if the revenue component of the PFI was developed on an accrual basis, then it likely would be appropriate to include the deferred revenue as a component of working capital. Alternatively, one could remove from the PFI the deferred revenue and accrual-based expenses associated with generating that revenue. In addition to the consideration of a deferred revenue adjustment to the overall PFI, an adjustment to the required level of net working capital would also need to be considered. The key to any adjustment is to avoid either double-counting or undercounting any revenue, expense, or profit.

6.40 When assessing the required level of working capital, the valuation specialist would need to determine whether deferred revenue may be included as a component of working capital. When making this determination, it is important to understand the underlying accounting for revenue recognition. For example, in the software industry, in which revenue recognition accounting[3] is based on vendor-specific objective evidence as provided in FASB ASC 985-605, deferred revenue may not correspond with the remaining legal performance

---

[3] The Financial Accounting Standards Board (FASB) and the International Accounting Standards Board are currently working on a joint revenue recognition project, which may modify this and other industry-specific revenue recognition guidance. An exposure draft of the proposed standard was originally issued in June 2010. However, the proposed standard was reexposed in November 2011 to provide interested parties with an opportunity to comment on revisions that have been made since the publication of the exposure draft in June 2010. The latest information on the status of this joint project is available at www.fasb.org/cs/ContentServer?c=FASBContent_C&pagename=FASB%2FFASBContent_C%2FProjectUpdatePage&cid=900000011146.

obligation associated with services to be provided, in which case, the valuation specialist would need to measure the fair value of the remaining legal performance obligation associated with the deferred revenue.

6.41 To the extent that the valuation specialist does not receive sufficient support for particular PFI assumptions, the valuation specialist would need to investigate other records of the reporting entity, as well as documents from external sources, in an effort to obtain corroborating objective support for each material assumption. If conflicting data exists, the task force believes that the valuation specialist should discuss with management the need to either further support its assumptions or change those assumptions to be consistent with the objective evidence.

Step 3: Ensure That the Assumptions Made in the Development of the PFI Are Consistent With Those of Market Participants

6.42 FASB ASC 820-10-35-9 provides that a reporting entity should measure the fair value of an asset or a liability using the assumptions that market participants would use in pricing the asset or liability, assuming that market participants act in their economic best interest. Therefore, when analyzing the assumptions underlying the selected PFI, the valuation specialist would need to ensure that, consistent with FASB ASC 820, the anticipated future performance reflects market participant assumptions. To the extent that relevant observable inputs are not available, FASB ASC 820 allows for the use of unobservable inputs to measure fair value. However, as indicated in FASB ASC 820-10-35-53, the fair value measurement objective remains the same, that is, an exit price at the measurement date from the perspective of a market participant that holds the asset or owes the liability. According to FASB ASC 820-10-35-54A, a reporting entity should develop unobservable inputs using the best information available in the circumstances, which might include the reporting entity's own data. However, as indicated in FASB ASC 820-10-35-53, unobservable inputs should reflect the assumptions that market participants would use when pricing the asset or liability, including assumptions about risk. When differentiating between entity-specific and market participant PFI, factors to consider may include, but are not limited to, the following:

- The reporting entity's strategies and objectives, which underlie the PFI, and how these strategies and objectives shaped the assumptions within the PFI

- The extent to which the reporting entity's expectations are consistent with the forecasts of industry analysts and market experts

- The level of revenue and cost synergies reflected within the PFI and whether those synergies would be available to a market participant

- Whether the PFI assumes use of the assets being valued that differs from their highest and best use

6.43 One of the most common areas in which the distinction between entity-specific and market participant assumptions arises relates to the inclusion of synergies within the PFI. Synergies unique to the combined enterprise should not be considered when measuring fair value of assets. It may be necessary to adjust the prospective revenue or expenses by revising the revenue, revenue growth, expenses, cost savings rates, and so forth from those used in the selected PFI to those that would reasonably be expected by market participants.

6.44 In addition to performing an analysis of synergies, the valuation specialist would confirm that the selected PFI assumes the highest and best use of the assets being valued. This usage determination should, again, be consistent with the assumptions made by a market participant.

Examples

6.45 *Eliminating entity-specific cost synergies.* Company A acquired Company T in a business combination. Selling costs for Company T are 40 percent of revenues, and the rate representative of performance of market participants is 30 percent of revenues. Due to the unique size and efficiency of its distribution channel, selling costs for Company A are 20 percent (also the rate used by Company A in its PFI that was used to negotiate the final purchase price). Selling costs in the PFI would be adjusted up to 30 percent, the rate representative of market participants, to eliminate a synergy specific to the acquiring company.

6.46 *Eliminating entity-specific revenue synergies.* Company A acquired Company T in a business combination. Company T's product complements Company A's product. Upon acquisition, Company A's combined product offering will be unique in the market, and Company A believes that it can derive 10 percent more in revenues from both products than it or market participants could if they were to sell either product on a separate stand-alone basis. The PFI used to measure fair value of Company T's product should exclude all revenues attributable to Company A's preexisting product and the incremental 10-percent increase in revenues derived from Company T's product, which resulted from having a combined product offering.

6.47 *Eliminating entity-specific income tax synergies.* Company A acquired Company T in a business combination. Company A currently does not pay income taxes because of considerable net operating loss carryforwards and, thus, does not expect to pay income taxes in the foreseeable future (whereas market participants are typically tax-paying entities.) In the PFI that Company A provides to the valuation specialist for use in valuing certain IPR&D assets, management of Company A does not include any anticipated income tax payments resulting from the cash flows attributable to the acquired assets. In other words, in the PFI prepared by Company A's management, the present value of the future cash flows attributed to the acquired assets is the same on a pretax basis as on an after-tax basis because no income tax payments are anticipated. The valuation specialist would adjust the PFI to include an estimate of the anticipated tax payments that market participants would expect to pay on the future cash flows attributable to the acquired assets. The "favorable" tax attributes of Company A is an entity-specific synergy and, therefore, is eliminated from the PFI used to value the acquired assets.

Step 4: Isolate the PFI Related to the IPR&D Assets

6.48 Once the final market participant PFI and purchase price has been identified for the subject business as a whole, the valuation specialist would attempt to isolate those revenues and expenses related to the IPR&D assets from those of other business activities. For example, maintenance, consulting, installation, implementation services, and other ancillary revenues and costs would be considered individually by the valuation specialist to determine whether these economic benefits are directly related to the IPR&D assets. Only those ancillary revenues and costs directly related to the IPR&D assets would be considered when valuing these assets. For example, a software-related IPR&D project expected to generate revenue from both the upfront licensing agreement, as well as ongoing maintenance contracts, would be valued using both sources of revenue and their associated costs. Sales of complementary hardware products, however, would not necessarily be considered in the valuation of the software IPR&D asset because these sales are not directly related to the subject asset.

6.49 The final PFI would extend only for the estimated useful life of the IPR&D assets. For example, the useful life of a pharmaceutical patented compound that will be marketed as a drug upon successful completion of development generally may be the longer of patent life or the period of market exclusivity, or it may be longer if it is not cost beneficial for generics to enter the market (assuming a more successful drug does not deplete market share prior to expiration of the patent or exclusivity period).

6.50 The final PFI may be disaggregated into various subcomponents, including patents, software copyrights, enabling technology,[4] developed product technology, specific IPR&D projects,[5] technical drawings or manuals, and general intellectual know-how. Each subcomponent generally would be separately recognized and valued (provided that the subcomponent meets the applicable recognition criteria for recognition apart from goodwill). Typically, discussions with engineers and technical teams provide information on the appropriate categories to be valued based on how technology is deployed. However, if there is no basis for disaggregating (for example, cash flows attributable to patents from cash flows attributable to related technological know-how [including potentially proprietary technology]), then patents may not be valued separately from related technological know-how.

6.51 *Enabling technology.* For purposes of this guide, *enabling technology* is defined as the underlying technology that has value through its continued use or reuse across many products or product families (product family represents many generations of a singular product). Effectively, enabling technology represents shared technology with multiple uses across many products or product families. Given that useful life, growth, risk, and profitability behaviors of enabling technology may be different from those of the products in which it is utilized, assuming that the enabling technology meets the accounting criteria for recognition apart from goodwill, it may be appropriate to value enabling technology separately. However, even if enabling technology is valued

---

[4] See the glossary and paragraphs 6.51–.58 for a description of enabling technology.

[5] As discussed in the "Unit of Account" section in paragraphs 2.18–.24, in some cases, a reporting entity may conclude that a single IPR&D project represents several individual units of account (for example, a pharmaceutical company that is working on a project to develop a drug for which it will seek regulatory approval in several jurisdictions may conclude that it is appropriate to account for certain jurisdictions as separate units of account). When the unit of account is disaggregated in this manner, it is important to ensure that individual units of account are properly valued. To accomplish that, a valuation specialist would need to understand how costs and revenues or profits will be allocated among different units of account and ensure that no unit of account unduly bears costs or unduly receives the benefit of revenues or profits. In this situation, costs and revenues or profits would need to be allocated consistent with assumptions of independent third-party market participants. This would not be an issue when the unit of account is aggregated across several jurisdictions.

separately, enabling technology may not necessarily represent a separate unit of account from an accounting perspective (see paragraph 6.53 for a discussion of unit of account considerations.) Examples of enabling technology include, but are not limited to, a portfolio of patents, a software object library, or an underlying form of drug delivery technology.

6.52   The existence of enabling technology is dependent on facts and circumstances. In some cases, companies may "in-license" technology that serves as enabling technology for their product development efforts or as the base for technology migration.[6] In other cases, enabling technology may not exist at all, such as when each new product is developed from a new or novel technology platform.

6.53   The task force does not intend to imply that enabling technology would always represent a separate unit of account. Items viewed as enabling technology would be recognized as separate assets only if they meet the applicable recognition criteria at the measurement date (which would be, for example, the acquisition date, in the case of a transaction). (For an in-depth discussion of recognition criteria and unit of account considerations, please refer to chapter 2.) Furthermore, enabling technology is not merely a balance sheet caption, but rather, a description of how technology is used. Therefore, the use of enabling technology might be encompassed within other specific technologies or as a separately recognized shared technology asset.

6.54   *Question 1:* Company A acquired Company T, which had developed a delivery mechanism for the delivery of Drug 1 and Drug 2. The delivery mechanism has been approved by the U.S. Food and Drug Administration (FDA) for the delivery of Drug 1, and Company T has been selling that product for 2 years. In addition, Company T has commenced clinical trials for delivery of Drug 2 via the same delivery mechanism in anticipation of applying to the FDA for approval for such use. Significant R&D costs were incurred to customize the delivery mechanism technology to accommodate the unique characteristics of Drug 2 before beginning clinical trials for delivery of Drug 2. Those clinical trials are approximately 50 percent complete, but the FDA has not approved delivery of Drug 2. Furthermore, because the delivery mechanism technology requires significant customization in order to be utilized in delivery of any other drug, presume for purposes of this question that the delivery mechanism technology cannot be outlicensed to other pharmaceutical companies. Do the technological processes and institutional knowledge represented by the delivery mechanism used for the delivery of Drug 1 represent enabling technology? If so, should this enabling technology be recognized as a separate asset?

Answer: The task force believes that the technological processes and institutional knowledge represented by the delivery mechanism used for the delivery of Drug 1 that currently is marketed would represent enabling technology because this technology is shared between Drugs 1 and 2 and potentially other future drugs. However, the characteristics of Drugs 1 and 2 are different, and the design of a delivery mechanism for each drug must reflect those different characteristics. Therefore, the delivery mechanism for Drug 2 does not use the design of the delivery mechanism for Drug 1 as it existed at the transaction date. Given this, and the related inability to outlicense the delivery mechanism

---

[6] See the glossary and paragraphs 6.59–.70 for a description of technology migration.

technology discussed previously, in this fact pattern, the enabling technology would not be recognized as a separate asset because it does not meet the criteria of being *identifiable* as defined in the FASB ASC glossary (it is not separable and does not arise from contractual rights.) Therefore, in this case, the value of enabling technology would be subsumed into other asset categories (including the developed technology surrounding Drug 1 and IPR&D technology surrounding Drug 2.) This situation is demonstrated on the left side of the figure in paragraph 6.57.

6.55 *Question 2:* Assume the same facts as in question 1, except for the following: In this scenario, the delivery mechanism technology does not require significant alterations in order to be utilized in delivery of Drug 2, and, as a result of not requiring significant alterations, Company T is also considering outlicensing delivery mechanism technology to other pharmaceutical companies. Therefore, in this example, the delivery mechanism technology is being utilized by an existing product, products under development, and, potentially, products developed by third parties. Does the delivery mechanism used for the delivery of Drug 1 represent enabling technology that should be recognized as a separate asset?

Answer: Yes. In this situation, because the delivery mechanism technology can be outlicensed, it meets the separability criterion in FASB ASC 805 and, therefore, represents an identifiable intangible asset. The task force believes that these kinds of circumstances (that is, the delivery mechanism technology being utilized by an existing product, products under development, and, potentially, products developed by third parties) would lead to a situation in which enabling technology represented by the delivery mechanism technology would meet the criteria for separate recognition. This situation is demonstrated on the right side of the figure in paragraph 6.57.

6.56 *Question 3:* Company A acquired Company T, which had a portfolio of patents. Company T has been using patented technology covered by these patents in its developed products and in its ongoing R&D activities across different product categories. Company T is also outlicensing this patented technology to other companies. Therefore, in this example, the patented technology is being utilized by an existing product, products under development, and products developed by third parties. Does this patented technology represent enabling technology that should be recognized as a separate asset?

Answer: Yes. In this situation, because the patented technology is outlicensed, it meets the separability criterion in FASB ASC 805 and, therefore, represents an identifiable intangible asset. The task force believes that these kinds of circumstances (that is, the patented technology being utilized by an existing product, products under development, and products developed by third parties) would lead to a situation in which enabling technology represented by the patented technology would meet the criteria for separate recognition. This situation is demonstrated on the right side of the figure in paragraph 6.57. However, circumstances described in questions 2 and 3 are not intended to be all-inclusive, nor are they all required to be present in order for enabling technology to be recognized as a separate asset. Please note that the fact pattern in this example is similar to the fact pattern used in the "Comprehensive Example" section of this chapter, which, among other things, addresses patented technology (see paragraphs 6.189–.190 and schedule 6-3, "Patents").

6.57 The following figure illustrates the concept of the enabling technology. It presents two scenarios:

On the left side	On the right side
Enabling technology is being used *across* multiple assets.	Enabling technology is being used *across* multiple assets.
However, it does *not* meet the recognition criteria.	And it does meet the recognition criteria.
Therefore, it is subsumed into other assets.	Therefore, it is recognized as a separate unit of account.

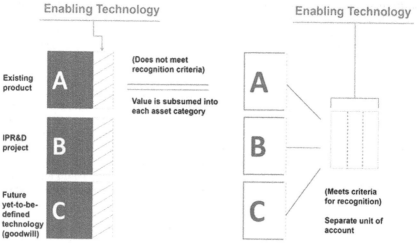

Note: This figure is not drawn to scale.

Relative value attributed to existing products, IPR&D projects, and future yet-to-be-defined technology will depend on specific facts and circumstances. Future yet-to-be-defined technology that does not meet the criteria for separate recognition would be subsumed in goodwill. However, enabling technology would not be expected to significantly contribute to the amount recognized as goodwill.

6.58 It is important to point out that the enabling technology concept is not synonymous with the concept of core or base technology, which was discussed in the original practice aid. The original practice aid defined *core* or *base technology* as "[t]hose technical processes, intellectual property, and the institutional understanding that exist within an organization with respect to products or processes that have been completed and that will aid in the development of future products, services, or processes that will be designed in a manner to incorporate similar technologies." The task force believes that this definition was overly broad and was applied inconsistently in practice. The task force believes that enabling technology is a subset of items that used to be viewed as core technology because enabling technology will only exist when certain conditions, such as those described in questions 2 and 3 in paragraphs 6.55–.56, are met. Therefore, the task force believes that enabling technology will be recognized as a separate asset less frequently than core technology had been previously recognized. (See the "Core Technology" section in paragraphs 2.25–.27 for further discussion.)

6.59 *Technology Migration.* Enabling technology is different from technology migration which, for purposes of this guide, is defined as the process by which certain elements of technology are used or reused within a product or product family from one product generation to the next. In other words, technology migration represents reuse of "old" technology in combination with "new" IPR&D technology or "new" future yet-to-be-defined technology. In contrast to enabling technology, technology migration is only shared within a product or product family. Values of different stages of technology within the technology migration concept would be encompassed either in developed products (for developed technology), in IPR&D (for *future technology* that is under development), or in goodwill[7] (for future yet-to-be-defined technology.) Therefore, the process of technology migration would generally not result in separate recognition of assets. For example, technology migration in the software and electronic devices industries might be represented by Version 1 being modified and partly reused in Version 2, whereas in the life science industry, it may be the use of a particular small molecule for one indication that is later enhanced and reintroduced.

6.60 *Question 1:* Company A acquired Company T in a business combination. At the acquisition date, Company T was selling engineering design software as "Version 1." In addition to the completed Version 1, Company T was actively developing significant improvements to Version 1 that they expected to include and sell as "Version 2." Further, although not under development, Company T had identified further enhancements that were expected to be included in "Version 3." Does the technology present in Version 1 that will serve as a base or foundation for subsequent versions of the software represent technology migration?

Answer: Yes. The task force believes that the technology present in Version 1 that will serve as a base or foundation for subsequent versions of the software would demonstrate technology migration because this technology will be used or reused within this engineering design software product family from one product generation to the next product generation. This technology would not be recognized as a separate asset because it does not meet the criteria of being *identifiable* as defined in the FASB ASC glossary (it is not separable and does not arise from contractual rights.) However, its value would be encompassed in the asset recognized for Version 1 existing technology (for further discussion on how technology migration affects valuation, see example in paragraphs 6.66–.70).

6.61 Two primary stratifications of technology to consider are (*a*) type (or subcomponents) and (*b*) stage. For type of technology, an example is enabling technology (such as an operating system) versus product technology (such as application software to be used with the operating system). Although a given software product may use both types of technology, these technologies are distinct in that they may become obsolete over different time periods because enabling technology typically decays more slowly than product technology. For stage of technology, it should be noted that both enabling and product technology may have developed versions, versions under development, or future

---

[7] Similar to enabling technology, technology migration would not be expected to significantly contribute to the amount recognized as goodwill.

yet-to-be-started versions. The following paragraph further discusses the interplay between type and stage of technology.

6.62 A current product's attributes and characteristics (known as *functionality*) are often the result of the functionality of prior versions or releases of the product (referred to as *technology migration*) and the functionality that was added as a result of the release of the current product (collectively referred to as *developed product technology*). As future versions of the products are released, the revenue generated by those future products also will be a result of R&D that is undertaken in the future (referred to as *future R&D* or *future technology*). On occasion, there may be a direct correlation between a technology project and a new product offering. When the subcomponents of technologies used in R&D activities are used by many product offerings, or when the subcomponents will be used over numerous generations of product offerings, the valuation specialist would need to assign a portion of the revenue or cash flow stream from each product offering to the subcomponents. The assigning of cash flows to the subcomponents would consider the relative contribution of enabling technology, developed product technology, current R&D projects, and future technology over successive releases of products that incorporate these subcomponents. When determining the contribution of each subcomponent of technology, the task force recommends evaluating factors that may include the following:

- Historical cost to develop the subcomponent

- Dates that the development of the subcomponent began and was completed

- Economic useful life of the subcomponent

- Relative complexity of technical issues addressed and resolved by the subcomponent

- Whether the subcomponent represents unique or proprietary technology or an alternative solution to other technologies in the marketplace

- Whether the subcomponent is (or could be) protected by patents and, if so, the difficulty of designing around the patented technology of the subcomponent

- Whether the technology in the subcomponent allows the company to generate larger PFI, either through the ability to charge premium prices for the product, sell larger volumes of the product, or increase the economic life of the product

- Other factors, depending on specific facts and circumstances

6.63 The following figure illustrates the contribution of the technology subcomponents to the prospective revenue included in the final PFI. In year 1 (the year immediately following the valuation date), a significant portion of the prospective revenue is attributed to the developed product technology (that is, the products that existed at the date of valuation) with assistance from the enabling technology, whereas in year 5, a significant portion of the prospective revenue is attributed to R&D that will be performed subsequent to the date of valuation, which, outside of existing IPR&D projects, does not relate to a recognizable asset.

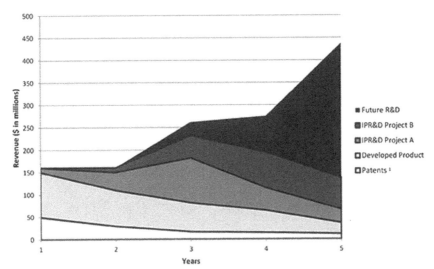

¹ Please note that patents would be viewed in this diagram as meeting the recognition criteria and qualifying as a separate unit of account and would be defined as a form of enabling technology.

6.64 The valuation of the various subcomponents of a business, such as those shown in the preceding figure, may be performed by using the following methodologies:

- Adjustments to revenues and costs to eliminate everything but revenues and costs associated with a specific IPR&D asset (known as revenue, cash flow, or profit splitting).

- Contributory asset charges related to developed product technology and enabling technology (charges that may decrease over time) and future technology (charges that may increase over time). This technique is associated with the application of the multiperiod excess earnings method and will be described further in this section.

- Other appropriate methods, when applicable.

6.65 The revenue, cash flow, or profit-splitting method may be appropriate in circumstances in which a company has one of the following: numerous separable businesses, products, or services or, in the case of technology, numerous subcomponents, such as enabling technology, developed product technology, IPR&D, and future technology. When the subject assets (or some subset thereof) produce measurable economic benefit only in combination with one another, the task force believes that the best way to isolate individual asset values is through a revenue, cash flow, or profit-splitting exercise. The task force believes that the splitting of revenues, cash flows, or profits in this fashion for technology may be a preferable alternative, when applicable, to that of applying contributory asset charges (or economic rents) for the use of enabling or developed technologies. Contributory asset charges are discussed in detail in paragraphs 6.82–.98.

6.66 *Example—Technology migration.* Assume the same facts as in question 1 in paragraph 6.60. Furthermore, Company T releases annually a major new version of its software products. Historically, each release has doubled the functionality of the product, and Company A expects this to continue. The relative contributions over multiple releases (that is, the technology migration) are estimated as illustrated in table 6-1.

Table 6-1

	PFI Year				
	1	2	3	4	5
Developed product technology (underlying Version 1)	100.0%	50.0%	25.0%	12.5%	6.0%
IPR&D (underlying Version 2)	0.0%	50.0%	25.0%	12.5%	6.0%
Future technology (underlying Version 3 and other future versions)	0.0%	0.0%	50.0%	75.0%	88.0%
Total	**100.0%**	**100.0%**	**100.0%**	**100.0%**	**100.0%**

6.67 Upon acquisition, Company A recognizes a technology asset (assets) for Version 1; an IPR&D asset related to the current state of development of new technology to be included in Version 2; and no asset would be recognized for Version 3 due to a lack of substance. Accordingly, the percentage of annual prospective revenues attributable to the IPR&D subcomponent of the product (that is, Version 2) would be only 50 percent of the prospective revenues for year 2 (the year in which Version 2 is initially released), 25 percent of the prospective revenues for year 3, and so forth. Therefore, technology migration affects the revenue estimate for an IPR&D asset being valued.

6.68 As indicated in table 6-1, the value of the technology underlying Version 1 would capture revenue stream attributable to Version 1, as well as portions of revenue streams attributable to Version 2, Version 3, and other future versions to the extent those versions will leverage the technology that is embedded in Version 1. Because the technology present in Version 1 will persist in future versions, the technology asset underlying Version 1 would be assigned a useful life that is longer than just the product life of Version 1. With respect to amortization, FASB ASC 350-30-35-6 provides that the method of amortization should reflect the pattern in which the economic benefits of the intangible asset are consumed or otherwise used up. In this case, given that contribution to revenue of the technology underlying Version 1 will be declining with the release of each future version, it may be appropriate to use an accelerated method of amortization.

6.69 In this example, no revenue is presumed to be assigned to enabling technology in the revenue split. In cases in which enabling technology is present and when the valuation specialist is using the multiperiod excess earnings method, the cash flows attributable to the IPR&D asset would include a contributory asset charge associated with the enabling technology used by, or incorporated in, the IPR&D asset. The multiperiod excess earnings method and contributory asset charges are discussed in detail in the following sections.

6.70 A number of factors would need to be considered by Company A when estimating the relative contributions of the subcomponent technologies (for example, the number of lines of code added or changed) and the functionality of the product that was added or changed by each subcomponent. The valuation specialist would gather the underlying support for the assigned revenue split percentages based on discussions with management, which may include representatives from R&D, marketing and sales, finance, operations, and others, regarding historical and future expectations of relative subcomponent contributions, through industry data, and the valuation specialist's experience with similar companies and technologies.

6.71 Even when using a valuation model that splits revenues, it may be necessary to separately recognize and value enabling technology because it meets the recognition criteria and derives its economic value from its use with many products or product families, as well as ongoing developmental efforts. Strictly speaking, such technology no longer exhibits the one-to-one correspondence that a single-product technology migration model might indicate. The consideration of a simulated or implicit royalty is one alternative to a revenue split model because it effectively "profit-splits" the income stream. That royalty also may be applied against future revenues to capture continued reuse of the enabling technology. It should be noted that in a valuation model that splits revenues, cash flows, or profits, it is important to properly consider all completed technology, both enabling and developed product technology. In the valuation of an IPR&D project, if the split includes a category that properly comprises both enabling and developed product technology, then no further disaggregation may be necessary. However, if the split of revenue or profits considers only the migration of developed product technology, then, to the extent that enabling technology exists, it may be necessary to provide for a separate category comprising enabling technology.

6.72 A common approach to valuing technology is to start with an aggregate prospective revenue that includes the contribution of both enabling and product technologies. That portion of the aggregate revenue stream attributable to enabling and product technology, respectively, may decay at different rates. Product revenue streams would then be split between the stage of technology (that is, developed, IPR&D, and future R&D) within each type of technology. If revenue associated with enabling technology is not separately split out, then a simulated or implicit royalty can be used to isolate the profits or cash flows to be associated with enabling technology, when applicable.

6.73 From a unit of account perspective, the use of two categories of technology (enabling/developed and in-process) versus three categories of technology (enabling, developed, and in-process) is significant if the categories of enabling and developed product technology have different economic useful lives. (As stated previously, if a category of technology meets the applicable criteria for separate recognition from goodwill, then the category of technology would be valued, recognized, and amortized.) However, if the useful lives are the same, then when valuing an IPR&D project, developed product technology and enabling technology may be combined into one category in a valuation model that "splits" revenues, cash flows, or profits among developed technology, IPR&D, and future technology.

6.74 Once the prospective revenues attributable to a specific IPR&D asset have been properly isolated, the valuation specialist would also need to isolate those expenses related specifically to that asset. These expenses include costs of sales, selling and marketing expenses, general and administrative expenses,

R&D costs to complete the development of the IPR&D asset, maintenance R&D costs (including only ongoing changes to debug or maintain technology once complete), any one-time rollout or launch costs, and income taxes. Unrelated expenses, including costs of financing and future developmental R&D, are not deducted when arriving at after-tax cash flows. The following is a brief discussion of some of the expenses that may need to be reflected in the PFI and related considerations:

- *R&D expense attributable to IPR&D.* In the case of an IPR&D asset, there is generally a significant upfront expense related to R&D costs to complete. Also, there are typically ongoing expenses that may be incurred by the R&D staff subsequent to project completion that may relate to maintenance, debugging, postmarket approval surveillance, and other activities. The product roadmap of the subject company, combined with R&D budgeting documents, will often serve as primary source material evidencing appropriate levels of costs to complete and ongoing expenditures. A useful cross-check is to compare all project costs-to-complete and ongoing expenditures per year with the total R&D budget or R&D expense as a percentage of sales historically for the subject company, reporting entity, or both, and for market participants, when relevant data is available.

- *Technical support expense attributable to IPR&D.* In many industries, technical support is provided as part of product sales or in exchange for product maintenance fees. To the extent that such fee revenues are included in the future cash flows attributable to specific IPR&D projects, it would be appropriate for the associated expense to be included in the future cash flows. Often, technical services cannot be unbundled from the product sale and, therefore, the appropriate level of expense would need to be reflected in the PFI.

- *Tax expense attributable to IPR&D.* When choosing the appropriate tax rate, it is important to ensure that it does not reflect specific tax circumstances of the subject company, reporting entity, or both, which may occur by consideration of net operating loss carryforwards, tax penalties, special payments, and so forth. Instead, industry data demonstrating the tax rates experienced by market participants would need to be considered and compared with company-specific data and statutory rates. Further, companies that are engaged in R&D activities often operate in numerous tax jurisdictions. When choosing the appropriate tax rate, such companies would need to consider tax rates, ability to deduct amortization in various jurisdictions, and whether market participants would be expected to repatriate offshore profits into the United States. See paragraphs 6.122–.131 for guidance on the impact of income taxes on the determination of fair value of subject assets.

Step 5: Compare the PFI Attributable to the IPR&D Assets to the PFI for the Overall Entity

6.75 When comparing the PFI attributable to various IPR&D assets to the PFI of the overall entity, certain expenses related to liabilities separately recognized in the overall business PFI would need to be removed from the cash flows related to a specific IPR&D asset. For instance, cash flows related to contingent assets or liabilities, such as potential legal settlements, pension accruals, warranty accruals, and the like, would also need to be removed from the cash flows. If the prospective cash flows of such contingencies are not removed from the cash flows used to measure the fair value of IPR&D assets, the contingency may be double-counted in the analysis when those same cash flows are used to value the contingent asset or liability itself. However, there may be similar expenses that are not related to a separately recognized liability that would need to be included in the specific IPR&D asset's cash flows.

6.76 As mentioned previously, some IPR&D assets may have related liabilities that may need to be considered separately from an accounting perspective. When the risk associated with such assets diverges from that of related liabilities, the valuation specialist needs to reflect differences in risk profiles in the respective measurements of the associated units of account.

6.77 Management may provide separate PFI attributable to specific IPR&D projects, which, when aggregated with all assets, may not add up to the PFI for the overall entity. Such differences would need to be documented and reconciled by management. For instance, one outcome of this process could be that the overall or individual PFI, or both, may need to be reconsidered.

6.78 Once the revenue and expenses related to IPR&D activities have been appropriately isolated and compared to the overall PFI, the result can be used to value IPR&D assets by applying various income-based valuation methods, such as the multiperiod excess earnings method, relief from royalty method, decision tree analysis, or the real options method, many of which are discussed in detail in the following sections.

Application of the Multiperiod Excess Earnings Method to IPR&D Assets

Overview

6.79 The multiperiod excess earnings method is one of the methods used by valuation specialists to measure fair value of IPR&D assets acquired in a business combination, asset acquisition, or, subsequently, for impairment testing and measurement purposes.

6.80 In cases in which there is an identifiable stream of cash flows associated with more than one asset, a multiperiod excess earnings method may provide a reasonable indication of the value of a specific asset. Under this method, the value of an intangible asset is equal to the present value of the after-tax cash flows attributable solely to the subject intangible asset, after making adjustments for the required return *on* and *of* (when appropriate) the other associated assets.

6.81 Once the PFI related to IPR&D activities has been isolated (as discussed in the "Use of Prospective Financial Information" section in paragraphs 6.26–.78), the application of the multiperiod excess earnings method generally involves the following steps:

- Step 1: Apply contributory asset charges for assets that contribute to the generation of cash flows.

- Step 2: Calculate the present value of the cash flows using a discount rate appropriate for the specific IPR&D asset being valued.[8]

- Step 3: Compute and add the related income tax benefits resulting from the amortization of the IPR&D asset for income tax purposes.[9]

- Step 4: In the case of a transaction, evaluate the overall reasonableness of the asset's fair value relative to the other assets acquired and the overall purchase price. In other circumstances, compare the fair value of individual IPR&D assets to the overall fair value of the entity and the fair value of the other assets owned by the entity.

Steps

Step 1: Apply Contributory Asset Charges for Assets That Contribute to the Generation of Cash Flows[10]

6.82 Specifically, under the multiperiod excess earnings method, the estimate of an intangible asset's fair value starts with the PFI[11] associated with a collection of assets, rather than a single asset. *Contributory asset charges*, also referred to as *economic rents* or *capital charges*, are then commonly deducted from the net cash flows for the collection of the associated assets to isolate "excess earnings" attributable solely to the intangible asset being valued. The contributory asset charge is a deduction for the contribution of supporting assets (for example, net working capital, fixed assets, customer relationships, trade names, and so forth), as required by market participants, to the generation of the prospective cash flows attributable to the particular asset being valued. An asset charge is applied for each asset, including other intangible assets, which contribute to the generation of the prospective cash flows. The contributory asset charges are based on the fair values of the contributing assets (for example, fixed assets). After-tax cash flows of the collection of assets are often charged after-tax amounts representing a return *of* and a return *on* (when appropriate) these contributory assets, based on the fair values of such contributory assets, to estimate the fair value of the subject asset. The excess cash flows, net of the charges for contributory assets, are then discounted to a present value.

6.83 The principle behind a contributory asset charge is that each IPR&D asset "rents" or "leases" from a hypothetical third party all the assets it requires to produce the cash flows resulting from its development; each project rents only

---

[8] Some have suggested that a variant of this step would be to apply different discount rates depending on the risk profile of upfront expenses versus future benefits. See paragraph 6.138 for further discussion.

[9] The need to include the benefits of tax amortization will depend on which tax jurisdiction the intangible asset is located, or would be located, from a market participant perspective.

[10] For further information on contributory asset charges, see the Appraisal Foundation document setting forth best practices for *The Identification of Contributory Assets and the Calculation of Economic Rents* (the Appraisal Foundation document), which is available at the Appraisal Foundation's website at https://appraisalfoundation.sharefile.com/d/s80f9c7da9e744de9.

[11] The nature of cash flows used in the prospective financial information (conditional versus expected) may affect the determination of contributory asset charges. In the case of conditional cash flows, which assume commercial success, it may be necessary to make appropriate adjustments to the level of contributory assets. For further discussion, please refer to paragraphs 1.3, 3.1.09, and section 3.6 in the Appraisal Foundation document.

those assets it needs and not the ones that it does not need; and each project pays the owner of the assets a fair return *on* (and *of*, when appropriate) the value of the rented assets.[12] Thus, any net cash flows remaining after such charges are attributable to the subject IPR&D asset.

6.84 The contributory assets for which a charge should be taken include not only assets purchased in the specific transaction or existing in a particular point in time, but all assets that would be required by market participants to generate the overall cash flows of the collection of assets. The reporting entity already may own some of these assets or may need to purchase them in a separate transaction, if they are necessary to generate the future cash flows in the aggregate. For example, in the case of a transaction, the acquiring company may plan not to use the trade name of the subject company but replace it with a newly developed name. In this case, provided such plans are consistent with market participant assumptions, a contributory asset charge for use of the newly developed name would need to be applied despite the fact that the acquired name will no longer be used. Additionally, if the acquiring company plans not to use the acquired trade name and sell only unbranded products, but market participants would choose to maximize cash flows by using a trade name in their marketing of the product, a contributory asset charge for use of the trade name would be applied in order to perform the valuation on a market participant basis.

6.85 *Types of contributory assets.* Contributory asset charges would need to be made for all assets or elements of goodwill that contribute to the realization of the future cash flows. Similarly, contributory asset charges would not be made for assets that do not contribute to the future cash flows (for example, land held for investment would not be considered as a basis for a charge if it is not necessary for the generation of future cash flows).

6.86 Assets contribute to future cash flows by supporting the realization of those cash flows. Examples of assets that may be charged for and the type of contributions that they make include the following:

- *Working capital.* Realizing cash flows from the commercialization of a new product or service requires working capital for net investment in receivables, inventory, and other short-term assets. Working capital makes a contribution to the project by allowing and supporting the normal business cycle. The required level of working capital represents the level that market participants would consider appropriate to support the subject intangible asset. Because working capital supports business operation without loss in value due to economic depreciation, only a return *on* working capital would be considered in contributory asset charge calculation. Note that the composition and level of working capital may change as an asset moves from development to production and, therefore, the level of charge could be different year by year over the prospective period.

- *Fixed assets.* Fixed assets allow for the physical production of products; the workspace for the marketing, sales, and logistics

---

[12] From the perspective of an investment in contributory assets, an owner of such assets would require an appropriate return on investment, which consists of a pure investment return (referred to as return *on*) and a recoupment of the original investment amount (referred to as return *of*). (This explanation is based on the explanation in paragraph 1.6 of the Appraisal Foundation document.)

functions for both tangible and intangible products; and the facilitation of general management functions and corporate overhead. Although the exact nature of the contribution of a particular desk to a specific IPR&D project is most likely unknowable, a reasonable estimation would be used (for example, assigning fixed asset charges on the basis of revenue). Fixed assets mostly are "wasting" assets that require replacement or replenishment, or both, to sustain their productive capacity. Both return *of* and return *on* fixed assets would be charged to the intangible assets that those fixed assets support. Note that similar to net working capital, the composition and required level of fixed assets may change as an asset moves from development to production and, therefore, the level of charge could be different year by year over the prospective period.

- *Intangible assets.* In addition to the preceding, business combinations may include other assets. Paragraphs 11–45 of FASB ASC 805-20-55 include examples of intangible assets that meet the criteria for recognition as a separate asset apart from goodwill, including marketing-related intangible assets, customer-related intangible assets, artistic-related intangible assets, contract-based intangible assets, and technology-based intangible assets. In addition, certain elements of a business may make a contribution to future cash flows, even if they are not recognizable as intangible assets under FASB ASC 805, such as assembled workforce and trained staff. In all cases, required levels of intangible assets would serve as a basis for applying contributory asset charges. For further discussion about the potential for applying contributory asset charges for elements of goodwill other than recognizable intangible assets, refer to paragraphs 2.2.14–.16 in the Appraisal Foundation document.

6.87 The task force believes that when calculating the contributory asset charge associated with self-created assets (such as customer lists, assembled workforce, or trade names), it is often appropriate to assume that costs to maintain and enhance intangible assets (that is, return *of* those intangible assets) are part of the operating expense structure of the entity's business and, as such, only return *on* contributory intangible assets will be charged to the subject intangible asset. Prospective expenses would need to be analyzed to determine the appropriate level of maintenance and enhancement costs included in relation to the full return *of* the subject assets. For example, maintenance R&D expense, as opposed to total R&D (that is, maintenance and developmental R&D) expense, would be considered in the analysis.

6.88 Note that the approach outlined previously is deemed reasonable for intangible assets that are valued on a replacement cost basis (that is, their value is replenished based on a prospective expense or cost). However, for self-created assets that generate an excess return, the prospective expense may only capture the maintenance expense, which may lead to a potential understatement of the charge for the asset. For example, for a trade name, which may be valued using the relief from royalty method, the royalty rate is typically a portion of profit after deducting the maintenance expense. In other words, the royalty rate captures the excess profit from the trade name above and beyond the maintenance cost and, therefore, is assumed to incorporate both the return *on* and *of* that asset. In such cases, prospective expenses may also need to be adjusted downward to avoid a duplicate charge for the return *of*. For further discussion, see paragraph 3.5.03 in the Appraisal Foundation document.

6.89 As with working capital and fixed assets, a return would be charged for the use of each intangible asset as appropriate. However, a careful analysis would be made to determine which assets contribute to which projects. Many contributory assets benefit most or all projects, including current technologies. The total return earned by an asset would need to be assigned across the projects that benefit from that asset. For example, a project that uses twice as much of a contributory asset than another project would incur twice the contributory asset charge. When objective information is available, it would provide the basis for assigning contributory asset charges. In the absence of reliable data, reasonable assumptions would be used. Although contributory asset charges generally are assigned to projects based on the relative revenue of each project, this approach may not always be correct. For example, IPR&D projects may not generate revenue in the first few years of the prospective period. In such cases, relative expenses of each subject intangible asset each year may represent a more appropriate assignment basis. When an asset is not expected to contribute to a particular project, its return is not charged against that project (its return is, however, charged against all the projects to which it does make a contribution).

6.90 *Basis for determining charges*. Contributory asset charges are based on the concept that the owner of that asset reasonably expects to get a return *on* and *of* the fair value of the asset that is commensurate with the risk of that asset and the returns earned by market participants on similar assets. The valuation specialist should take care to note circumstances when the carrying amount of the asset is not the same as its fair value, the latter of which should be the base for contributory asset charge.

6.91 The required level of contributory assets may be expected to remain relatively constant over time. For example, working capital may be assumed to remain a constant percentage of sales and, therefore, would be expected to change as the level of prospective sales changes.

6.92 The valuation specialist would also need to consider the possibility that the level of required contributory assets may change over time. For example, a technology-based business may have high scalability relative to fixed assets and possibly other assets (for example, a software company may be able to grow revenue ten-fold without significantly increasing its fixed assets). Thus, applying a stable charge for the entirety of the prospective period would not be appropriate in this case. In summary, the capacity and current asset usage expected by market participants would need to be considered when determining the required amount of each contributory asset over the life of the subject asset.

6.93 The required rates of return for the contributory assets need to be commensurate with the relative risk associated with investment in each particular asset. The level of debt financing that could be secured for a particular asset can serve as a proxy for the risk level associated with that asset. One can then estimate the market participant cost of equity and the cost of debt related to financing the subject asset. From that, the valuation specialist may use a loan-to-value ratio approach when developing the required return *on* specific classes of assets. The valuation specialist would need to evaluate how specific assets would be financed by market participants and the respective risks and rates of returns associated with those assets, rather than how the overall entity may be financed.

6.94 The following table provides examples of assets typically charged for and the commonly considered basis for determining the fair return, and in many cases, the return *of* the asset is reflected in the operating costs when applicable (for example, intangible assets valued under the cost approach). The contributory asset charge is the product of the asset's fair value and the *required rate of return on* the asset (and *of* the asset, in cases when investment recapture is not part of the operating costs). For each asset listed in the following table, the valuation specialist may consider the level of debt and equity financing required to fund that specific asset.

Asset	*Commonly Considered Basis of Charge*
Working capital	Blend of short-term borrowing rates (for example, working capital lines or short-term revolver rates) and cost of equity for market participants.
Fixed assets (for example, property, plant, and equipment)	Blend of a borrowing rate[13] for similar assets for market participants (for example, terms offered by vendor financing, rates on longer term borrowings, or rates implied by operating leases, capital leases, or both (typically segregated between return *of* [that is, recapture of investment] and return *on* asset), and cost of equity.
Workforce (which is not recognized separate from goodwill), customer lists, trademarks, and trade names	Frequently, the weighted average cost of capital (WACC) (may be lower than discount rate applicable to a particular project).
Patents, including other types of enabling technology	Frequently, the WACC (may be lower than discount rate applicable to a particular project). In cases when risk of realizing economic value of the patent is close to, or the same as, risk of realizing a project, rates would be equivalent to that of the project. Additionally, when a contributory asset is itself valued using a relief from royalty method (which is commonly the case with patents and enabling technology), the royalty rate assumed is, in essence, a substitute for a contributory asset charge (economic rent for the use of the asset). In other words, the royalty rate can be assumed to incorporate the return *on* and *of* that asset. Thus, the contributory asset charge for use of that asset would be set equal to its royalty rate multiplied by the relevant revenue amount (adjusted for taxes if contributory charges are taken against after-tax cash flows).

---

[13] For further discussion regarding borrowing rates, see paragraph 4.2.06 in the Appraisal Foundation document.

Asset	Commonly Considered Basis of Charge
Other intangibles	Rates appropriate to the risk of the subject intangible. Market evidence would be used whenever available. In other cases, rates would need to be consistent with the relative risk of other assets in the analysis, with rates being higher for riskier assets. Additionally, intangible assets typically are not financed with significant debt and, therefore, would require a higher proportion of equity financing.

6.95 When the asset is unique to the entity and has limited value on a standalone basis, the required return would likely be closer to the overall *weighted average cost of capital* (WACC) or even the entity's cost of equity than when the asset is easily liquidated and more generic in nature. For example, tangible assets specifically used in a utility company may have a risk profile similar to the overall entity's risk, thereby warranting a rate of return closer to the WACC; whereas tangible assets not unique to a particular industry would likely have lower risk relative to that of the overall entity. Generally, the risk associated with specialized inventory, fixed assets without alternative uses, and intangibles would be considered similar to the risk of the overall entity and, therefore, a return closer to the WACC would be applied.

6.96 *Contribution for elements of goodwill.* The general principle of contributory asset charges is to provide a return on the fair value of all assets necessary for the realization of the cash flows. In order to avoid capturing elements of goodwill in the fair value of a specific intangible asset (such as an IPR&D asset), some valuation specialists have argued that taking contributory asset charges for elements of goodwill would serve as a remedy. However, although the task force acknowledges that taking a contributory asset charge for an element of goodwill that contributes to the generation of cash flows has conceptual merit, the task force believes that only in very limited circumstances would an element of goodwill be identifiable and reliably measurable (such as assembled workforce).

6.97 *Period of charge.* Contributory asset charges are applied over the period that the subject project requires such assets. For example, if a project requires an asset that has an economic life of three years but the project has a life of six years and requires the use of the contributory assets for the entire project life, the contributory asset charge would be applied over the entire six years. The assumption is that the investment in that asset is replaced over time as the asset is depreciated or amortized and that the subsequent new investment requires the same type of return as was required by the original investment. This would not be the case, however, for assets that are not otherwise replaced and simply expire (for example, a covenant not to compete).

6.98 *Tax amortization benefit.* As discussed further in this chapter, when measuring the fair value of intangible assets, current practice is to include a tax amortization benefit (TAB) for assets, regardless of whether they were acquired in a taxable or nontaxable transaction. Because the goal of fair value measurement is to determine an exit price for the asset, the fair value of the asset itself would be expected to include its inherent tax benefits of amortization or depreciation. Further, charges for contributory assets should be based on the fair value of assets inclusive of those same tax benefits of depreciation or amortization because the resulting fair value would be the basis for economic rent if such contributory assets were to be truly leased.

Step 2: Calculate the Present Value of the Cash Flows Using a Discount Rate Appropriate for the Specific IPR&D Asset Being Valued

6.99 Conceptually, a *discount rate* represents the expected rate of return (that is, yield) that an investor would expect from an investment. The magnitude of the discount rate depends on the perceived risk of the cash flows being discounted. Theoretically, investors are compensated, in part, based on the degree of inherent risk and, therefore, would require additional compensation in the form of a higher rate of return for investments bearing additional risk.

6.100 FASB Concepts Statement No. 7, *Using Cash Flow Information and Present Value in Accounting Measurements*,[14] and paragraphs 5–20 of FASB ASC 820-10-55 provide a framework for determining the appropriate discount rate for cash flows with a specific risk profile. They describe two basic techniques: the *discount rate adjustment* (formerly referred to as *traditional*) technique (DRAT) and the *expected present value* (or, expected cash flow) technique (EPVT). As indicated in FASB ASC 820-10-55-10, the DRAT "uses a single set of cash flows from the range of possible estimated amounts, whether contractual or promised...or most likely cash flows. In all cases, those cash flows are conditional upon the occurrence of specified events." For example, the cash flows may reflect a single "most likely" or "promised" cash flow scenario that contains an assumption about the outcome of an uncertain future event, such as FDA approval. The EPVT, however, represents a probability-weighted average of all possible outcomes. Because expected cash flows incorporate expectations of all possible outcomes, expected cash flows are not conditional on particular events or outcomes. However, as indicated in FASB ASC 820-10-55-18

> to apply the expected present value technique, it is not always necessary to take into account distributions of all possible cash flows using complex models and techniques. Rather, it might be possible to develop a limited number of discrete scenarios and probabilities that capture the array of possible cash flows. For example, a reporting entity might use realized cash flows for some relevant past period, adjusted for changes in circumstances occurring subsequently (for example, changes in external factors, including economic or market conditions, industry trends, and competition as well as changes in internal factors affecting the reporting entity more specifically), taking into account the assumptions of market participants.

6.101 In either case, the overriding principle contained in those techniques is that the discount rate used to discount the prospective cash flows should reflect assumptions that are consistent with the risks inherent in the cash flows. Conditional cash flows are discounted using a conditional rate, and expected cash flows are discounted using an expected rate. In theory, the two techniques consider the same risks; the DRAT reflects the risk through

---

[14] It should be noted that the FASB Concepts Statements were not codified. However, the IPR&D Task Force (task force) believes that FASB Concepts Statement No. 7, *Using Cash Flow Information and Present Value in Accounting Measurements*, provides relevant guidance and, therefore, included references to it in this guide. The FASB Concepts Statements are available at www.fasb.org/jsp/FASB/Page/SectionPage&cid=1176156317989.

adjustments to the discount rate,[15] whereas the EPVT primarily reflects this risk in the expected cash flows.

6.102   There are two methods under the EPVT, which are described in paragraphs 13–20 of FASB ASC 820-10-55. Method 1 of the EPVT (subsequently referred to as *EPVT Method 1*) adjusts the expected cash flows of an asset for systematic (that is, market) risk by subtracting a cash risk premium (that is, risk-adjusted expected cash flows). In contrast, method 2 of the EPVT (subsequently referred to as *EPVT Method 2*) adjusts for systematic (that is, market) risk by including a risk premium in the discount rate. The discount rate in EPVT Method 2 is generally equivalent to the WACC.

6.103   EPVT Method 1 is the appropriate technique when the expected cash flows have been adjusted to arrive at certainty equivalents, allowing the results to be discounted at an appropriate risk-free rate. However, aside from techniques, such as Black-Scholes, that use a risk neutral framework, the task force believes that method 1 is rarely used in practice. EPVT Method 2 is the appropriate technique when the expected cash flows represent the probability-weighted cash flows from multiple scenarios, which address risks, except for those that are systematic in nature. Such probability-weighted cash flows are discounted at a rate of return that includes a premium for systematic risk.

6.104   FASB ASC 820-10-55-16 suggests that, all else equal, the DRAT discount rate is likely to be higher than the EPVT Method 2 rate, assuming that conditional cash flows may contain an element of risk that is eliminated when probability-weighted cash flows are employed. Because it is applied to a certainty-equivalent cash flow, the risk-free rate developed pursuant to EPVT Method 1 would be lower than either of these other two techniques. A summary follows:

- Likely the highest rate: DRAT (conditional)[16]
- Mid-rate: EPVT Method 2 (systematic risk)
- Lowest rate: EPVT Method 1 (certainty equivalent)

6.105   It is important to note, as further discussed in paragraph 6.107, that FASB ASC 820 does not limit the use of present value techniques to measure fair value to these three choices. There are many elements of risk that may be handled by adjusting either the level of expected cash flows or the discount rate, or both. For example, if the most likely scenario is not explicitly conditional, but the prospective cash flows in this scenario are greater than the probability-weighted cash flows would be, then the appropriate discount rate would likely be based on a "mixed" model, lower than a DRAT rate, higher than an EPVT Method 2 rate, and utilizing elements from both techniques. This could be the case in situations in which the distribution of expected cash flows, including the most likely scenario, is "skewed to the right" as opposed to being symmetrical.

6.106   "Mixed" models are often employed in the pharmaceutical industry in situations when technical risks, such as risk of receiving FDA approvals,

---

[15] Adjustments to discount rates are beyond the scope of this guide because this topic is not unique to IPR&D assets. However, various resources exist in general valuation literature discussing derivation of discount rates.

[16] The discount rate chosen for the discount rate adjustment technique (DRAT) would relate to the riskiness of the cash flows to which it is applied.

may already be considered in the PFI, whereas probabilities associated with the timing of the approvals may not be explicitly factored into the PFI development. Both elements associated with approvals and timing of such approvals can have a meaningful effect on value. In addition, commercialization risks, such as market acceptance risks, also may not have been explicitly considered in the PFI. In such circumstances, a mixed model would be used in the determination of an appropriate discount rate whereby certain adjustments to components of the WACC or the asset-specific discount rate may be warranted to account for the uncertainty with respect to the timing of approval or commercialization risks, or both.

6.107 To offer some historical perspective, FASB Concepts Statement No. 7, issued in 2000, provides guidance for using present value techniques to measure fair value. (However, as noted in footnote 14 in paragraph 6.100, FASB Concepts Statement No. 7 was not codified.) FASB Statement No. 157, *Fair Value Measurements* (codified in FASB ASC 820), issued in 2006, clarified that guidance in its appendix B. In FASB Concepts Statement No. 7, FASB expressed a preference for the use of EPVTs in connection with the measurement of nonfinancial assets and liabilities for which no market for the item or a comparable item exists (see paragraphs 44–45 of FASB Concepts Statement No. 7). However, appendix B of FASB Statement No. 157 indicates that it

> neither prescribes the use of one specific present value technique nor limits the use of present value techniques to measure fair value to the techniques discussed herein. The present value technique used to measure fair value will depend on facts and circumstances specific to the asset or liability being measured (for example, whether comparable assets or liabilities can be observed in the market) and the availability of sufficient data (see paragraph B1 of FASB Statement No. 157).

6.108 Furthermore, in paragraph C61 of FASB Statement No. 157, FASB acknowledged inconsistencies between FASB Concepts Statement No. 7 and FASB Statement No. 157 and stated its decision not to revise FASB Concepts Statement No. 7 at that time to conform it to FASB Statement No. 157. However, FASB indicated that it would consider in the future the need to revise FASB Concepts Statement No. 7. Although FASB Concepts Statements have not been codified, appendix B of FASB Statement No. 157 has been codified in paragraphs 4–20 of FASB ASC 820-10-55 (the language from paragraph B1 of FASB Statement No. 157 quoted previously appears in FASB ASC 820-10-55-4).

6.109 Generally, if applied properly, both the DRATs and EPVTs would be expected to produce consistent results. The task force believes that use of the EPVT would provide added transparency for valuing assets used in IPR&D given the nature of these assets and their associated cash flows. For example, for assets related to IPR&D projects that are still in trial stages and subject to risks, such as the risk of reaching the necessary scale of operation, the risk of obtaining the necessary regulatory approval, or the uncertainty associated with meeting sales targets once requisite approvals have been obtained, it is often more straightforward to model these risks directly in the cash flows, rather than in adjustments to the discount rates. The task force also recognizes that valuation specialists are often faced with a single scenario with respect to PFI and that scenario may have additional risks that would be best accounted for under the DRAT or a mixed model (described previously).

6.110 Both the DRAT and EPVT involve subjectivity either in selecting an appropriate discount rate or in assigning probabilities to cash flow outcomes. The DRAT implies that a similar asset with similar cash flow characteristics exists in the marketplace, and the rate of return implicit in its market price may be derived. However, the task force observes that for many unique nonfinancial assets, including IPR&D, it may be difficult to identify exact comparables in the marketplace and, thus, in order to apply the DRAT, it may be necessary to derive a discount rate from observable data for similar assets or entities.[17] Although both the DRAT and EPVT involve subjectivity in selecting certain inputs, the EPVT requires the consideration of the various risk factors that may affect cash flows in the future. Some believe that there may be more and better support about the distribution of possible outcomes than there is to support the magnitude of a risk adjustment to the discount rate.

6.111 The task force believes that the valuation report should include a description of the nature of the PFI employed (for example, conditional, probability-weighted, and so forth) and the type of discount rate selected (conditional versus expected).

6.112 *Return of the overall entity.* As a starting point for estimating the rate of return warranted by specific assets, the valuation specialist would begin by analyzing the return expected to be earned from the overall entity. In order to derive this entity return, the valuation specialist would generally start by calculating an industry WACC. The WACC should reflect the weighted-average rate of return on debt and equity as required within the industry, adjusted to reflect return requirements of market participants.

6.113 As a helpful diagnostic, the valuation specialist would also look to the internal rate of return (IRR) implied by the acquisition (in the case of an acquisition of a business) to obtain an additional indication of the overall entity's return. The IRR is derived by equating the sum of the prospective cash flows on a present-value basis to the consideration transferred. An alternative would be to adjust the PFI to a market participant level (that is, entity-specific synergies have been removed) and compare it to the fair value of the entity acquired, which may or may not be equal to the consideration transferred. Because PFI generally represents the cash flows anticipated from the acquiree's operating assets and liabilities, the calculation of the IRR would also need to consider adjustments when nonoperating assets or liabilities exist. In the case of an acquisition of assets that do not constitute a business, a use of the IRR calculation as a diagnostic may be difficult. The IRR can also be used to assess the calculation accuracy of the WACC. However, valuation specialists should be careful to not use it simply to adjust the WACC calculation because under certain circumstances, such as bargain purchases, IRR and WACC may deviate from each other.

---

[17] The task force recognizes that in connection with DRAT, FASB ASC 820-10-55-10 requires the use of the "discount rate...derived from observed rates of return for comparable assets or liabilities that are traded in the market." As indicated in paragraph 6.110, it may be difficult to identify exact comparables in connection with IPR&D assets from which to derive observed rates of return. Also, FASB ASC 820-10-55-11 provides that "if a single comparable asset or liability does not fairly reflect the risk inherent in the cash flows of the asset or liability being measured, it may be possible to derive a discount rate using data for several comparable assets or liabilities in conjunction with the risk-free yield curve (that is, using a build-up approach)." Therefore, when valuing IPR&D assets, valuation specialists derive rates of return by using the internal rate of return, single technology companies' rates of return, returns required by investors given prospective cash flows, diagnostics such as comparison of weighted average cost of capital and weighted-average return on assets and so on.

6.114 Conceptually, the IRR should be consistent with the WACC. This should be the case for all types of PFI, such as conditional, probability-weighted, and PFI with mixed attributes, as discussed previously. If the implied IRR and WACC differ, it may be an indication that entity-specific synergies are included in the PFI, cash flows are not consistent with the expectations of market participants, or the price paid for the business was not representative of its fair value. If such a scenario exists, the valuation specialist would analyze the assumptions in the PFI to ensure that only market participant assumptions are reflected (that is, excludes entity-specific synergies or biased PFI) to derive anticipated cash flows for the overall entity and asset. Alternatively, or additionally, if there is evidence of the price not reflecting fair value, the valuation specialist would need to impute fair value for the acquisition if that imputed value is to be used in WACC-WARA-IRR comparison.

6.115 The following summarizes the relationship between the IRR and WACC and the implications for the selection of PFI in the instance of a business combination:

IRR = WACC	Indicates that the PFI likely properly reflects market participant assumptions, and the transaction consideration is likely representative of the fair value.
IRR > WACC	Indicates that the PFI may include some or all of the impact of entity-specific synergies, may reflect an optimistic bias, may reflect a bargain purchase, or all three. May also indicate that market participant synergies have not been adjusted by the probability of occurrence (that is, market participant synergies are riskier than the overall projections excluding the synergies).
IRR < WACC	Indicates that the PFI may exclude some or all of the impact of market participant synergies, may reflect a conservative bias, may reflect an overpayment, or all three.

6.116 Once the WACC (and IRR, when appropriate) has been determined, the valuation specialist would assess the risk profile of the various assets being valued relative to that of the overall entity. To the extent that the cash flows identified for a given asset are subject to more risk than those of the overall entity, that asset would warrant a discount rate higher than the WACC. Conversely, assets whose cash flows are subject to less risk would warrant a discount rate below the WACC.

6.117 IPR&D assets may be subject to greater risk than those assets related to other, more established business activities. There may be instances when the required rate of return for an IPR&D project may not be significantly different than the rate for existing technology, if, for instance, it was building off similar existing technology. The valuation specialist would assess the level of risk to be reflected in probability adjustments to the PFI and the remaining level of risk to be reflected in increases to the discount rate used to discount prospective cash flows. Specifically, the valuation specialist would need to consider whether the cash flows associated with the underlying IPR&D assets being valued reflect expected cash flows or conditional cash flows because their rates of return may be different. Generally, IPR&D assets valued using expected cash flows would have a lower required rate of return than the same assets valued using conditional cash flows because conditional cash flows include additional uncertainty. Either way, significant professional judgment is required to determine the appropriate discount rates.

6.118 As a means of testing the relative consistency of the rates of return for the various assets, a useful diagnostic is to perform a calculation of the weighted-average return on assets (WARA). Such a calculation provides an indication of the return for the overall entity implied by the weighted-average rate of return assigned to various assets that make up the business. The purpose of the WARA calculation is to assess the reasonableness of the asset-specific returns for identified tangible and intangible assets and the implied (or calculated) return on goodwill. Because the WARA and WACC are indicators of the market participant expected return of the overall entity, the two metrics can be compared and contrasted to identify any adjustments required to the discount rates assigned to the various assets. In the case of an acquisition of assets that do not constitute a business, a use of WARA calculation as a diagnostic may be difficult.

6.119 Table 6-2 illustrates the calculation of a WARA. As shown in this table, rates of return are assigned to each asset in accordance with the asset's risk profile. The weighted-average return of all the assets provides another method of observing the return of the overall entity.

Table 6-2

Assets	Fair Value	% of Total	After-Tax Rate of Return	Weighted Average Rate of Return
Net working capital	$40.0	8.9%	4.0%	0.4%
Fixed assets	60.0	13.3%	7.0%	0.9%
Trademarks/trade names	30.0	6.7%	12.0%	0.8%
Customer relationships	40.0	8.9%	12.0%	1.1%
Developed technology	50.0	11.1%	12.0%	1.3%
IPR&D	80.0	17.8%	14.0%	2.5%
Assembled workforce	10.0	2.2%	12.0%	0.3%
Residual goodwill	140.0	31.1%	18.0%[1]	5.6%
Entity's fair value	**450.0**	**100.0%**		**12.8%**

[1] Please note that the after-tax rate return on goodwill can be either derived on an implied basis or qualitatively estimated by a valuation specialist.

6.120 When measuring the fair value of an entity using expected cash flows, the discount rate would typically reflect the WACC of this particular entity. Historically, IPR&D assets, unlike other intangible assets, were often valued based on conditional cash flows, as opposed to expected cash flows, and were discounted at a rate of return that is commensurate with the riskiness of the conditional IPR&D cash flows (known as the DRAT). The WACC is consistent with the conceptual framework of expected cash flows and expected returns. The reconciliation of the WARA to the WACC implies that the returns used in the WARA should be based on expected returns for each asset as well. Because the WACC is an average expected return, implicitly, rates of return applied to individual assets must be their respective expected rates of return. However, if the discount rate for the IPR&D asset is developed for use with conditional cash flows, and the overall entity PFI was determined to be expected cash flows, then such a discount rate would not be consistent with the WACC or WARA's conceptual framework of an expected return. In the case of a transaction, the overall purchase price is often based not on conditional but on expected cash flows. The IPR&D cash flows can be adjusted for the probability of completion or weighted with downside cash flows that reflect potential development failure. If all risks, except for systematic risks, have been captured in the PFI, then a discount rate closer to the IRR or WACC, or both, may be warranted. As a result, probability-weighted cash flows generally would be consistent with the overall WACC conceptual framework.

6.121   A decision tree analysis can be used to estimate probability-adjusted cash flows, discussed in greater detail in the "Application of Decision Tree Analysis to IPR&D Assets" section in paragraphs 6.154–.170. The "Comprehensive Example" section in paragraphs 6.185–.199 provides an example of the application of the EPVT in a pharmaceutical setting.

Step 3: Compute and Add the Related Income Tax Benefits Resulting From the Amortization of the IPR&D Asset for Income Tax Purposes

6.122   The task force believes that the fair value of an intangible asset valued using an income approach would include (*a*) the expected tax payments resulting from the cash flows attributable to the intangible asset, and (*b*) the tax benefits resulting from the amortization of that intangible asset for income tax purposes. These tax benefits would need to be based on assumptions related to the tax impacts a market participant buyer would encounter (see paragraph 6.123). For example, if the market participant would be able to absorb the losses, a negative tax expense may be appropriate. Including this TAB is common in the application of the income approach. It is not typical in the market approach because any tax benefits would already be factored into the quoted market price through negotiation between market participants. (See footnote 9 in paragraph 6.81 for further discussion of market participant tax assumptions.)

6.123   In the case of a taxable transaction, practice typically includes the associated tax benefits in the fair value of the assets acquired because it is assumed that the assets acquired will be amortizable for tax purposes. When a stock sale occurs without a corresponding change in the bases of assets acquired and liabilities assumed for tax purposes, some have argued that no tax benefit should be included in the fair value of the intangible assets acquired because the buyer will not amortize the intangible assets acquired for income tax reporting purposes. However, under FASB ASC 820, the fair value of the asset is an exit price that maximizes the economic benefit to market participants, which bears no relation to the manner in which the asset was purchased. The task force believes that the exit price should include the tax benefit because individual assets generally would be sold among market participants in a taxable transaction.

6.124   This issue should not be confused with the need to apply taxes to pretax income streams to apply a particular income-based valuation method, such as a discounted cash flow method (presuming an after-tax analysis is applied). A market participant would factor into the amount that it would be willing to pay to acquire all incremental cash flows that inure to the benefit of that market participant. Those incremental cash flows would be reduced by expected income tax payments using appropriate tax rates. The task force believes that the determination of fair value would take into account future income taxes that a market participant purchasing the asset would be expected to pay, without regard to how a transaction would be structured at the entity level for income tax reporting purposes (that is, whether a transaction would be structured to result in a change in bases of assets acquired and liabilities assumed for income tax reporting purposes). As discussed previously, the task force also believes that the fair value of an intangible asset would include the value of the tax benefit resulting from the amortization of that asset, when appropriate. If the value of the tax benefit resulting from the amortization of that asset were not included in the fair value of the intangible asset, it would have the impact of stating that asset on the balance sheet "net of tax." The task force believes that only after the fair value is determined would the asset's assigned value be subjected to the deferred tax accounting requirements of FASB ASC 740, *Income Taxes*. That is, the deferred tax calculation is performed only after the fair value is estimated and accounted for separately, when applicable.

6.125 The value of this TAB (when using straight-line amortization) can be calculated using the following formula:

TAB $= \text{PVCF} \times [1/(1\text{-}PVA*T) - 1]$

Where:

PVCF $=$ Present value of cash flows excluding amortization of the asset

N $=$ Tax amortization period and is used to determine PVA (see the following)

PVA $=$ Present value of an annuity of 1/N paid over the tax amortization period

T $=$ Tax rate

6.126 Table 6-3 illustrates the calculation of the TAB for an asset with a straight-line tax amortization period of 15 years (as would be the case under the current U.S. tax law, presuming Internal Revenue Code Section 197 treatment). In this calculation, the total value of the asset is inclusive of the TAB itself.

Table 6-3

Assumptions

Present value of asset cash flows	$10,000.0
Tax amortization period (years)	15.0
Tax rate:	40.0%
Discount rate	15.0% [1]

Year	Period	Midpoint of Period	Present Value Factor	1 / Period	Present Value of Amortization
1	1.0000	0.5	0.9325	0.067	0.0622
2	1.0000	1.5	0.8109	0.067	0.0541
3	1.0000	2.5	0.7051	0.067	0.0470
4	1.0000	3.5	0.6131	0.067	0.0409
5	1.0000	4.5	0.5332	0.067	0.0355
6	1.0000	5.5	0.4636	0.067	0.0309
7	1.0000	6.5	0.4031	0.067	0.0269
8	1.0000	7.5	0.3506	0.067	0.0234
9	1.0000	8.5	0.3048	0.067	0.0203
10	1.0000	9.5	0.2651	0.067	0.0177
11	1.0000	10.5	0.2305	0.067	0.0154
12	1.0000	11.5	0.2004	0.067	0.0134
13	1.0000	12.5	0.1743	0.067	0.0116
14	1.0000	13.5	0.1516	0.067	0.0101
15	1.0000	14.5	0.1318	0.067	0.0088

Present value of the annuity (PVA)	**0.4180**
Tax amortization benefit PVCF x [1/(1 – PVA*T) – 1]	**$ 2,007.9**
Present value of asset cash flows	10,000.0
Fair value of asset	**$ 12,007.9**

[1] For ease of demonstration in this example, the same discount rate was used for the tax amortization benefit and the underlying intangible asset. The task force notes that there is some discussion in the valuation profession regarding whether different discount rates may apply for the TAB versus the underlying intangible asset.

Questions and Answers—Income Tax Benefits

6.127 *Question 1:* Company A acquires the assets of Company T in a business combination structured as an asset acquisition for income tax reporting purposes resulting in an increase in the tax basis of the asset, and for financial reporting purposes, the fair value of an intangible asset is measured using a discounted cash flow method. Would the expected future income taxes to be paid resulting from the pretax expected future cash inflows to be generated by the acquired intangible asset be deducted from the pretax cash flows when calculating the fair value of the acquired intangible asset?

Answer: Yes. As discussed in paragraph 6.124, the application of the discounted cash flow method would capture after-tax cash flows resulting from ownership of the subject asset being valued.

6.128 *Question 2:* Assume the same set of facts as in question 1. In addition, the acquired intangible asset is deductible for income tax reporting purposes on a straight-line basis over a 15-year life. Company A values the acquired intangible assets using a discounted cash flow method with a 15-percent discount rate.[18] Further, assume the following regarding the acquired intangible asset:

	Year 1	Year 2	Year 3
Estimated:			
Pretax cash flows	$1,000	$1,000	$1,000
Income taxes at 40%	400	400	400
After-tax cash flows	600	600	600
Present value factor at 15%	.8696	.7561	.6575
Present value of estimated after-tax cash flows	522	454	395
Sum			$1,370

This $1,370 of discounted cash flows also generates an income tax benefit from its tax amortization over a 15-year period. The present value of that benefit has been calculated to be $274, giving rise to an overall value for the asset of $1,644. Should the fair value of the intangible be $1,370, representing its value before consideration of tax deductibility, or $1,644, representing the value assuming the acquired intangible asset is amortizable for income tax reporting purposes?

Answer: $1,644. As discussed in paragraph 6.122, the fair value of an intangible asset would include the tax benefits resulting from the amortization of that intangible asset for income tax reporting purposes.

6.129 *Question 3:* Assume the same facts as in questions 1 and 2, except that the transaction was structured as a nontaxable business combination. Because the transaction was structured as nontaxable instead of taxable, no

---

[18] For ease of demonstration in this example, the same discount rate was used for the tax amortization benefit (TAB) and for the underlying intangible asset. The task force notes that there is some discussion in the valuation profession regarding whether different discount rates may apply for the TAB versus the underlying intangible asset.

change occurs in the bases of the assets acquired for income tax reporting purposes. The intangible asset under analysis has no tax basis to this buyer in this transaction. Should the fair value of the intangible asset be $1,370, representing its value without assuming tax deductibility (that is, reflecting that no tax benefits will result from the asset), or $1,644, representing the value assuming the acquired intangible asset is amortizable for income tax reporting purposes irrespective of the asset's actual tax attributes?

Answer: $1,644. As discussed in paragraph 6.122, the fair value of an intangible asset would include the tax benefits resulting from the amortization of that intangible asset for income tax reporting purposes. In addition, as discussed in paragraph 6.124, the tax benefits associated with the amortization of that intangible asset would be included in the fair value of the intangible asset without regard to whether the transaction was structured as a taxable (that is, change in tax bases of assets acquired) or nontaxable business combination (that is, no change in tax bases of assets acquired). This is because the exit value to a market participant buyer of the asset would include consideration of the tax deductibility of the asset.

6.130 *TAB effect on WARA in a taxable versus nontaxable transaction.* When calculating the WARA when the TAB is not reflected in the overall PFI (for example, a nontaxable transaction), an adjustment should be incorporated into the total consideration used in the WARA calculation in order to properly reconcile asset values, including the inherent TAB, to the total consideration that is otherwise based on overall cash flows that do not reflect a TAB. If this adjustment is not applied, the potential exists to understate the implied *economic goodwill* and, therefore, distort the stratification of the discount rates and reconciliation of the WARA to the WACC and IRR. For further discussion, see paragraphs 4.3.03 and 4.3.08 in the Appraisal Foundation document.

6.131 *Example of total consideration adjustment.* This example assumes a total consideration of $710 million and $620 million for a hypothetical taxable transaction and nontaxable transaction, respectively. For purposes of this example, it is assumed that there are no other differences between the two scenarios. Further, assume the calculated value of the assets, including their respective TAB values, is $600 million. In the hypothetical taxable transaction, the implied economic goodwill (residual approach) is $110 million. When measuring the fair value of intangible assets, common practice is to include, as part of the intangible asset's fair value, a TAB value for both taxable and nontaxable transactions. However, the TAB value is generally realizable only in taxable transactions. Following this practice, in a nontaxable transaction in which the TAB value is included in the value of the acquired assets ($600 million) but not reflected in the PFI that supports the total consideration of $620 million, the accounting goodwill is only $20 million prior to the calculation of any deferred tax liability or other purchase price adjustments. In the nontaxable transaction, there is an implicit mismatch of cash flows (specifically with regard to the effect of taxes) between the PFI supporting the total consideration of $620 million and the PFI supporting the value of the acquired assets of $600 million. Because the PFI supporting the total consideration of $620 million excludes the incremental cash flows associated with the tax savings that a buyer would realize in a taxable transaction (essentially, the economic underpinning of the TAB value calculation), an adjustment of $90 million should be added to the total consideration for use in the WARA calculation to arrive at the true economic goodwill of $110 million associated with the nontaxable transaction as adjusted. Without this adjustment to the total consideration, as shown in table 6-4, the required rate of return on the residual goodwill may be distorted due to its proportionate undervaluation. Furthermore, this same adjustment can be applied in the calculation of the IRR (together with the inclusion of the incremental cash flows associated with the tax savings in the PFI), which can then be used as a diagnostic, for comparison purposes, to both the WACC and the WARA.

Table 6-4

	Taxable transaction	Nontaxable transaction
Transaction consideration	$710	$620
Asset fair value (including TAB)	600	600
Residual goodwill	110	20
Present value of TAB[1]	(included)	90
Adjusted transaction consideration	710 (unchanged)	710
Adjusted residual goodwill	110 (unchanged)	110

[1] Present value of TAB includes TAB on all intangible assets, including goodwill.

The concept of making an imputed adjustment to a nontaxable transaction price to arrive at a taxable transaction price equivalent involves considering all asset categories and comparing their fair values to their tax basis. The difference between fair values of the assets, including goodwill, and their tax bases would represent the foregone tax benefit that would be added as an adjustment to arrive at an imputed taxable value for the transaction.

Step 4: In the Case of a Transaction, Evaluate the Overall Reasonableness of the Asset's Fair Value Relative to the Other Assets Acquired and the Overall Purchase Price. In Other Circumstances, Compare the Fair Value of Individual IPR&D Assets to the Overall Fair Value of the Entity and to the Fair Value of the Other Assets Owned by the Entity

6.132 The task force believes that the valuation specialist should compare the individual asset valuations to the overall entity valuation (including the value of contingent consideration, if applicable) to ensure that assumptions are consistent or can be reconciled. It is important to solicit feedback from management and its advisers to establish that the valuation analysis is reasonable and consistent with the facts and circumstances as of the valuation date. To the extent that differences of opinion exist, they would need to be reconciled and documented in an objective and supportable fashion.

Additional Considerations for the Multiperiod Excess Earnings Method

6.133 Circumstances have arisen in which multiple assets of equal importance to the business, such as IPR&D assets and customer relationships, have overlapping revenues, and one of the assets does not readily lend itself to valuation by another technique. In such situations, some practitioners have chosen to value such assets simultaneously using the multiperiod excess earnings method with the use of circular cross-charges as an attempt to adjust for overlapping revenues and cash flows. The task force believes that the simultaneous use of two or more multiperiod excess earnings method models to value two or more intangible assets that, in combination, generate one cash flow stream does not represent best practice and should be avoided.

6.134 One method to remedy overlapping revenue and cash flows from two or more assets comprising a collection of assets would be to apportion (or "split") the PFI related to the assets so that each asset in the collection will have distinct PFI. Once the PFI has been apportioned to the distinct assets, contributory asset charges are not required because each asset will have its own PFI. Note that if the PFI is split between only two intangible assets (or asset groups), the multiperiod excess earnings model for each of these two assets will require charges for the contribution of other supporting assets, but not a cross-charge for the contribution of each to the other. Note that this "revenue, cash flow, or profit-split" method is best when an apportionment can be made in an objective and supportable manner. Further, comparing the asset revenues to the business enterprise revenues is a necessary element of the process to demonstrate that double counting has not occurred.

6.135 Another alternative method to remedy overlapping revenue and cash flows is to value one subject intangible asset using the multiperiod excess earnings method and the others using an alternative method (for example, relief from royalty, cost approach, Greenfield method, or "with and without" method). In this case, the asset valued using the multiperiod excess earnings method would be charged for the other assets to the extent that the other assets are contributory or to the extent that the other asset values are derived from overlapping revenues and cash flows.

6.136 The qualitative factors of each intangible asset that affect the overall profitability of a business would need to be taken into consideration when applying either the revenue, cash flow, or profit-split method to apportion the PFI among the subject intangible assets or in the application of independent valuation techniques to value the subject intangible assets.

Illustrative Example: Multiperiod Excess Earnings Method

6.137 Table 6-5 provides an example of the application of the multiperiod excess earnings method. In this example, the IPR&D asset being valued is entering phase II clinical trials. The valuation specialist has identified four potential scenarios for the success of the asset through clinical trials and commercialization, ranging from failure of phase II trials through a highly successful commercial launch. Each scenario includes corresponding prospective revenues and expenses, as well as an assessment of the probability of occurrence. For example, the scenario in which phase II, but not phase III trials, are successful shows significant expenses during the trial periods but no revenue thereafter. This scenario is assigned a probability of 20 percent. The probability-weighted pretax profit from these various scenarios is tax-effected, and contributory asset charges are applied for the use of net working capital, fixed assets, and the assembled workforce to arrive at the cash flows attributable specifically to the subject asset. The contributory asset charges are applied based on the probability-weighted PFI.

6.138 Because the cash flows within this analysis are expected rather than conditional in nature, an expected rate of return is used to discount those cash flows to present value. A TAB appropriate for the specific jurisdiction in which the asset is held is then added to arrive at the concluded value. It should be noted that in order to simplify this example, a single rate of return has been applied to discount the prerevenue cash outflows, which are at the discretion of management, as well as the future cash inflows, which are expected to result from operations during the subsequent revenue-generating periods. In reality, the risk profile of the prerevenue versus postrevenue expected cash flows can vary significantly, and the valuation specialist may want to consider developing a separate risk-adjusted rate to discount the prerevenue cash outflows.

Table 6-5[1]

Year	1 Phase II	2 Phase III	3 Commercial Launch	4	5	6	7	8	9	10 Patent Expiration
Revenue Scenarios										
Failed Phase II trials	$ —	$ —	$ —	$ —	$ —	$ —	$ —	$ —	$ —	$ —
Successful Phase II but failed Phase III	—	—	—	—	—	—	—	—	—	—
Successful commercial launch	—	—	50.0	65.0	75.0	70.0	60.0	40.0	20.0	5.0
Highly successful commercial launch	—	—	100.0	120.0	150.0	150.0	110.0	70.0	30.0	10.0
Operating Expense Scenarios										
Failed Phase II trials	7.0	—	—	—	—	—	—	—	—	—
Successful Phase II but failed Phase III	7.0	15.0	—	—	—	—	—	—	—	—
Successful commercial launch	7.0	15.0	42.0	51.0	49.0	46.0	40.0	29.0	15.0	4.0
Highly successful commercial launch	7.0	15.0	80.0	90.0	93.0	91.0	70.0	48.0	20.0	7.0
Pretax Income Scenarios										
Failed Phase II trials	(7.0)	—	—	—	—	—	—	—	—	—
Successful Phase II but failed Phase III	(7.0)	(15.0)	—	—	—	—	—	—	—	—
Successful commercial launch	(7.0)	(15.0)	8.0	14.0	26.0	24.0	20.0	11.0	5.0	1.0
Highly successful commercial launch	(7.0)	(15.0)	20.0	30.0	57.0	59.0	40.0	22.0	10.0	3.0

Probability-Weighted Pretax Income	Probabilities										
Failed Phase II trials	35.0%	(2.5)	—	—	—	—	—	—	—	—	—
Successful Phase II but failed Phase III	20.0%	(1.4)	(3.0)	—	—	—	—	—	—	—	—
Successful commercial launch	30.0%	(2.1)	(4.5)	2.4	4.2	7.8	7.2	6.0	3.3	1.5	0.3
Highly successful commercial launch	15.0%	(1.1)	(2.3)	3.0	4.5	8.6	8.8	6.0	3.3	1.5	0.5
Expected Pretax Income	**100.0%**	**(7.0)**	**(9.8)**	**5.4**	**8.7**	**16.4**	**16.1**	**12.0**	**6.6**	**3.0**	**0.8**
	Tax Rate										
Less: Taxes	40.0%	(2.8)	(3.9)	2.2	3.5	6.5	6.4	4.8	2.6	1.2	0.3
After-Tax Income		**(4.2)**	**(5.9)**	**3.2**	**5.2**	**9.8**	**9.6**	**7.2**	**4.0**	**1.8**	**0.5**
Contributory Asset Charges											
Net working capital		0.3	0.4	0.5	0.6	0.8	0.7	0.6	0.4	0.2	0.1
Fixed assets		0.4	0.5	0.6	0.8	0.9	0.9	0.7	0.5	0.2	0.1
Assembled workforce		0.2	0.3	0.4	0.5	0.6	0.6	0.5	0.3	0.1	0.0
Total Contributory Asset Charge		**0.9**	**1.2**	**1.5**	**1.9**	**2.3**	**2.2**	**1.7**	**1.1**	**0.5**	**0.2**
Excess Earnings Attributable to IPR&D		**(5.1)**	**(7.1)**	**1.7**	**3.3**	**7.6**	**7.5**	**5.5**	**2.8**	**1.3**	**0.3**
	Discount Rate										
Discount factor	13.0%	0.941	0.832	0.737	0.652	0.577	0.511	0.452	0.400	0.354	0.313
Present Value		**(4.8)**	**(5.9)**	**1.3**	**2.2**	**4.4**	**3.8**	**2.5**	**1.1**	**0.5**	**0.1**
Present value of cash flows	5.1										
Plus: Tax amortization benefit	1.1										
Fair Value	**$6.3**										

[1] Some totals in this table may not add due to rounding.

Application of Relief From Royalty to IPR&D Assets

Overview

6.139 As discussed in chapter 1, the relief from royalty method under the income approach is relatively specialized for use in measuring the fair value of those intangible assets that are often the subject of licensing, such as trade names, patents, and proprietary technologies.

6.140 The fundamental concept underlying this method is that ownership of the subject asset relieves the owner from the need to pay royalties for use of the asset to a hypothetical third-party owner. The fair value of the asset is the present value of the license fees avoided by owning the subject asset (that is, the royalty savings).

6.141 Application of the relief from royalty method generally involves the following steps:

- Step 1: Isolate the prospective revenue stream related to the subject asset.

- Step 2: Determine the appropriate hypothetical royalty rate for use of the subject asset.[19]

- Step 3: Calculate the present value of the after-tax cash flows using a discount rate appropriate for the specific asset being valued.

- Step 4: Compute the related income tax benefits resulting from the amortization of the IPR&D asset for income tax purposes.

- Step 5: In the case of a transaction, evaluate the overall reasonableness of the IPR&D asset's fair value relative to the other assets acquired and the overall purchase price.

Steps

Step 1: Isolate the Prospective Revenue Stream Related to the Subject Asset

6.142 The starting point for application of the relief from royalty method is to identify the revenue stream expected to be derived from use of the asset being valued based on probability-weighted revenues. The hypothetical royalty rate will be applied to this revenue stream.

6.143 The valuation specialist would need to consider all issues noted in the "Use of Prospective Financial Information" section in paragraphs 6.26–.78 (including consistency with market participant assumptions, apportionment of revenue to various assets, probability-weighting, technology migration, and so forth) when identifying the appropriate market participant level of anticipated revenues.

---

[19] This discussion presumes that royalty rates can be derived for similar stage IPR&D projects. To the extent that royalty rates cannot be derived for similar stage IPR&D projects but can only be found for completed projects, an alternative approach would include specific consideration of the costs to complete.

Step 2: Determine the Appropriate Hypothetical Royalty Rate for Use of the Subject Asset

6.144 To appropriately apply the relief from royalty method for valuing an IPR&D asset, it is critical to develop a hypothetical royalty rate that reflects the comprehensive rights of use by virtue of the ownership of the asset. As with the valuation of any other asset or liability and consistent with guidance in FASB ASC 820, development of inputs for this method using observed market data, such as observed royalty rates in actual arm's length negotiated licenses, is preferable to more subjective unobservable inputs, such as those that might be found in "rules of thumb."

6.145 Because most IPR&D assets have unique characteristics, the royalty rate selection process requires judgment. In certain instances, the underlying technology is often licensed or sublicensed to other third parties. The actual royalty rate charged by the company for use of the technology to other parties may be a reasonable proxy for the appropriate royalty rate to use within the valuation. However, in the absence of actual royalty rate transactions, market-based royalty rates for similar products are often used. Market royalty rates can be obtained from numerous third-party data vendors and publications.[20]

6.146 Based on the level of comparability, actual licensing fees or comparable market rates are adjusted to reflect the subject IPR&D asset being measured at fair value. Examples of such adjustments may include consideration to the usage of the subject asset in accordance with the expectations of market participants. For example, market royalty rates may reflect only limited usage of comparable assets, such as instances in which use is restricted to specific geographic locations, applications, or time periods. Other factors that may exist would also need to be considered. A market participant's use of the asset may differ from this type of limited use, thereby warranting an adjustment to the royalty rate.

6.147 The valuation specialist would also evaluate whether the observed rate reflects the all-inclusive rate commensurate to the complete set of rights associated with the subject asset. Frequently, a licensor may split the benefits associated with an asset with a licensee for a number of reasons. Truly comparable rates may be difficult to find for most technologies and, therefore, simulated or adjusted royalty rates taking into consideration qualitative value drivers of the subject intangible asset would be used.

Step 3: Calculate the Present Value of the After-Tax Cash Flows Using a Discount Rate Appropriate for the Specific Asset Being Valued

6.148 As with the multiperiod excess earnings method, the valuation specialist would select a discount rate for the avoided royalty payments, which is consistent with the risk inherent in those payments.

6.149 When selecting the appropriate discount rate, it is important to consider all issues discussed in paragraphs 6.99–.121 related to the discount rate selection within the multiperiod excess earnings method.

---

[20] As of the date of publication of this guide, third-party data vendors and publications included, but were not limited to, LexisNexis, RoyaltySource Online, ktMINE, and Licensing Economic Review.

Step 4: Compute the Related Income Tax Benefits Resulting From the Amortization of the IPR&D Asset for Income Tax Purposes[21]

6.150 As noted previously with regard to the multiperiod excess earnings method, the fair value of an asset valued using the relief from royalty method should incorporate the tax benefits resulting from the amortization of the intangible asset for income tax purposes. See paragraphs 6.122–.131 for a discussion of tax amortization benefits within the multiperiod excess earnings method.

Step 5: In the Case of a Transaction, Evaluate the Overall Reasonableness of the IPR&D Asset's Fair Value Relative to the Other Assets Acquired and the Overall Purchase Price

6.151 As discussed in paragraph 6.132, the valuation specialist should compare the individual IPR&D asset valuation to the value of the other assets acquired and the overall entity valuation of the acquired company (including the value of contingent consideration, if applicable) to ensure that assumptions are consistent or can be reconciled.

Illustrative Example: Relief From Royalty Method

6.152 Table 6-6 provides an example of the application of the relief from royalty method. The following were key inputs and assumptions used in the application of this method:

- Prospective revenue for the specific IPR&D project
- The proportion of revenue attributable to the subject asset in each year
- A pretax royalty rate based on an analysis of licensing agreements for comparable assets
- An effective tax rate for the royalty payments
- A discount rate commensurate with the specific risk of the subject asset's cash flows

---

[21] A valuation specialist would need to ensure that if tax benefits are separately valued as part of valuation methodology, they are not, in effect, double-counted if already considered in the royalty rate utilized.

Table 6-6[1]

Year	1	2	3	4	5	6	7	8	9	10
Overall revenue	$100.0	$105.0	$110.3	$115.8	$120.4	$125.2	$130.2	$134.1	$138.1	$142.3
Growth		5.0%	5.0%	5.0%	4.0%	4.0%	4.0%	3.0%	3.0%	3.0%
Percentage of revenue attributable to IPR&D	100.0%	90.0%	80.0%	70.0%	60.0%	50.0%	40.0%	30.0%	20.0%	10.0%
Revenue attributable to IPR&D	100.0	94.5	88.2	81.0	72.2	62.6	52.1	40.2	27.6	14.2
Royalties avoided	10.0	9.5	8.8	8.1	7.2	6.3	5.2	4.0	2.8	1.4
Less: Taxes	(4.0)	(3.8)	(3.5)	(3.2)	(2.9)	(2.5)	(2.1)	(1.6)	(1.1)	(0.6)
After-tax royalties avoided	**6.0**	**5.7**	**5.3**	**4.9**	**4.3**	**3.8**	**3.1**	**2.4**	**1.7**	**0.9**
Discount factor	0.941	0.832	0.737	0.652	0.577	0.511	0.452	0.400	0.354	0.313
Present value	**5.6**	**4.7**	**3.9**	**3.2**	**2.5**	**1.9**	**1.4**	**1.0**	**0.6**	**0.3**
Present value of cash flows	25.1									
Plus: Tax amortization benefit	5.6									
Fair value	**$30.7**									

Royalty Rate[1] 10.0%
Tax Rate 40.0%
Discount Rate 13.0%

[1] The royalty rate in this example is predicated on all expenses being at the licensee level. Thus, it represents a net royalty. Depending on the source of royalty rate data, certain expenses may be recognized at the licensor level and would need to be reflected in the relief from royalty calculation.

Additional Considerations for Relief From Royalty Method

6.153 In certain circumstances, if there are insufficient observable royalty transactions for comparable assets, the task force believes that the relief from royalty method may not be appropriate to value IPR&D assets. The approach may be suitable, however, as a means of measuring the value of contributory assets required to generate the anticipated cash flows from IPR&D projects (for example, royalties paid for the use of trade names, developed product technology, or enabling technology, subject to the points discussed in paragraph 1.23). See paragraphs 6.82–.98 for guidance on contributory asset charges.

Application of Decision Tree Analysis to IPR&D Assets

Overview

6.154 As noted in chapter 1, a *decision tree analysis* is an income-based method that explicitly captures the anticipated benefits, costs, and probabilities of contingent outcomes at future decision points, or nodes. In general, these nodes are points at which a major investment decision will be made, such as whether to embark on a phase III clinical trial. At that point, management can decide whether to make an additional investment based on the benefits and costs anticipated from that point forward. If the expected present value of the asset at that time is less than the required investment, then the investment is avoided. This is the key difference between decision tree analysis and the previously discussed methods—the ability to analyze future values, change course, and potentially avoid future investment costs that are not expected to produce an adequate return. Decision tree analysis is particularly applicable to the valuation of assets subject to risks that are not correlated with the market, such as the risk that a particular technology will succeed or fail. Risks that are correlated with external markets would need to be estimated discretely when a decision tree analysis is employed. In summary, the decision tree analysis provides the valuation specialist an ability to analyze cost at various stages, technological feasibility, and the value resulting from a successful outcome.

Pharmaceutical IPR&D Valuation Example: Decision Tree Analysis

6.155 Pharma Inc. acquired Company T, a developer, manufacturer, and marketer of pharmaceutical products. One of the assets acquired in the business combination was an in-process project involving a compound that has possible application in the treatment of certain cancers. At the acquisition date, the compound was entering phase II clinical testing in preparation for possible approval by the FDA. Two possible indications (tumor types) for the compound (that is, colorectal and prostate) were under development. The probabilities of success at each phase based on historical experience are provided in the following table. The probability of success for each indication is independent of the probability of success for the other, and neither indication has an alternative future use.

Development Phase	Probability of Advancing
Phase II	15%
Phase III	75%

Based on these indicators, the probabilities of reaching a commercial launch for each indication is 11.25 percent (15% × 75% = 11.25%).

6.156 Additional facts related to this example are as follows:

- Pharma Inc. acquired laboratory equipment and other tangible assets that are used in this project. These assets have an acquisition date fair value of $10.0 million.

- Pharma Inc. also acquired the project team (assembled workforce) with a value to be determined.

- The after-tax development costs for each indication are $5 million for phase II and $50 million for phase III.

- It is estimated that it will take one year to complete each phase, with all costs assumed to occur at the beginning of the period.

- The estimated net cash flows following a commercial launch for the two indications (assuming an eight-year commercial life) are summarized in table 6-7. All amounts are in millions of dollars after income taxes.

- The computation of the net present value (NPV) of those net cash flows is discounted using the risk-free rates of return applicable to the period (for simplicity, this has been assumed to be a single rate of 6 percent throughout the yield curve).[22] The NPV amounts are computed to the start date of the remaining development effort.

- For each indication, the probability of a high market potential is 30 percent, and a low market potential is 70 percent. The estimates for the probability of success were based on historical experience with similar compounds.

Table 6-7

	Postlaunch Year								
	1	*2*	*3*	*4*	*5*	*6*	*7*	*8*	*NPV*
Colorectal									
High	− 61	43	121	196	280	306	330	342	975
Low	− 50	34	80	100	161	180	190	190	554
Prostate									
High	− 68	47	135	217	311	339	366	379	1082
Low	− 56	39	90	105	166	190	205	210	593

---

[22] The use of the risk-free rates in this example is not intended to imply that the price for bearing uncertainty is captured solely in the expected cash flows. According to FASB ASC 820-10-55-6, a discount rate that is commensurate with the risk inherent in the expected cash flows should be used when estimating fair value.

6.157 The following tree diagram shows the present value of the net cash flows and related probabilities for the colorectal indication:

Colorectal Tree

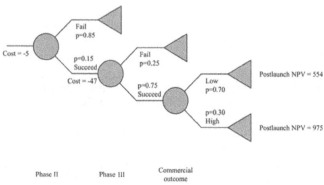

Phase II   Phase III   Commercial outcome

The probability-weighted present value of net cash flows for the colorectal indication equals $64.5 million.

6.158 The following tree diagram shows the present value of the net cash flows and related probabilities for the prostate indication:

Prostate Tree

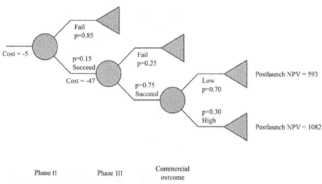

Phase II   Phase III   Commercial outcome

The probability-weighted present value of net cash flows for the prostate indication equals $71.2 million.

6.159 Because the probabilities and values associated with the two indications are independent of one another, the expected present value for the compound is the sum of the expected present value for each indication, or $135.7 million.

6.160 It is important to note that the preceding expected present values represent the incremental additional value of these growth opportunities to the market participant acquirer. In other words, these values include not just the value of the IPR&D asset itself, but the contribution to the asset's value from the acquirer's existing customer relationships, trade names, workforce, working capital, and so forth. The use of the preceding unadjusted values may, therefore, overstate the value of the IPR&D asset. In addition, all of the preceding calculations employed a simplified end-of-period discounting assumption for postlaunch cash flows. It is more reasonable to assume that such cash flows would be received ratably throughout each postlaunch period. A methodology for making these required adjustments to the colorectal indication is presented in the following paragraphs.

6.161 To isolate the IPR&D asset's value from that of the overall project, the first step is to develop an expanded analysis of each commercial outcome, beginning with the low (70-percent probability) case:

Table 6-8

	1	2	3	4	5	6	7	8	9	10
Revenues			50	200	300	325	400	400	400	400
Expenses			41.5	126	159	162.5	128	116	100	100
Pretax			8.5	74	141	162.5	272	284	300	300
Tax			3	30	56	65	109	114	120	120
Net income			5	44	85	98	163	170	180	180
Adjustments:										
Depreciation			30	40	40	40	40	40	40	40
Capital expenditures			− 70	− 35	− 35	− 35	− 35	− 30	− 30	− 30
Working capital			− 5	− 15	− 10	− 3	− 8	0	0	0
Net cash flow			− 40	34	80	100	161	180	190	190
Discount rate			0.8644	0.8155	0.7693	0.7258	0.6847	0.6460	0.6094	0.5749
Present value, net cash flows	579		− 34	28	61	73	110	117	116	109
Present value, ending working capital		22								
		601								

6.162 It should be noted that in preceding table 6-8 and tables 6-9–6-11 that follow, all net cash flows are discounted at the 6-percent rate assumed in paragraph 6.156 using the mid-year discounting convention. For example, the discount factor as of the end of year 3 is (1/1.062.5), or 0.8644. At the end of year 10, the product is expected to reach the end of its economic life. This may be due to expiry of a patent, expected introduction of competing products, or other factors. For simplicity purposes, the liquidation value of tangible assets is assumed to be *de minimis* at the end of this period. The net working capital balance of $41 million is assumed to be recovered by the end of year 10, and the assembled workforce of unspecified value will be redeployed to other activities.

6.163 The low case is then reevaluated using the multiperiod excess earnings method to isolate the IPR&D asset value from the value of other contributory assets, as follows:

Table 6-9

	1	2	3	4	5	6	7	8	9	10
Revenues			50	200	300	325	400	400	400	400
Expenses			41.5	126	159	162.5	128	116	100	100
Pretax			8.5	74	141	162.5	272	284	300	300
Tax			3	30	56	65	109	114	120	120
Net income			5	44	85	98	163	170	180	180
Adjustments:										
Contributory asset charges			− 3	− 10	− 15	− 16	− 20	− 20	− 20	− 20
Excess earnings			3	34	70	81	143	150	160	160
Discount rate			0.8644	0.8155	0.7693	0.7258	0.6847	0.6460	0.6094	0.5749
	528		2	28	54	59	98	97	98	92

6.164 A similar process is also applied to the high (30-percent probability) case:

Table 6-10

	1	2	3	4	5	6	7	8	9	10
Revenues			100	200	350	500	650	650	650	650
Expenses			69	128	140	165	175.5	156	117	97.5
Pretax			31	72	210	335	474.5	494	533	552.5
Tax			12	29	84	134	190	198	213	221
Net income			19	43	126	201	285	296	320	332
Adjustments:										
Depreciation			30	50	50	50	50	50	50	50
Capital expenditures			− 90	− 40	− 40	− 40	− 40	− 40	− 40	− 40
Working capital			− 10	− 10	− 15	− 15	− 15	0	0	0
Net cash flow			− 51	43	121	196	280	306	330	342
Discount rate			0.8644	0.8155	0.7693	0.7258	0.6847	0.6460	0.6094	0.5749
Present value, net cash flows	1,013		− 44	35	93	142	192	198	201	196
Present value, ending working capital	36									
	1,049									

6.165 Again, applying the multiperiod excess earnings method, the IPR&D asset value is isolated, as follows:

Table 6-11

	1	2	3	4	5	6	7	8	9	10
Revenues			100	200	350	500	650	650	650	650
Expenses			69	128	140	165	175.5	156	117	97.5
Pretax			31	72	210	335	474.5	494	533	552.5
Tax			12	29	84	134	190	198	213	221
Net income			19	43	126	201	285	296	320	332
Adjustments:										
Contributory asset charges			− 5	− 10	− 18	− 25	− 33	− 33	− 33	− 33
Excess earnings			14	33	109	176	252	264	287	299
Discount rate			0.8644	0.8155	0.7693	0.7258	0.6847	0.6460	0.6094	0.5749
	940		12	27	83	128	173	170	175	172

6.166 The IPR&D asset value of the two commercial outcomes has now been estimated. These results are summarized in table 6-12 that follows:

Table 6-12

	Low	High	Total
Value of opportunity	601	1,049	
Probability of outcome	.70	.30	
	421	315	736
Probability of success			.1125
			82.8
Cost of opportunity:			
Phase III (present value of 50 at 6%)	47		
Probability	.15		-7.1
Phase II			-5.0
Net present value of opportunity			70.7
Value of IPR&D asset	528	940	
Probability of outcome	.70	.30	
	370	282	652
Probability of success			.1125
			73.4
Cost of IPR&D asset:			
Phase III (present value of 50 at 6%)	47		
Probability	.15		-7.1
Phase II			-5.0
Net present value before TAB			61.3
TAB (35% tax rate over 15 years)			18.7
Fair value, IPR&D asset			80.0

6.167   It should be noted that the present value of the overall opportunity is $70.7 million. However, the value of the IPR&D asset, stripped of the impact of acquired contributory assets (tangible assets of $10.0 million plus the assembled workforce), is adjusted to $61.3 million. To arrive at fair value, the TAB is then added to this adjusted value to arrive at the final estimate of fair value, $80.0 million.

6.168   The preceding example is simplified in a number of ways:

- Both low and high outcomes are "in-the-money;" additional scenarios could be added that may imply it would be optimal to abandon R&D efforts associated with the project and avoid the costs of phase II or phase III, or both.

- The decisions themselves assume either success or failure, as determined at each decision point; more realistic scenarios might include partial failures (for example, phase II was not successful based on original time and cost estimates) but may be successful if additional efforts are made.

- Precommercialization contributory assets (other than the acquired tangible assets and assembled workforce discussed previously) and charges are assumed to be "purchased" by the IPR&D project: $5 to pay for phase II and $50 for phase III. Thus, they are implicitly accounted for in the cost estimates for each phase.

All of the preceding simplifications can be modeled in greater detail, but the basic concepts presented herein would not change.

Summary of Decision Tree Analysis

6.169   As discussed in chapter 1, the decision tree analysis is most applicable when the asset to be valued is subject to multiple risks and contingent outcomes. In the previous pharmaceutical case, the acquirer faces two types of risks:

- The market risks associated with achieving unit prices, sales volumes, operating margins, and so forth

- The technological (contingent) risks of achieving success in phases II and III

6.170   When commonly used methods are employed in the valuation of IPR&D assets such as these, both the market and technology risks are often captured in a single, combined risk-adjusted discount rate (see paragraphs 6.99–.121 for a detailed discussion of discount rates). Alternatively, these risks can be segregated and evaluated separately, as illustrated previously.

Other Methods

6.171   Chapter 1 discusses three valuation approaches (cost, market, and income) and various valuation methods under the income approach. However, this chapter demonstrates only three methods under the income approach (the multiperiod excess earnings method, the relief from royalty method, and decision tree analysis), which have been most commonly used in practice as of the writing of this guide. By not demonstrating the cost and market approaches or additional methods under the income approach, this guide is not intended to imply that these approaches and methods are not acceptable. The task force decided not to demonstrate the other approaches and methods due to their less common usage as of the writing of this guide.

6.172 As discussed in chapter 1, the cost approach is rarely used in practice to value IPR&D assets because generally, there is little or no relationship between cost and fair value. The market approach is used infrequently to value IPR&D assets due to lack of observable data. Furthermore, some of the more advanced methods under the income approach (such as the real options method or Monte Carlo simulation) are not demonstrated because their use has not become common as of the writing of this guide. However, these advanced methods may be increasingly used in the future, and this guide does not intend to foreclose their use.

Valuation Report Considerations

6.173 A valuation specialist will typically document the valuation conclusions in a written report. A written report serves as important documentation in memorializing the characteristics of the assets valued, including IPR&D assets, the methodologies and assumptions used in the valuation of the assets, and the conclusions of value. Most valuation specialists belong to professional organizations, such as the AICPA, which have published standards, as well as report requirements, related to performing a valuation engagement.

6.174 The AICPA's Statement on Standards for Valuation Services (SSVS) No. 1, *Valuation of a Business, Business Ownership Interest, Security, or Intangible Asset* (AICPA, *Professional Standards*, VS sec. 100),[23] provides guidance on the appropriate contents and other considerations associated with the preparation of the valuation report. Client personnel and non-CPA valuation specialists who do not work for a CPA firm are not subject to SSVS No. 1 requirements but may be subject to those of another professional organization.

6.175 Although a full discussion of the requirements of SSVS No. 1 is beyond the scope of this guide, the task force believes that there are certain items that are particularly important when documenting the valuation of IPR&D assets.

Identification and Description of IPR&D Assets

6.176 The task force recommends including the following items related to the identification of IPR&D assets in the valuation report:

- A description of the process used to identify IPR&D assets that meet the recognition criteria

- A discussion of the level of aggregation or disaggregation selected for subject assets, including assets to be used in R&D activities, given particular consideration to their highest and best use

- A description of how IPR&D assets are classified into appropriate subcomponents (for example, developed product technology and IPR&D projects)

---

[23] Other standards include those contained within the Uniform Standards of Professional Appraisal Practice as promulgated by the Appraisal Foundation and the Business Valuation Standards of the American Society of Appraisers, among others.

- A discussion of how technology migration or existence of enabling technology (that meets the applicable recognition criteria), or both, have been addressed

- Discussion of how the relevant accounting guidance, such as that discussed in chapters 2–4, has been considered

Valuation of IPR&D Assets

6.177 For IPR&D assets valued under the cost approach, the task force recommends including the following items in the valuation report:

- Sources of data (for example, acquiring company, acquired company, competitors)

- Nature of costs (reproduction versus replacement)

- Details of the method of cost aggregation (that is, actual application of the method or technique)

- Treatment of obsolescence

- Treatment of opportunity costs

- Treatment of taxes (if applicable)

- Treatment of TAB (if applicable)

- Rationale that led to selection of the cost approach

6.178 As discussed in chapter 1, the cost approach is rarely used in the valuation of intangible IPR&D assets because, generally, there is little or no relationship between cost and fair value.

6.179 For IPR&D assets valued under the market approach, the task force recommends including the following items in the valuation report:

- Sources of comparable data (acquiring company, acquired company, competitors, markets considered)

- Treatment of the adjustments to comparable data

- Details of the application of method or technique

- Treatment of discounts or adjustments to value indications

- Rationale that led to selection of the market approach

6.180 As discussed in chapter 1, with the exception of certain assets within limited industries (for example, pharmaceuticals), the market approach is rarely used in the valuation of IRP&D assets because comparable data is rarely available.

6.181 For IPR&D assets valued under the income approach, the task force recommends including the following items in the valuation report:

- Sources of PFI applicable to IPR&D assets (acquiring company, acquired company, financial advisers, or competitors)

- Details of the procedures performed to allow the valuation specialist to rely on and use the PFI, including, for example:

  — Nature, timing, and estimated costs of the efforts necessary to complete the IPR&D project and the anticipated completion date

— Risks and uncertainties associated with completing development on schedule and consequences if it is not completed on a timely basis

— Product launch timing

— Expected economic life of developed product

— Anticipated changes in growth (that is, volumes and pricing) and margins over the relevant product life cycle

- Treatment of adjustments made to PFI to eliminate entity-specific assumptions

- Details of the circumstances and procedures performed to identify and reflect technology migration and, if necessary, the existence and separate valuation of enabling technology and other contributory assets

- If necessary, sources of royalty rates applied within the analysis

- Treatment of appropriate tax rates, discount rates, and, if necessary, contributory asset charges

- Details of the application of the valuation method or technique

- Derivation of discount rate

- Treatment of TAB

- Rationale that led to selection of the income approach

6.182 The use of alternative methods under the income approach, such as real options, decision tree analysis, Monte Carlo analysis, and so forth, would likely require a discussion of additional assumptions that are particular to those methods and not included in the preceding list.

6.183 Regardless of the valuation methods or techniques used to value the assets, the valuation specialist would need to document the selection of all key assumptions considered most likely to be made by market participants that are not unique to the reporting entity. Management would document the process used to determine the market participant assumptions and the reasons for any differences between the market participant assumptions and the reporting entity's assumptions used in the fair value measurements. In addition, the valuation specialist would need to document the types of data sources used for valuation inputs related to the fair value hierarchy (that is, observable versus unobservable inputs).

Reconciliation of Value Estimates

6.184 If a valuation specialist uses multiple valuation methods or techniques to value an IPR&D asset, then the task force believes that it would be necessary to provide a reconciliation of the various estimates of value, which would include a discussion of the relative merits of each valuation method or technique and the basis for any weightings applied in the conclusion of value.

Comprehensive Example

Note: This example is provided only to demonstrate concepts discussed in the preceding chapters of this guide and is not intended to establish requirements. Furthermore, the assumptions and inputs used in this example are illustrative only and are not intended to serve as guidelines. Facts and circumstances of each individual situation should be considered when performing an actual valuation.

Overview

6.185 This section includes a comprehensive example of a valuation analysis used for measuring fair value of IPR&D assets. In this example, assume that Acquirer Company (Acquirer) acquired in a business combination (the transaction) Target Company (Target), a California-based software and professional services company. Acquirer's management has essentially identified the Target primarily as a technology company. All potential intangible assets of Target related to the transaction that may have existed at the date of valuation were initially considered in the valuation analysis. The purchase price is $75 million, and it is assumed to be a taxable transaction. As a result of the valuation specialist's review, the following intangible assets were ultimately valued in the analysis: (*a*) trade name, (*b*) patents, (*c*) customer relationships, (*d*) developed technology, and (*e*) IPR&D.

6.186 The following general assumptions were made in connection with this valuation:

- Certain assumptions were discussed with Target's and Acquirer's management to determine their reasonableness for use in the analysis. The PFI was also analyzed and discussed with Target's and Acquirer's management to confirm that the PFI utilizes market participant assumptions.

- Three approaches were considered in determining the fair value of the intangible assets: the income approach, the market approach, and the cost approach.

- The income approach was used to value the trade name, patents, customer relationships, developed technology, and IPR&D.

- The estimated WACC for use in the analysis is 15 percent.

Trade Name

6.187 The trade name is associated with Target's entire business and, based on discussions with Target's management, it was indicated that the trade name was expected to be used for approximately 10 years following the date of the transaction. When estimating the value of the trade name, the income approach (through the relief from royalty method) was employed. The forecasted revenue base used in the valuation of the trade name was the revenue related to Target's overall business. Based on research of comparable third-party licensing transactions, a 1.0-percent net implicit royalty rate was utilized in the analysis. However, it was determined that a 1.0-percent implicit royalty for the acquired trade name would only apply for the first 5 years after the transaction. Given the technology-related nature of the acquired trade name, it was estimated that the implicit royalty rate would decline to 0.5 percent for the remaining 5 years of the trade name's life.

6.188 After calculating pretax income based on the previously noted implicit royalty rates, a 40.0-percent tax rate was used to arrive at after-tax cash flow. After-tax cash flow was then discounted to present value utilizing a discount rate of 15.0 percent. The selected discount rate was based on the estimated risk associated with the trade name, which was assumed to be approximately equivalent with the overall business of Target. The present values of the after-tax cash flow and the amortization tax benefit were summed to arrive at the fair value of Target's trade name. Refer to schedule 6-2, "Acquired Trade Name," for additional detail.

Patents

6.189 When estimating the value of Target's patents, the income approach (through the relief from royalty method) was employed. Based on the terms of the existing patents, it was indicated that the patents would be valid for 7 years following the transaction. The forecasted revenue used in the valuation of the patents was the revenue related to the developed technology and IPR&D. Research of comparable third-party licensing transactions for similar technologies was performed to conclude on a 3.0-percent implicit royalty rate.

6.190 After calculating pretax income based on a net implicit royalty rate of 3.0 percent, a 40.0-percent tax rate was used to arrive at after-tax cash flow. After-tax cash flow was then discounted to present value utilizing a discount rate of 15.0 percent. The selected discount rate was based on the estimated risk associated with the patents, which was assumed to be approximately equivalent with the overall business of Target. The present value of the after-tax cash flow and the amortization tax benefit were summed to arrive at the fair value of Target's patents. Refer to schedule 6-3 for additional details.

Customer Relationships

6.191 When estimating the value of the customer relationships, the income approach (through the "with and without" method) was employed. Based on discussions with Target's management, it was indicated that the existing customer relationships were valuable to Target's business. The forecasted revenue base used in the valuation of the customer relationships was assumed to be the total revenues for the Target.

6.192 Target's management indicated that rebuilding the customer base would require approximately 2 years of effort and result in certain lost revenues during that time. Specifically, it was estimated that without the customers, Target would lose approximately 20.0 percent of its revenue in the first year and 5 percent of its revenue in the second year (while reestablishing its customer base). Cost of goods sold and other operating expenses were assumed to be variable in both scenarios. Utilizing a discount rate of 15.0 percent, the present values of the differences in net cash flows between the two scenarios were added to the amortization tax benefit to arrive at fair value for the customer relationships. The selected discount rate was based on the assumed equivalent risk of the customer relationships, as compared to the overall business of Target. Refer to schedule 6-4, "Customer Relationships," for additional details.

Developed Technology

6.193 When estimating the value of the developed technology, the income approach (through the multiperiod excess earnings method)[24] was employed. The forecasted revenue and expense margins used in the valuation of the developed technology were provided by management. After arriving at the estimated earnings before interest, taxes, depreciation, and amortization (EBITDA) level for the developed technology, depreciation expense and pretax contributory asset charges for the trade name and patents (based on implicit royalty rates of 1 percent and 3 percent, respectively) were applied to arrive at earnings before interest and taxes (EBIT). Pretax cash flows were then tax-effected utilizing a 40.0-percent tax rate to calculate net income.

6.194 Depreciation was then added back because it represents a noncash expense. Additionally, after-tax contributory asset charges (for fixed assets, the return *of* and *on*, and for net working capital, assembled workforce, and customer relationships, return *on*) were deducted to arrive at after-tax cash flow (that is, excess earnings). Excess earnings were then discounted to present value utilizing a discount rate of 15.0 percent. The selected discount rate was based on the estimated risk associated with the developed technology, which was assumed to be approximately equivalent to the overall business of Target. Finally, the present value of the excess earnings and the amortization tax benefit were summed to arrive at fair value for the developed technology. Refer to schedule 6-5, "Developed Technology," for additional details.

IPR&D

6.195 When estimating the value of the IPR&D, the income approach (through the multiperiod excess earnings method)[25] was employed. The forecasted revenue base, expense margins, and initial costs to complete used in the valuation of the IPR&D were provided by management. As of the date of valuation, it was estimated that the IPR&D required approximately $4 million in remaining costs before it was completed. After arriving at the estimated EBITDA level for the IPR&D, depreciation expense and pretax contributory asset charges for the trade name and patents (based on implicit royalty rates of 1 percent and 3 percent, respectively) were applied to arrive at EBIT. Note that during the first forecast year (*a*) the implicit royalty payment for the patent in year 1 is assumed to represent the contribution of the patents to the technology during the development phase; (*b*) a contributory asset charge was not applied for the trade name because the IPR&D is not expected to generate revenue until the second year; and (*c*) the charges for the patents and other contributory assets were approximated based on the ratio of the remaining costs to complete the IPR&D relative to total costs as multiplied by the dollar

---

[24] The multiperiod excess earnings method was also used to value the IPR&D in this example. However, this example does not demonstrate the simultaneous application of the multiperiod excess earnings method to multiple assets using a single revenue stream. The revenue has been split first, and then the multiperiod excess earnings method has been applied to each of the streams of revenue separately. Many believe that the simultaneous application of the multiperiod excess earnings method is not appropriate because it may be subject to theoretical and mathematical inaccuracy.

[25] The multiperiod excess earnings method was also used to value the developed technology in this example. However, this example does not demonstrate the simultaneous application of the multiperiod excess earnings method to multiple assets using a single revenue stream. The revenue has been split first, and then the multiperiod excess earnings method has been applied to each of the streams of revenue separately. Many believe that the simultaneous application of the multiperiod excess earnings method is not appropriate because it may be subject to theoretical and mathematical inaccuracy.

amount for the contributory asset charge for that first forecast year. EBIT was then tax effected utilizing a 40-percent tax rate to calculate net income.

6.196 Depreciation was then added back because it represents a noncash expense. Additionally, the return of fixed assets and other after-tax contributory charges (for net working capital, return on fixed assets, assembled workforce, and customer relationships) were deducted to arrive at excess earnings. Excess earnings were then discounted to present value utilizing a discount rate of 19.0 percent. The selected discount rate was based on the higher estimated risk associated with the IPR&D, as compared to the overall business of Target. Also note that the selected discount rate represents what some would believe to be a blended rate, combining the lower rate, which could be applicable to the costs to complete, and the higher rate, which could be applicable to the uncertain positive cash flows of the IPR&D. Finally, the present value of the excess earnings and the amortization tax benefit were summed to arrive at fair value for the IPR&D. Refer to schedule 6-6, "IPR&D," for additional detail.

6.197 As discussed previously, the multiperiod excess earnings method is employed in this example to determine the value of the IPR&D. Although this method is frequently considered to be the preferred, best practices method for valuing such assets, other methods may also be acceptable in some circumstances, including decision tree analysis, the Greenfield method, and so forth. An example of an IPR&D asset valuation using a decision tree analysis is included in the "Application of Decision Tree Analysis to IPR&D Assets" section in paragraphs 6.154–.170.

Additional Analysis

6.198 The following are additional observations in connection with this valuation:

- The assembled workforce of Target was valued using the cost approach to calculate a contributory asset charge. (In this example, the cost approach was applied on a pretax basis. See paragraph 1.07 for further discussion.) Refer to schedule 6-7, "Assembled Workforce," for additional detail.

- The calculated contributory asset charges are shown in schedule 6-8, "Contributory Charges." For further detail related to the calculation of contributory asset charges, refer to the Appraisal Foundation document.

- he detailed revenue assumptions related to Target's technology, as forecasted by Target's management, are included in schedule 6-9, "Revenue Detail."

- Based on the forecast provided by Target's management, an IRR was calculated using a business enterprise valuation approach. The estimated IRR of 15.0 percent is detailed in schedule 6-10, "Business Enterprise Valuation and Internal Rate of Return."

- Schedule 6-11, "Summary of Assets," represents a summary of the assets considered in this analysis.

- WARA and reconciliation between the WARA, WACC, and IRR are included in schedule 6-12, "Weighted Average Return on Assets."

6.199 For purposes of this example, the relief from royalty method was used to value the trade name and patents, the "with and without" method was used to value the customer relationships, and the multiperiod excess earnings method was used to value the developed technology and IPR&D. However, it should not be assumed that this is the only combination of methodological selections that could be made. For example, there could be circumstances in which it is more appropriate to use the multiperiod excess earnings method for valuing customer relationships and the relief from royalty method for valuing developed technology and IPR&D. The valuation specialist would need to select the combination of methods that is the most representationally faithful to measuring fair value in accordance with FASB ASC 820.

Schedules[26]
6.200

Overview of Assumptions and Inputs

(000's)

Overall	2X11	2X12	2X13	2X14	2X15	2X16	2X17	2X18	2X19	2X20
Total revenue	$100,000	$109,000	$116,500	$122,000	$127,100	$130,913	$134,840	$138,886	$143,052	$147,344
Revenue growth	—	9.0%	6.9%	4.7%	4.2%	3.0%	3.0%	3.0%	3.0%	3.0%
Margins										
Cost of goods sold	65.0%	65.0%	65.0%	65.0%	65.0%	65.0%	65.0%	65.0%	65.0%	65.0%
Operating expenses[1]	13.4%	13.3%	13.2%	13.0%	12.9%	13.9%	13.7%	13.6%	13.6%	13.5%
Research & development (R&D)	7.0%	7.0%	7.0%	7.0%	7.0%	7.0%	7.0%	7.0%	7.0%	7.0%
Maintenance R&D[2]	1.8%	1.8%	1.8%	1.8%	1.8%	1.8%	1.8%	1.8%	1.8%	1.8%
Depreciation	1.6%	1.7%	1.8%	2.0%	2.1%	1.1%	1.3%	1.4%	1.4%	1.5%

Terminal year growth rate	3.0%
Income tax rate	40.0%
Working capital % of revenue	5.0%
Amortization period	15.0

Trade name assumptions	2X11	2X12	2X13	2X14	2X15	2X16	2X17	2X18	2X19	2X20
Revenue related to trade name	100,000	109,000	116,500	122,000	127,100	130,913	134,840	138,886	143,052	147,344
Implicit royalty rate	1.0%	1.0%	1.0%	1.0%	1.0%	0.5%	0.5%	0.5%	0.5%	0.5%

Discount rates	
Trade Name	15.0%
Patents	15.0%
Customer relationships	15.0%
Developed technology	15.0%
IPR&D	19.0%
Workforce	15.0%
Goodwill	20.0%
WACC	15.0%

(continued)

[26] Some totals in these tables may not add due to rounding.

Overview of Assumptions and Inputs—continued

(000's)

	2X11	2X12	2X13	2X14	2X15	2X16	2X17	2X18
Patents assumptions								
Revenue related to patents	60,000	67,400	73,200	77,100	81,000	59,290	26,280	0
Revenue growth	—	12.3%	8.6%	5.3%	5.1%	– 26.8%	– 55.7%	– 100.0%
Implicit royalty rate	3.0%							
Customers	2X11	2X12	2X13	2X14	2X15			
Revenue without customers, as a % of revenue with customers	80.0%	95.0%	100.0%	100.0%	100.0%			
Increase in expenses, as a % of revenue	1.0%	0.5%	0.0%	0.0%	0.0%			
Developed Technology	2X11	2X12	2X13	2X14				
Revenue related to technology	60,000	40,440	18,300	0				
Cost of goods sold	67.0%	72.0%	72.0%	72.0%				
IPR&D	2X11	2X12	2X13	2X14	2X15	2X16	2X17	
Revenue related to technology	0	26,960	54,900	77,100	81,000	59,290	26,280	
Cost of goods sold	NMF³	68.0%	64.0%	62.0%	62.0%	65.0%	69.0%	
Cost to complete	4,000							
Workforce								
See schedule 6-7 for assumptions								

1 Operating expenses are 15.0% of total revenues less applicable depreciation expense.
2 Maintenance R&D expenses are 25.0% of total R&D expenses.
3 NMF stands for "not meaningful."

Schedule 6-1

Target Company
Valuation Summary

Intangible Assets		*Fair Value (000's)*
Trade name		$3,800
Patents		6,400
Customer relationships		3,000
Developed technology		6,100
IPR&D		12,900
	Total Identifiable Intangible Assets	$32,200

Schedule 6-2

Target Company
Acquired Trade Name

(000's)

For the fiscal years ending		2X11	2X12	2X13	2X14	2X15	2X16	2X17	2X18	2X19	2X20
Revenue		$100,000	$109,000	$116,500	$122,000	$127,100	$130,913	$134,840	$138,886	$143,052	$147,344
Implicit royalty payment		1,000	1,090	1,165	1,220	1,271	655	674	694	715	737
Pretax income		1,000	1,090	1,165	1,220	1,271	655	674	694	715	737
Income tax expense	40.0%	400	436	466	488	508	262	270	278	286	295
After-tax cash flow		600	654	699	732	763	393	405	417	429	442
Discount period		0.50	1.50	2.50	3.50	4.50	5.50	6.50	7.50	8.50	9.50
Present value factor	15.0%	0.9325	0.8109	0.7051	0.6131	0.5332	0.4636	0.4031	0.3506	0.3048	0.2651
Present value of after-tax cash flow		560	530	493	449	407	182	163	146	131	117
Sum, present value of interim cash flows		3,177									
Tax amortization benefit		638									
Fair value		3,815									
Fair value (rounded)		$3,800									
Selected Assumptions											
Life		10 years									
Implicit royalty rate		1.0%	1.0%	1.0%	1.0%	1.0%	0.5%	0.5%	0.5%	0.5%	0.5%

Schedule 6-3
Target Company
Patents (shared by both developed technology and IPR & D)

(000's)

For the fiscal years ending		2X11	2X12	2X13	2X14	2X15	2X16	2X17	2X18
Revenue		$60,000	$67,400	$73,200	$77,100	$81,000	$59,290	$26,280	$0
Implicit royalty payment[1]		1,935	2,022	2,196	2,313	2,430	1,779	788	0
Pretax income		1,935	2,022	2,196	2,313	2,430	1,779	788	0
Income tax expense	40.0%	774	809	878	925	972	711	315	0
After-tax cash flow		1,161	1,213	1,318	1,388	1,458	1,067	473	0
Discount period		0.50	1.50	2.50	3.50	4.50	5.50	6.50	7.50
Present value factor	15.0%	0.9325	0.8109	0.7051	0.6131	0.5332	0.4636	0.4031	0.3506
Present value of after-tax cash flow		1,083	984	929	851	777	495	191	0
Sum, present value of interim cash flows		5,309							
Tax amortization benefit		1,066							
Fair value		6,375							
Fair value (rounded)		$6,400							
Selected Assumptions									
Implicit royalty rate		3.0%	3.0%	3.0%	3.0%	3.0%	3.0%	3.0%	3.0%

[1] For 2X11 only: Implicit royalty payment is based on the sum of the percentage of revenue ($1,800 for developed technology plus the percentage of cost ($135 for IPR&D).

Schedule 6-4
Target Company
Customer Relationships[1]

(000's)

	2X11	2X12	2X13	2X14	2X15
For the fiscal years ending					
Revenue					
With customers	$100,000	$109,000	$116,500	$122,000	$127,100
Without customers	80,000	103,550	116,500	122,000	127,100
Difference in revenue	20,000	5,450	0	0	0
Cost of goods sold and operating/research and development expenses					
With customers	87,000	94,830	101,355	106,140	110,577
Without customers	70,400	90,606	101,355	106,140	110,577
Difference in operating expenses	16,600	4,224	0	0	0
EBIT[2]					
With customers	13,000	14,170	15,145	15,860	16,523
Without customers	9,600	12,944	15,145	15,860	16,523
Difference in EBIT	3,400	1,226	0	0	0

Income tax expense						
With customers		5,200	5,668	6,058	6,344	6,609
Without customers		3,840	5,178	6,058	6,344	6,609
Difference in income taxes	40%	1,360	491	0	0	0
Debt-free cash flow						
With customers		7,800	8,502	9,087	9,516	9,914
Without customers		5,760	7,766	9,087	9,516	9,914
Difference in debt-free net cash flow		2,040	736	0	0	0
Discount period		0.50	1.50	2.50	3.50	4.50
Present value factor	15.0%	0.9325	0.8109	0.7051	0.6131	0.5332
Present value of after tax cash flow		1,902	597	0	0	0
Sum, present value of interim cash flows		2,499				
Tax amortization benefit		502				
Fair value		3,001				
Fair value (rounded)		$3,000				

1 This schedule illustrates a simplified version of the "with and without" method; it is not intended to demonstrate details and complexities that are typically involved in this analysis (for example, the effect of fixed versus variable costs).

2 EBIT stands for "earnings before interest and taxes."

Selected Assumptions

Revenue differential (loss)	20,000	5,450	0	0	0
Expense differential (increase)	1.0%	0.5%	0.0%	0.0%	0.0%

Schedule 6-5

Target Company
Developed Technology

(000's)

For the fiscal years ending		2X11	2X12	2X13	2X14
Revenue		$60,000	$40,440	$18,300	$0
Cost of goods sold		40,200	29,117	13,176	0
Gross profit		19,800	11,323	5,124	0
Operating expenses		8,027	5,373	2,412	0
Research and development—maintenance		1,050	708	320	0
Total operating expenses		9,077	6,081	2,732	0
EBITDA[1]		10,723	5,242	2,392	0
Depreciation		973	693	333	0
Implicit royalty payment—trade name		600	404	183	0
Implicit royalty payment—patents		1,800	1,213	549	0
EBIT[2]		7,350	2,932	1,327	0
Income tax expense	40.0%	2,940	1,173	531	0
Net income (loss)		4,410	1,759	796	0
Add: Depreciation		973	693	333	0
Less: Return of fixed assets		973	693	333	0
Less: Other after-tax contributory charges		618	417	189	0
Excess earnings		3,792	1,343	608	0
Discount period		0.50	1.50	2.50	3.50
Present value factor	15.0%	0.9325	0.8109	0.7051	0.6131
Present value of after tax cash flow		3,536	1,089	428	0

Sum, present value of interim cash flows	5,053			
Tax amortization benefit	1,015			
Fair value	6,068			
Fair value (rounded)	$6,100			

Selected Assumptions

Cost of goods sold	67.0%	72.0%	72.0%	72.0%
Gross margin	33.0%	28.0%	28.0%	28.0%
Operating expenses	13.4%	13.3%	13.2%	13.0%
Research and development—maintenance	1.8%	1.8%	1.8%	1.8%
EBITDA margin	17.9%	13.0%	13.1%	NMF[3]
Depreciation	1.6%	1.7%	1.8%	2.0%
Implicit royalty rate—trade name	1.0%	1.0%	1.0%	1.0%
Implicit royalty rate—patents	3.0%	3.0%	3.0%	3.0%
Charge for the use of contributory assets	1.0%	1.0%	1.0%	1.0%

[1] EBITDA stands for "earnings before interest, taxes, depreciation, and amortization."

[2] EBIT stands for "earnings before interest and taxes."

[3] NMF stands for "not meaningful."

Schedule 6-6

Target Company
IPR&D

(000's)

For the fiscal years ending	2X11	2X12	2X13	2X14	2X15	2X16	2X17
Revenue	$0	$26,960	$54,900	$77,100	$81,000	$59,290	$26,280
Cost of goods sold	0	18,333	35,136	47,802	50,220	38,539	18,133
Gross profit	0	8,627	19,764	29,298	30,780	20,752	8,147
Operating expenses	0	3,582	7,235	10,057	10,452	8,234	3,598
Cost to complete	4,000	0	0	0	0	0	0
Research and development—maintenance	0	472	961	1,349	1,418	1,038	460
Total operating expenses	4,000	4,054	8,196	11,407	11,870	9,271	4,058
EBITDA[1]	(4,000)	4,573	11,568	17,891	18,910	11,480	4,089
Depreciation	318	462	1,000	1,508	1,698	660	344
Implicit royalty payment—trade name	0	270	549	771	810	593	263
Implicit royalty payment—patents[2]	135	809	1,647	2,313	2,430	1,779	788
EBIT[3]	(4,453)	3,033	8,372	13,300	13,973	8,449	2,694
Income tax expense 40.0%	(1,781)	1,213	3,349	5,320	5,589	3,380	1,077
Net income (loss)	(2,672)	1,820	5,023	7,980	8,384	5,069	1,616
Add: Depreciation	318	462	1,000	1,508	1,698	660	344
Less: Return of fixed assets	318	462	1,000	1,508	1,698	660	344
Less: Other after-tax contributory charges[4]	48	278	566	794	834	611	271
Excess earnings	(2,720)	1,542	4,458	7,186	7,549	4,458	1,345
Discount period	0.50	1.50	2.50	3.50	4.50	5.50	6.50
Present value factor 19.0%	0.9167	0.7703	0.6473	0.5440	0.4571	0.3841	0.3228
Present value of after-tax cash flow	(2,494)	1,188	2,886	3,909	3,451	1,713	434

Sum, present value of interim cash flows		11,087
Tax amortization benefit		1,832
	Fair value	12,919
	Fair value (rounded)	$12,900

Selected Assumptions

Cost of goods sold		NMF[5]	68.0%	64.0%	62.0%	62.0%	65.0%	69.0%
	Gross margin	NMF	32.0%	36.0%	38.0%	38.0%	35.0%	31.0%
Operating expenses		13.4%	13.3%	13.2%	13.0%	12.9%	13.9%	13.7%
Research and development—maintenance		1.8%	1.8%	1.8%	1.8%	1.8%	1.8%	1.8%
	EBITDA margin	NMF	17.0%	21.1%	23.2%	23.3%	19.4%	15.6%
Depreciation		1.6%	1.7%	1.8%	2.0%	2.1%	1.1%	1.3%
Implicit royalty rate—trade name		1.0%	1.0%	1.0%	1.0%	1.0%	1.0%	1.0%
Implicit royalty rate—patents		3.0%	3.0%	3.0%	3.0%	3.0%	3.0%	3.0%
Charge for the use of contributory assets		1.0%	1.0%	1.0%	1.0%	1.0%	1.0%	1.0%

[1] EBITDA stands for "earnings before interest, taxes, depreciation, and amortization."

[2] For 2X11 only:
(Costs to complete / (Technology cost of goods sold + Total technology operating expenses + Costs to complete)) * (Implicit patent royalty rate * Technology revenue)
The implicit charge for the patents is deducted to represent the contribution of the patents to the technology during the development phase.

[3] EBIT stands for "earnings before interest and taxes."

[4] For 2X11 only: (Costs to complete / (Cost of goods sold + total operating expenses)) * (Contributory charge * total revenue)

[5] NMF stands for "not meaningful."

Schedule 6-7
Target Company
Assembled Work Force

Salary Data

Category	Number of Employees	Average Annual Salary (without burden)	Burden Rate (%)	Average Annual Salary (with burden)	Average Weekly Salary (with burden)
Engineering	35	$65,000	25%	$81,250	$1,563
Sales	12	55,000	15%	63,250	1,216
Administrative	25	45,000	20%	54,000	1,038

Training Cost Data

Category	Weeks of Training	Percent of Time Spent Training	Training Cost	Explicit Training Cost	Total Training Cost
Engineering	4	100%	6,250	1,000	7,250
Sales	4	100%	4,865	750	5,615
Administrative	2	50%	1,038	0	1,038

Pretax Cost per Employee

Category	Search	Interview	Training	Total Acquisition Cost	Number of Employees	Total Pretax Cost
Engineering	3,000	1,500	7,250	11,750	35	411,250
Sales	2,500	1,500	5,615	9,615	12	115,385
Administrative	1,000	1,000	1,038	3,038	25	75,962
				Indication of value		602,596
				Indication of value (000's and rounded)		$600

Schedule 6-8

Target Company
Contributory Charges

(000's)

Asset		2X11	2X12	2X13	2X14	2X15	2X16	2X17
Net working capital								
Charge (after-tax rate)	4.6%							
as a percentage of total revenue		$232	$253	$270	$283	$295	$304	$313
		0.2%	0.2%	0.2%	0.2%	0.2%	0.2%	0.2%
Normalized level		0.2%						
Fixed assets (return on only)								
Charge (after-tax rate)	5.8%							
as a percentage of total revenue		440	439	426	403	369	369	400
		0.4%	0.4%	0.4%	0.3%	0.3%	0.3%	0.3%
Normalized level		0.3%						
Assembled work force								
Charge (after-tax rate)	15.0%							
as a percentage of total revenue		90	90	90	90	90	90	90
		0.1%	0.1%	0.1%	0.1%	0.1%	0.1%	0.1%
Normalized level		0.1%						
Customer relationships								
Charge (after-tax rate)	15.0%							
as a percentage of total revenue		450	450	450	450	450	450	450
		0.5%	0.4%	0.4%	0.4%	0.4%	0.3%	0.3%
Normalized level		0.4%						
Aggregate after-tax charge for the use of contributory assets		1.0%						
Trade name								
Pretax contributory charge as a percentage of total revenue		1.0%						
Patents								
Pretax contributory charge as a percentage of total revenue		3.0%						

Schedule 6-9

Target Company
Revenue Detail

(000's)

For the fiscal years ending	2X11	2X12	2X13	2X14	2X15	2X16	2X17	2X18	2X19	2X20
Revenue	$100,000	$109,000	$116,500	$122,000	$127,100	$130,913	$134,840	$138,886	$143,052	$147,344
Revenue attributable to										
Technology	60,000	67,400	73,200	77,100	81,000	84,700	87,600	90,200	92,900	95,700
Other revenue	40,000	41,600	43,300	44,900	46,100	46,213	47,240	48,686	50,152	51,644
Total	100,000	109,000	116,500	122,000	127,100	130,913	134,840	138,886	143,052	147,344
Revenue attributable to										
Technology, as a % of revenue	60%	62%	63%	63%	64%	65%	65%	65%	65%	65%
Other, as a % of revenue	40%	38%	37%	37%	36%	35%	35%	35%	35%	35%
Total	100%	100%	100%	100%	100%	100%	100%	100%	100%	100%
Technology revenue										
Developed	100%	60%	25%	0%	0%	0%	0%	0%	0%	0%
IPR&D	0%	40%	75%	100%	100%	70%	30%	0%	0%	0%
Future yet-to-be-defined	0%	0%	0%	0%	0%	30%	70%	100%	100%	100%
Total	100%	100%	100%	100%	100%	100%	100%	100%	100%	100%
Technology revenue										
Developed	60,000	40,440	18,300	0	0	0	0	0	0	0
IPR&D	0	26,960	54,900	77,100	81,000	59,290	26,280	0	0	0
Future yet-to-be-defined	0	0	0	0	0	25,410	61,320	90,200	92,900	95,700
Total	60,000	67,400	73,200	77,100	81,000	84,700	87,600	90,200	92,900	95,700

Schedule 6-10
Target Company
Business Enterprise Valuation and Internal Rate of Return

(000's)

For the fiscal years ending		2X11	2X12	2X13	2X14	2X15	2X16	2X17
Revenue		$100,000	$109,000	$116,500	$122,000	$127,100	$130,913	$134,840
Cost of goods sold		65,000	70,850	75,725	79,300	82,615	85,093	87,646
Gross profit		35,000	38,150	40,775	42,700	44,485	45,820	47,194
Operating expenses		13,379	14,482	15,354	15,914	16,401	18,180	18,462
Research and development		7,000	7,630	8,155	8,540	8,897	9,164	9,439
Total operating expenses		20,379	22,112	23,509	24,454	25,298	27,344	27,901
EBITDA[1]		14,621	16,038	17,266	18,246	19,187	18,476	19,294
Depreciation		1,621	1,868	2,121	2,386	2,664	1,457	2,200
EBITA[2]		13,000	14,170	15,145	15,860	16,523	17,019	17,094
Income tax expense	40.0%	5,200	5,668	6,058	6,344	6,609	6,807	6,837
Debt-free net income		7,800	8,502	9,087	9,516	9,914	10,211	10,256
Add: Depreciation		1,621	1,868	2,121	2,386	2,664	1,457	2,200
Add/(Less): Changes in debt-free net working capital		0	(450)	(375)	(275)	(255)	(191)	(196)
Less: Capital expenditures		(1,700)	(1,750)	(1,800)	(1,900)	(2,000)	(2,100)	(2,200)
Debt-free cash flow		7,721	8,170	9,033	9,727	10,323	9,378	10,060
Discount period		0.50	1.50	2.50	3.50	4.50	5.50	6.50
Present value factor (Internal Rate of Return)	17.2%	0.9237	0.7881	0.6724	0.5737	0.4895	0.4176	0.3563
Present value of after-tax cash flow		7,132	6,439	6,074	5,580	5,053	3,916	3,585

(continued)

Target Company
Business Enterprise Valuation and Internal Rate of Return—continued

(000's)

For the fiscal years ending	2X11	2X12	2X13	2X14	2X15	2X16	2X17
Terminal year growth rate and value	3.0%						
Sum of present values	$63,772					72,944	
						Total purchase consideration	
Plus: Tax amortization benefit[3]	11,228						
Total	$75,000						

Total purchase consideration		$75,000	
Less: Net working capital		5,000	
Less: Fixed assets		7,500	
Less: Other assets		—	
Total implied goodwill and intangibles		$62,500	
Tax amortization benefit		11,228	

Selected Assumptions

	2X11	2X12	2X13	2X14	2X15	2X16	2X17
Revenue growth	—	9.0%	6.9%	4.7%	4.2%	3.0%	3.0%
Cost of goods sold	65.0%	65.0%	65.0%	65.0%	65.0%	65.0%	65.0%
Gross profit	35.0%	35.0%	35.0%	35.0%	35.0%	35.0%	35.0%
Operating expenses	13.4%	13.3%	13.2%	13.0%	12.9%	13.9%	13.7%
Research and development	7.0%	7.0%	7.0%	7.0%	7.0%	7.0%	7.0%
EBITDA	14.6%	14.7%	14.8%	15.0%	15.1%	14.1%	14.3%
Depreciation and amortization	1.6%	1.7%	1.8%	2.0%	2.1%	1.1%	1.6%
EBIT	13.0%	13.0%	13.0%	13.0%	13.0%	13.0%	12.7%
Federal and state tax rate	40.0%	40.0%	40.0%	40.0%	40.0%	40.0%	40.0%
Net working capital as a % of revenue	5.0%	5.0%	5.0%	5.0%	5.0%	5.0%	5.0%

[1] EBITDA stands for "earnings before interest, taxes, depreciation, and amortization."

[2] EBITA stands for "earnings before interest, taxes, and amortization."

[3] This transaction has been structured as an asset sale, therefore, a tax amortization benefit has been added for the step-up in basis.

Schedule 6-11

Target Company
Summary of Assets

Identified Assets	Fair Value (000's)	Percent of Total
Total current assets	$10,000	12.5%
Property and equipment, net	7,500	9.4%
Other assets	0	0.0%
Subtotal, current and tangible assets	17,500	21.9%
Trade name	3,800	4.8%
Patents	6,400	8.0%
Customer relationships	3,000	3.8%
Developed technology	6,100	7.6%
IPR&D	12,900	16.1%
Subtotal, intangible assets	32,200	40.3%
Assembled work force	600	0.8%
Implied goodwill	29,700	37.1%
Total transaction value (detail below)	80,000	100.0%
Consideration paid	75,000	
Liabilities assumed	5,000	
Total	$80,000	

Schedule 6-12

Target Company
Weighted Average Return on Assets

Assets	Fair Value (000's)	After-Tax Return	Weighted Return	
Net working capital	$5,000	4.6%	0.3%	
Property and equipment, net	7,500	5.8%	0.6%	
Other assets	0	5.8%	0.0%	
Trade name	3,800	15.0%	0.8%	
Patents	6,400	15.0%	1.3%	
Customer relationships	3,000	15.0%	0.6%	
Developed technology	6,100	15.0%	1.2%	
IPR&D	12,900	19.0%	3.3%	
Assembled work force	600	15.0%	0.1%	
Implied goodwill	29,700	20.0%	7.9%	
Total	$75,000		16.1%	Weighted Average Return on Assets
			15.0%	Weighted Average Cost of Capital
			17.2%	Internal Rate of Return

Company A Supporting Schedule
Target Company
Fixed Asset Additions and Depreciation

($000's)

	2X11	2X12	2X13	2X14	2X15	2X16	2X17	2X18	2X19	2X20
Opening net fixed asset balance	$7,500	$7,579	$7,461	$7,139	$6,654	$5,989	$6,632	$7,068	$7,404	$7,750
Capital expenditures (additions)	1,700	1,750	1,800	1,900	2,000	2,100	2,200	2,300	2,400	2,500
Depreciation										
Opening balance	$1,500	$1,500	$1,500	$1,500	$1,500	$0	$0	$0	$0	$0
Additions, period 1	121	243	243	243	243	243	243	121	0	0
Additions, period 2		125	250	250	250	250	250	250	125	0
Additions, period 3			129	257	257	257	257	257	257	129
Additions, period 4				136	271	271	271	271	271	271
Additions, period 5					143	286	286	286	286	286
Additions, period 6						150	300	300	300	300
Additions, period 7							157	314	314	314
Additions, period 8								164	329	329
Additions, period 9									171	343
Additions, period 10										179
Subtotal	1,621	1,868	2,121	2,386	2,664	1,457	1,764	1,964	2,054	2,150
Ending net fixed asset balance	$7,579	$7,461	$7,139	$6,654	$5,989	$6,632	$7,068	$7,404	$7,750	$8,100
Average net fixed assets	$7,539	$7,520	$7,300	$6,896	$6,321	$6,311	$6,850	$7,236	$7,577	$7,925
Revenue	$100,000	$109,000	$116,500	$122,000	$127,100	$130,913	$134,840	$138,886	$143,052	$147,344
Average net fixed asset turnover[1]	13.3	14.5	16.0	17.7	20.1	20.7	19.7	19.2	18.9	18.6
Average remaining lives (net fixed assets)										
Opening balance	5 years									
New asset additions	7 years									
Depreciation, as a % of revenue	1.6%	1.7%	1.8%	2.0%	2.1%	1.1%	1.3%	1.4%	1.4%	1.5%

[1] Defined as total revenue divided by average net fixed assets.

AAG-RDA 6.200

Glossary

This glossary contains terms from the following sources, when indicated:

- *International Glossary of Business Valuation Terms* (IGBVT), which has been adopted by a number of professional societies and organizations, including the AICPA

- Financial Accounting Standards Board (FASB) *Accounting Standards Codification* (ASC)

- Statement on Standards for Valuation Services (SSVS) No. 1, *Valuation of a Business, Business Ownership Interest, Security, or Intangible Asset* (AICPA, *Professional Standards*, VS sec. 100)

active market. A market in which transactions for the asset or liability take place with sufficient frequency and volume to provide pricing information on an ongoing basis. (FASB ASC Master Glossary)

asset resulting from research and development (R&D) activities. Completed asset produced by R&D activities (for example, a software program released for sale).

collaborative arrangement. A contractual arrangement that involves a joint operating activity (see FASB ASC 808-10-15-7). These arrangements involve two (or more) parties that meet both of the following requirements:

 a. They are active participants in the activity (see FASB ASC 808-10-15-8 through 15-9).

 b. They are exposed to significant risks and rewards dependent on the commercial success of the activity (see FASB ASC 808-10-15-10 through 15-13).

 (FASB ASC Master Glossary)

conditional cash flows. Cash flows that are conditional upon the occurrence of specified events. (FASB ASC 820-10-55-10) For example, for IPR&D assets, the condition generally relates to the commercial success of the IPR&D project being valued.

cost approach. A valuation technique that reflects the amount that would be required currently to replace the service capacity of an asset (often referred to as *current replacement cost*). (FASB ASC Master Glossary)

A general way of determining a value indication of an individual asset by quantifying the amount of money required to replace the future service capability of that asset. (IGBVT)

decision tree analysis. An income-based method that explicitly captures the expected benefits, costs, and probabilities of contingent outcomes at future decision points, or nodes.

defensive intangible asset. An acquired intangible asset in a situation in which an entity does not intend to actively use the asset but intends to hold (lock up) the asset to prevent others from obtaining access to the asset. (FASB ASC Master Glossary)

developed product technology. Technology as it exists in a current product(s) offering. Today's developed product technology may be tomorrow's enabling technology.

discount rate. A rate of return used to convert a future monetary sum into present value. (IGBVT)

discount rate adjustment technique. A present value technique that uses a risk-adjusted discount rate and contractual, promised, or most likely cash flows. (FASB ASC Master Glossary)

discounted cash flow (DCF) method. A method within the income approach whereby the present value of future expected net cash flows is calculated using a discount rate. (IGBVT)

EBIT. Earnings before interest and taxes.

EBITDA. Earnings before interest, taxes, depreciation, and amortization.

EITF. Emerging Issues Task Force of the Financial Accounting Standards Board.

economic goodwill. For purposes of this guide, economic goodwill is defined as the residual goodwill that would result from subtracting fair value of assets and liabilities from the fair value of the acquired entity as opposed to from the purchase price.

enabling technology. For purposes of this guide, enabling technology is defined as the underlying technology that has value through its continued use or reuse across many products or product families (product family represents many generations of a singular product). Effectively, enabling technology represents shared technology with multiple uses across many products or product families.

expected cash flow. The probability-weighted average (that is, mean of the distribution) of possible future cash flows. (FASB ASC Master Glossary)

expected present value technique. The expected present value technique uses as a starting point a set of cash flows that represents the probability-weighted average of all possible future cash flows (that is, the expected cash flows). The resulting estimate is identical to expected value, which, in statistical terms, is the weighted average of a discrete random variable's possible values with the respective probabilities as the weights. Because all possible cash flows are probability-weighted, the resulting expected cash flow is not conditional upon the occurrence of any specified event (unlike the cash flows used in the discount rate adjustment technique). (FASB ASC 820-10-55-13)

fair value. The price that would be received to sell an asset or paid to transfer a liability in an orderly transaction between market participants at the measurement date. (FASB ASC 820, *Fair Value Measurement*)

FASB. Financial Accounting Standards Board.

future R&D (or **future technology**). R&D that will be undertaken in the future.

income approach. Valuation techniques that convert future amounts (for example, cash flows or income and expenses) to a single current (that is, discounted) amount. The fair value measurement is determined on the basis of the value indicated by current market expectations about those future amounts. (FASB ASC Master Glossary)

A general way of determining a value indication of a business, business ownership interest, security, or intangible asset using one or more methods that convert anticipated economic benefits into a present single amount. (IGBVT)

Also known as *income-based approach*.

in-process R&D (IPR&D) asset. Intangible asset that is to be used or is used in R&D activities, including a specific IPR&D project. In other words, an IPR&D project is an example of an IPR&D asset. However, in some cases, an IPR&D project may comprise several IPR&D assets.

indefinite-lived IPR&D asset. Intangible asset acquired in a business combination that is to be used in R&D activities. Such assets are not subject to amortization until the completion or abandonment of the associated R&D efforts.

IPR&D project. R&D project that has not yet been completed. IPR&D project is an example of an IPR&D asset.

market approach. A valuation technique that uses prices and other relevant information generated by market transactions involving identical or comparable (that is, similar) assets, liabilities, or a group of assets and liabilities, such as a business. (FASB ASC Master Glossary)

A general way of determining a value indication of a business, business ownership interest, security, or intangible asset by using one or more methods that compare the subject to similar businesses, business ownership interests, securities, or intangible assets that have been sold. (IGBVT)

Also known as *market-based approach*.

market participants. Buyers and sellers in the principal (or most advantageous) market for the asset or liability that have all of the following characteristics:

    a. They are independent of each other, that is, they are not related parties, although the price in a related-party transaction may be used as an input to a fair value measurement if the reporting entity has evidence that the transaction was entered into at market terms

    b. They are knowledgeable, having a reasonable understanding about the asset or liability and the transaction using all available information, including information that might be obtained through due diligence efforts that are usual and customary

    c. They are able to enter into a transaction for the asset or liability

    d. They are willing to enter into a transaction for the asset or liability, that is, they are motivated but not forced or otherwise compelled to do so.

    (FASB ASC Master Glossary)

multiperiod excess earnings method. A specific application of the discounted cash flow method, which is more broadly a form of the income approach. The most common method used to estimate the fair value of an intangible asset.

outlicensing arrangement. For purposes of this guide, outlicensing arrangement is defined as an arrangement in which a transferor, such as a pharmaceutical company, transfers (outlicenses) its rights to a previously identified and measured IPR&D asset to a third party (transferee). The intangible asset transferred is commonly known as the *outlicensed asset*. It should be noted that there are other types of outlicensing arrangements that involve internally developed IPR&D assets; however, these arrangements are not addressed in this guide.

prospective financial information (PFI). Any financial information about the future. The information may be presented as complete financial statements or limited to one or more elements, items, or accounts. (AICPA Guide *Prospective Financial Information*)

related parties. Related parties include the following:

   a. Affiliates of the entity

   b. Entities for which investments in their equity securities would be required, absent the election of the fair value option under the "Fair Value Options" subsection of FASB ASC 825-10-15, to be accounted for by the equity method by the investing entity

   c. Trusts for the benefit of employees, such as pension and profit-sharing trusts that are managed by or under the trusteeship of management

   d. Principal owners of the entity and members of their immediate families

   e. Management of the entity and members of their immediate families

   f. Other parties with which the entity may deal if one party controls or can significantly influence the management or operating policies of the other to an extent that one of the transacting parties might be prevented from fully pursuing its own separate interests

   g. Other parties that can significantly influence the management or operating policies of the transacting parties or that have an ownership interest in one of the transacting parties and can significantly influence the other to an extent that one or more of the transacting parties might be prevented from fully pursuing its own separate interests.

   (FASB ASC Master Glossary)

relief from royalty method. A valuation method used to value certain intangible assets (for example, trademarks and trade names) based on the premise that the only value that a purchaser of the assets receives is the exemption from paying a royalty for its use. Application of this method usually involves estimating the fair market value of an intangible asset by quantifying the present value of the stream of market-derived royalty payments that the owner of the intangible asset is exempted from or "relieved" from paying. (Appendix C, "Glossary of Additional Terms," of SSVS No. 1)

replacement cost new. The current cost of a similar new property having the nearest equivalent utility to the property being valued (IGBVT). Also known as *current replacement cost* or *replacement cost*.

required rate of return. The minimum rate of return acceptable by investors before they will commit money to an investment at a given level of risk. (IGBVT)

SSVS. Statement on Standards for Valuation Services, issued by the AICPA and available as VS section 100, *Valuation of a Business, Business Ownership Interest, Security, or Intangible Asset* (AICPA, *Professional Standards*).

synergy. Used mostly in the context of mergers and acquisitions, the concept that the value and performance of two entities combined will be greater than the sum of the separate individual parts. In the context of developing prospective financial information, synergies may account for some of the difference between the assumptions used to estimate cash flows that are unique to an entity and the assumptions that would be used by market participants.

technology migration. For purposes of this guide, technology migration is defined as the process by which certain elements of technology are used or reused within a product or product family from one product generation to the next. In other words, technology migration represents reuse of "old" technology in combination with "new" IPR&D technology or "new" future yet-to-be-defined technology.

unobservable inputs. Inputs for which market data are not available and that are developed using the best information available about the assumptions that market participants would use when pricing the asset or liability. (FASB ASC Master Glossary)

valuation specialist. An individual recognized as possessing the abilities, skills, and experience to perform valuations. A valuation specialist may be external or internal. When referring to the valuation specialist in this guide, it is commonly presumed that it is an external party but, if individuals within the entity possess the abilities, skills, and experience to perform valuations, they can also serve in the capacity of a valuation specialist.

weighted average cost of capital (WACC). The cost of capital (discount rate) determined by the weighted average, at market value, of the cost of all financing sources in the business enterprise's capital structure. (IGBVT)

Index of Pronouncements and Other Technical Guidance

A

Title	Paragraphs
APB Opinion No. 17, *Intangible Assets*	4.45
Appraisal Foundation *The Identification of Contributory Assets and the Calculation of Economic Rents*	1.21, 1.27, 6.39, 6.86, 6.88, 6.130, 6.198

F

Title	Paragraphs
FASB ASC	
250, *Accounting Changes and Error Corrections*	4.57
250-10-10-45	4.50
323, *Investments—Equity Method and Joint Ventures*	2.66, 3.31
323-10-15-10	2.66
323-10-35-13	2.66
323-10-35-32A	2.66
323-10-45-1	2.66
350, *Intangibles—Goodwill and Other*	2.58, 4.57
350-20	4.71, 4.77
350-20-40	4.77
350-30	2.11, 3.01, 4.03, 4.06, 4.32, 4.39, 4.71, 4.77, 4.86
350-30-35	2.11, 2.22, 2.30, 3.10, 3.20, 3.29, 4.07, 4.11, 4.15, 4.39, 4.86
350-30-35-1	4.37, 6.17
350-30-35-1C	4.37
350-30-35-2	4.38
350-30-35-3	4.40
350-30-35-5A	2.32

Title	Paragraphs
350-30-35-5B	2.32
350-30-35-6	4.43, 6.68
350-30-35-9	4.38
350-30-35-14	4.70
350-30-35-16	4.86
350-30-35-17	4.14
350-30-35-17A	2.10–.11, 2.31, 2.36, 2.67, 4.14, 4.24, 4.86
350-30-35-18B	4.12
350-30-35-18C	4.13
350-30-35-19	4.15, 4.18
350-30-45-2	4.23
350-30-50-1(c)	5.08
350-40	2.42
360, *Property, Plant and Equipment*	2.10, 4.06, 4.14, 4.24
360-10	2.27, 4.51, 4.71, 4.77
360-10-35	4.07, 4.54, 4.68
360-10-35-20	4.70
360-10-35-21	4.56
360-10-35-22	4.57
360-10-35-23	4.58, 4.67
360-10-35-27	4.71
360-10-35-28	4.55, 4.73
360-10-35-30	4.60, 4.62, 4.67
360-10-35-31	4.63
360-10-35-32	4.65
360-10-35-33	4.66
360-10-35-39	4.77
360-10-35-40	4.76, 4.78
360-10-35-43	4.75–.76
360-10-35-47	2.10, 4.24, 4.27, 4.51
360-10-35-49	2.10, 4.24
360-10-45-4	4.69

Title	Paragraphs
360-10-45-9	2.28, 4.52, 4.74
360-10-45-11	4.74
360-10-45-12	2.28
360-10-45-15	4.28, 4.51
360-10-55-20	4.73
450, *Contingencies*	3.10
450-20-05	3.10
450-20-30-1	3.10
730, *Research and Development*	5.08
730-10	2.04, 2.08, 2.17, 2.42, 2.56–.57, 2.62, 3.10, 3.12
730-10-15	2.08, 2.39
730-10-15-4(f)	2.39
730-10-25-2	3.02, 3.12–.13
730-10-25-2(a)	3.27
730-10-25-2(c)	6.03
730-10-55	2.39
730-10-55-1	2.39, 2.43, 2.60, 4.36
730-10-55-1(e)	2.43
730-10-55-2	2.41, 2.60, 4.36
730-10-55-2(d)	2.41
740, *Income Taxes*	6.124
740-25-47	4.82
805, *Business Combinations*	2.01, 2.15, 2.19, 2.23, 2.25–.26, 2.28, 2.58–.59, 2.67, 3.01, 3.03, 3.10, 3.30, 5.02, 5.04, 6.03, 6.55–.56, 6.86
805-10-25	2.06
805-10-25-13	2.65
805-10-25-13 through 25-14	2.65
805-10-25-17	2.65
805-10-25-23	3.10

Title	Paragraphs
805-10-50	5.02
805-10-50-1(c)	5.01
805-10-50-6	2.65
805-10-55-16	2.65, 5.04
805-10-55-27	2.65
805-20	2.04, 2.67
805-20-25	2.06, 2.67, 3.10
805-20-25-19	3.10
805-20-25-20	3.10
805-20-30-6	6.17
805-20-50	5.02
805-20-50-1(c)	5.04
805-20-55	6.86
805-20-S99-3	1.34
805-30-25-5	3.10
805-30-35-1	3.10
805-30-50	5.02
805-40-50	5.02
805-50	3.11
805-50-25-1	3.11
805-50-30-1	3.11
805-50-30-2	3.10, 3.11
805-50-30-3	3.10, 3.11, 3.20
805-50-35-1	3.11, 4.84
815, *Derivatives and Hedging*	3.10
820, *Fair Value Measurement*	2.28, 4.19, 6.01, 6.03–.21, 6.42, 6.105, 6.107, 6.123, 6.144, 6.199
820-10	6.04
820-10-15-1	2.28
820-10-35-5	6.04
820-10-35-9	6.04, 6.09, 6.42
820-10-35-10B	6.15

Title	Paragraphs
820-10-35-10E	6.04, 6.15
820-10-35-24	1.02–.03
820-10-35-24A	6.04
820-10-35-53	6.42
820-10-35-54A	6.08, 6.42
820-10-55	1.06, 1.28, 6.04, 6.16, 6.100, 6.102, 6.108
820-10-55-3A	1.10
820-10-55-3F	1.13
820-10-55-4	6.108
820-10-55-10	6.100
820-10-55-16	6.104
820-10-55-18	6.100
820-10-55-32	6.18–.19, 6.21
820, *Fair Value Measurement*	
820-10	6.04
820-10-35-9	6.04, 6.09, 6.42
820-10-35-10B	6.15
820-10-35-10E	6.04, 6.15
820-10-35-24A	6.04
820-10-35-54A	6.08
820-10-53	6.42
820-10-55	6.04, 6.100, 6.108
820-10-55-4	6.108
820-10-55-10	6.100, 6.110
820-10-55-11	6.110
820-10-55-16	6.104
820-30-30-6	6.17
820-30-35-1	6.17
Appendix B	6.107
855, *Subsequent Events*	2.67
985, *Software*	
985-20	2.42, 2.61

Subject Index